COMMUNISM IN THE ARAB EAST

The Lebanese Crisis, 1958 (1965)

COMMUNISM
IN THE ARAB EAST

M. S. AGWANI
Professor of West Asian Studies
Indian School of International Studies

Issued under the Auspices of the
Indian School of International Studies

ASIA PUBLISHING HOUSE

BOMBAY • CALCUTTA • NEW DELHI • MADRAS
LUCKNOW • BANGALORE • LONDON • NEW YORK

© 1969 M. S. AGWANI (1928)
Mohammed Shafi Agwani

PRINTED IN INDIA
BY P. K. GHOSH AT EASTEND PRINTERS, 3 DR SURESH
SARKAR ROAD, CALCUTTA-14 AND PUBLISHED BY
P. S. JAYASINGHE, ASIA PUBLISHING HOUSE, BOMBAY

PREFACE

THIS is not a comprehensive history of the Communist movement in the Arab East. What I have sought to do here is, firstly, to describe and evaluate the more significant stages in the development of Arab Communist parties and their ceaseless interaction with rival political groups. I have laid greater emphasis on the post-war period for the obvious reason that it was only in the later years of the war that Communism registered its first breakthrough in the region. This forms the subject of the first two parts of the study. The rest seeks to illuminate the differences as well as the common ground between Communism and nationalism, the strategy and tactics of the Communist movement, and the impact of Sino-Soviet discord on the Arab East and, in particular, on the fortunes of Arab Communism. This study was completed before the Arab-Israeli conflict of June 1967, which necessitated the inclusion of a postscript reflecting on the immediate and long-range implications of this new development.

I should like to express my gratitude to numerous friends in Egypt, the Lebanon, Syria, Iraq, and Jordan who contributed facts, insights, and focus to this study but whose names should remain unmentioned. They are, of course, in no way responsible for the shortcomings of this book.

During my visit to the Arab East in 1963, and again in 1968, I profited by the collection of the library of the American University of Beirut; and I take this opportunity to record my grateful appreciation of the generous assistance extended to me by Mr Jibran Bikhazi and his library staff. I am also indebted to the staff of the Sapru House library, especially to Mr Girja Kumar, Mrs C. Andrade, Miss Shanta Sehgal, and Dr A. R. Bedar, who treated my endless demands with cheerful indulgence; to Mr A. S. Hebbar, who edited the manuscript in a helpful and imaginative way; to Messrs A. L. Anand and B. L. Pahwa, who shared in the final typing; and to Mr S. L. Manchanda, who helped me in proof-reading and preparing the index.

Owing to some unavoidable technical difficulties I have not been able to transliterate Arabic names, terms, and titles. But I have transcribed them in a simple yet consistent way. Commonly accepted English forms of some Arabic names have been retained.

31 May 1968   M. S. AGWANI

CONTENTS

Preface   v

PART ONE: THE PRE-SUEZ ERA

I   THE EARLY PHASE   3
II   EXPANSION AND CONSOLIDATION: 1941-1945   21
III COMMUNISTS AND THE PARTITION OF PALESTINE   36
IV   STRUGGLE FOR POWER IN EGYPT: 1945-1956   44
V   UPS AND DOWNS IN SYRIA AND THE LEBANON:
     1946-1956   52
VI   IRAQ: FRUITS OF REPRESSION   64
VII JORDAN: YEARS OF FERMENT   71

PART TWO: THE POST-SUEZ ERA

VIII EGYPT: PRECARIOUS PARTNERSHIP   79
IX   SYRIA: FAILURE OF FRONT TACTICS   87
X   LEBANON: THE EMERGING TRIBUNE   106
XI   IRAQ: TRIUMPH AND REBUFF   113
XII JORDAN: THE CHRONIC STALEMATE   150

PART THREE: THE IDEOLOGICAL ISSUES

XIII COMMUNISM AND NATIONALISM   161
XIV IDEOLOGY, STRATEGY, AND TACTICS   177
XV   THE IMPACT OF THE SINO-SOVIET RIFT   196
XVI CONCLUSION   220
     POSTSCRIPT   227
     Select Bibliography   233
     Index   243

PART ONE
THE PRE-SUEZ ERA

CHAPTER ONE

THE EARLY PHASE

THE initiation and spread of Communist ideas and activities in the Arab East did not follow the process outlined by the Marxian textbooks. Arab interest in Communism started somewhat abruptly and superficially. The Bolshevik Revolution in Russia created a stir in parts of the Arab East when the region was still in the throes of the First World War. The four-century-old Ottoman order had crumbled under the impact of the war and was about to pass into history. But the outlines of the new order were still far from being distinct. There were, of course, a few straws in the wind such as President Woodrow Wilson's Fourteen Points and the British promise to the Sharif of Mecca for an Independent Arab State. But the formidable presence of alien forces in the Arab lands created a feeling of uncertainty about the future. The seizure of power by the Bolsheviks and their loud pledges of sympathy for the exploited people of the East, therefore, had a balmy effect on minds agitated by gnawing doubts about the shape of things to come. Even so, Communism in the Arab East, at this stage, was strictly a political reflex rather than a reality. A few modern industries had appeared in Egypt and in the Levant, but a class-conscious industrial proletariat was still practically non-existent. Agricultural labour, though numerically strong, was weak, unorganized, and politically inarticulate. In short, political and economic conditions in the Arab East were not conducive to the growth of an indigenous Communist movement. None the less, there were tiny groups of intellectuals in Cairo, Alexandria, and Beirut whose curiosity was deeply roused by the triumph of Communism in Russia. And they formed the nuclei of the Communist movements that cropped up in the region during the following decade.

Communism in Egypt

In the fall of 1920 a small group of revolutionary intellectuals, including Salama Musa, Muhammad 'Abdullah al-'Inani, and Husni al-'Urabi, founded the Socialist Party of Egypt. Salama Musa narrates its brief career thus:

The imperialists gave us a long rope in order to gauge the extent of our activity and the degree of popular response to it. In fact, the response was good; and it appeared that we were proceeding with moderation avoiding conflicts.... Then all of a sudden one of us, Husni al-'Urabi, became impatient with our slow pace. He went to Alexandria and announced the formation of the Communist (*ibahi*) Party.... Many young men who defected from us to join the new party took away the records of the (Socialist) Party and destroyed it.[1]

The Communist Party of Egypt joined the Comintern in 1923.

Although the Party appeared on the scene immediately after the nation-wide nationalist upsurge led by the emergent urban middle class of professionals and backed by large sections of people in towns as well as in the countryside, it was not a direct outcome of the latter. Rather it was a precocious offspring of the revolutionary effervescence generated by the Bolshevik Revolution. And to this the Egyptian Communists owed their theoretical preference for the proletarian and instinctive suspicion of the broad-based Wafdist nationalists.

The innate proclivities of the Egyptian Communists found expression in their first Party Manifesto of 22 December 1921.[2] The party styled itself the "standard bearer of the proletariat and party of the class struggle" pledged to fight "against the Egyptian capitalist tyrants and oppressors, accomplices and associates of the tyrannic foreign domination". It also made no secret of its distaste for the means adopted by the Wafd to advance the cause of Egypt's freedom. "It is not by diplomatic steps and negotiations between Ministers or delegations which do not represent the wishes of the people that independence can be obtained", said the Manifesto. The party believed that "only the conscious and organized workers and peasants can achieve it".

Two years later the party framed a slightly more realistic programme which, barring a few exceptions, was strikingly close to the Wafdist platform. It called for progressive labour legislation, eight-hour working day, recognition of trade unions, equal pay for Egyptian and European workers, and formation of producers' and

[1] Salama Musa, *Tarbiya Salama Musa* (Cairo, n.d.), p. 165.
[2] Text of the Manifesto in *Labour Monthly* (London), vol. 2 (March, 1922), pp. 276-9.

consumers' co-operatives. For the first time the party also gave careful attention to the peasant front and called for the abolition of the existing farm tenure system which had brought hardships upon the peasantry, cancellation of debts of peasants owning less than 30 feddans (1 feddan=1.036 acres), and abrogation of land taxation for peasants possessing less than 10 feddans. The party, of course, stood for the restoration of Egypt's sovereignty, abolition of the capitulations, and union of the Sudan with Egypt. On two important points, however, the Communist programme outstripped the Wafd. First, it demanded confiscation of holdings of over 100 feddans and distribution of the surplus land among the landless peasantry—a measure directed against the 13,000 rich landlords of Egypt who nearly owned half the cultivated land in the country; and second, it called for the nationalization of the Suez Canal. A generation hence these radical demands were to be ardently championed and realized by an Egyptian nationalism rekindled by youthful but non-Marxist army officers. In the twenties, however, they sounded too revolutionary, and moderate nationalists carefully side-tracked them. To the Communists, however, the new programme signified only "provisional half measures", the ultimate goal being the complete socialization of land and other means of production.[3]

Notwithstanding this seemingly broad-based programme, the founders of the Egyptian Communist Party—Husni al-'Urabi, Joseph Rosenthal, and Antun Marun—dogmatically emphasized the need to make it a predominantly workers' party. The doctrinaire obsession with the proletariat, which was in any case numerically weak and politically inarticulate, naturally hampered the development of the party. Ironically, in the party itself, there was not a single manual worker at the level of leadership, which wholly consisted of middle class or well-to-do intellectuals.[4] The Communists nevertheless took earnestly to trade union work. By 1923 a Communist-oriented Confederation of Trade Unions was created. And this brought the Communist Party into a head-on clash with the first Wafdist Government in 1924. The labour strikes in Alexan-

---

[3] G. A. Hutt, "Egyptian Nationalism and the Class Struggle", *Labour Monthly*, vol. 4 (April 1923), pp. 295-6.

[4] One of them, Joseph Rosenthal, belonged to a rich jeweller's family of Alexandria. See Walter Z. Laqueur. *Communism and Nationalism in the Middle East* (London, 1957), p. 31, pp. 37-8.

dria and other industrial centres master-minded by Antun Marun were not exactly to the liking of foreign or Egyptian capital; and the Wafd could not afford to be unmindful of the interests particularly of the emergent Egyptian investors whose moral and material support it greatly cherished.

Zaghlul's Wafdist Government promptly suppressed the strikes and rounded up its leaders including Antun Marun, who died in prison the same year. The Government also disbanded the Confederation of Trade Unions and sponsored a nationalist labour organization under the leadership of Wafdist lawyers, M. Thabit and Zuhayr Sabri. These drastic measures set the pattern of the Egyptian nationalist movement's relationship with the extreme Left and vice versa. In any case, the Communists had always been sceptical about the Wafd's revolutionary potentialities. They believed that it represented the interests of the capitalist class and as such was "fundamentally" opportunist and that Sa'd Zaghlul, its leader, was an "Anglophile constitutional agitator". They charged that the Wafd had used the revolt of 1919 as a means to force a compromise on the British Government. For had not Zaghlul announced soon after his release from prison on 30 March, 1923 that the "aspirations of Egypt are not in contradiction with the protection of foreign interests"?[5] After the showdown of 1924 the Communists virulently denounced Zaghlul as "a retrograde of the worst type".[6]

Although the Communists had from the very beginning dubbed the Wafd a political organ of the Egyptian national *bourgeoisie*, they also emphasized the conflict of interest between the Egyptian and foreign capital—a conflict which justified a tactical cooperation between the workers' party and the national *bourgeoisie*. In 1925 Stalin theorized at length on the subject. He contended that "a single and all embracing colonial East no longer exists". He put the colonies of the East into three broad categories: colonies totally devoid of the national *bourgeoisie* and the industrial proletariat (e.g. Morocco); colonies which were industrially developed, but in which the national *bourgeoisie* was already divided between a revolutionary party and a compromising party, the latter having not yet come to terms with imperialism (e.g. Egypt and China);

---

[5] Hutt, n. 3, p. 298.
[6] J. Crossley, "Egypt at the Crossroads", *Labour Monthly*, vol. 8 (January 1926), p. 52.

and highly developed colonies where the compromising section of the national *bourgeoisie* had struck a deal with the imperialists (e.g. India). Stalin argued that each category had to be treated differently from the others for the purpose of revolutionary struggle. In the most backward colonies the Communists should go for a united national front of all classes of people. In countries like Egypt and China they must go forward to form a revolutionary bloc of the workers and the petty *bourgeoisie*. In the case of an advanced colony like India Stalin recommended a relentless war upon the national *bourgeoisie*.[7]

Needless to add that Stalin's thesis was invalidated by subsequent developments. In Egypt the stage for an alliance between the Communists and the national *bourgeoisie* was not reached until after the Second World War. But what forced the Comintern to review the entire situation was the Chinese Communists' disenchantment with the Kuomintang in the late twenties. The new thesis adopted by the Sixth Congress of the Comintern (1928) declared that the Chinese national *bourgeoisie* had "passed over finally into the camp of counter-revolution". Egypt was now lumped together with India as colonial prototypes where the national *bourgeoisie*, notwithstanding its "negative features", could still exert a certain accelerating influence "on the process of the political awakening of the wide masses of toilers". The Wafd was assailed for having "more than once betrayed the nationalist emancipatory struggle"; at the same time, the Egyptian Communists were reassured that the national *bourgeoisie* had not yet finally passed over to the counter-revolutionary camp in the manner of the Kuomintang.[8] The Congress also chided the Communists for confining their activities "exclusively" to the urban workers and emphasized the need to draw "the masses of agricultural workers" into the revolutionary struggle and to devote special attention to the building up of the party itself, "which is still very weak".[9]

Whatever remained of the Egyptian Communist Party after the 1924 suppression was too weak, numerically and organizationally,

[7] Joseph V. Stalin, *Marxism and the National and Colonial Question* (London, 1947), pp. 216-8.

[8] *Revolutionary Movement in the Colonies and Semi-Colonies: Thesis Adopted by the Sixth Congress of the Communist International, 1928* (Bombay, 1948), pp. 33-5.

[9] Ibid., p. 58.

to carry out the tasks outlined by the Comintern. Indeed the late twenties and thirties were utterly barren years for the Communists. The economic unrest resulting from the world economic crisis of the late twenties tempted some Communists to compare Zaghlul's successor Nahas to Kerensky. They also toyed with the idea of creating a revolutionary workers' army that would put the Wafd into power after having cured it of the fatal disease of compromise.[10] A manifesto[11] published in the early thirties proclaimed:

> The direct and immediate purpose of the anti-imperialist and anti-feudal revolution in Egypt is the overthrowing of the imperialist yoke and the reactionary monarchy, the winning of complete independence for Egypt, an agrarian peasant revolution, an eight-hour working day, and a radical improvement in the condition of the workers, the establishment of the revolutionary and democratic dictatorship of the working class and peasantry in the form of Soviet workers' and peasants' government.

The ambitious blueprints, wholly unrelated to the actual capabilities of the Communist Party, were symptomatic of a feeble mind prone to idle day-dreaming.

During the inter-war years the Communists were no match for the Wafd, which dominated the entire political scene. Also during this period the Egyptian *bourgeoisie* began to come into its own. The spurt in cotton prices during the First World War had induced many big landowners to invest their surplus earnings in commerce and industry. The League of Egyptian Industries was set up to protect the rights of indigenous capital. Established in 1927, the Bank Misr soon made an appreciable dent into the cotton weaving and spinning, silk and fishing industries. These developments, while lending strength to the nationalist movement, also created openings for the Communists. Moreover, the deepening international crisis of the thirties and the steady decline in the prestige of the Wafd following the Anglo-Egyptian Treaty of 1936 created new tensions and divisions in the body politic which the Communists would

[10] "J. B.", "The New Wave of Revolt in Egypt", *Labour Monthly*, vol. 12 (December 1930), pp. 748-9.

[11] Text in Ivar Spector, *The Soviet Union and the Muslim World 1917-56* (Washington, D.C., mimeographed, 1956), pp.82-91.

presently turn to account and with a greater measure of success than in the early twenties.

Palestine

The rise of Communist movement in Palestine was attended by extraordinary circumstances created by the Balfour Declaration (1917) and its subsequent incorporation into the framework of the British Mandate. With the opening up of Palestine to Jewish immigration came the first wave of settlers from Eastern Europe. This group contained a sprinkling of Communist elements which formed the nucleus of the prospective Communist Party of Palestine. The first Communist organization called *Mifleget Poalim Sozialistim Ivrin* (Jewish Socialist Workers' Party) was formed in 1920. The supporters of this organization, also known as *Mopsi*, belonged originally to the Left wing of *Poale Zion* (Workers of Zion).

The Jewish Socialist Workers' Party attracted public attention on May Day 1921, when it openly clashed with its moderate socialist rival *Achduh Avodah* (Unity of Work). It is alleged that the former organized the entire operation at Trotsky's instance. It was a clash between two wholly Jewish groups; and there were no casualties. But some discontented Arabs subsequently attacked Jewish immigrants leading to 314 wounded or killed on both sides. The British promptly suppressed the *Mopsi*.[12]

The *Mopsi's* initial handicap was that in a predominantly Arab country[13] its following consisted entirely of European Jews. Then it was organically linked to the Zionist movement to which it aspired to give a proletarian orientation. A small faction of the party was, however, in favour of totally repudiating Zionism; and this faction got the upper hand in 1922 which paved the way for the formation of the Communist Party of Palestine (CPP) the same year. It was admitted to the Comintern in 1924.

Henceforth, the Communists set out to purge their ranks of Zionist elements and canvass Arab support. The party took the line that it would resist all attempts to transform Palestine into a Jewish National Home and that the salvation of the Jews did not lie

---

[12] Christopher Sykes, *Cross Roads to Israel* (London, 1965), pp. 69-70; A. B. Magil, *Israel in Crisis* (New York, 1950), p. 131.

[13] In 1922, the population of Palestine was 750,000, of which 660,000 were Arabs.

in Zionism. The immediate result of this drastic change of policy was that the Communists became highly unpopular among the Jews. They were brusquely expelled from the *Histadrut* (General Confederation of Jewish Labour), and there were some desertions from the party itself. What was an even more serious set-back, the Communists registered no compensating gain on the Arab front either.[14]

All Communist efforts during the twenties to enlist Arab support came to naught, and for good reasons. The influx of the Jews into Palestine gave rise to certain political, economic, and psychological tensions which had a deep impact on all sections of Palestinian Arabs. The fear of the entire country being turned into a Jewish land in the long run was widespread. Added to this were the serious economic injuries inflicted upon the Arab peasantry by the sponsors of Jewish agricultural settlements who bought groups of villages from rich Arab landowners and proceeded to squeeze Arab cultivators out of these lands. Arab workers, too, nursed enmity towards Jewish workers, first because the doors of new Jewish industrial enterprises were closed on them; and secondly because of the considerable differential between the Arab and Jewish workers' wages.

Towards the end of the decade, however, Communism succeeded in making a little headway among Arab community, particularly among its newly educated *élite*. Early in 1929 the CPP took a sharp turn to the Left in its tactics towards "Anglo-Zionist oppression" on the one hand and Arab nationalist groups on the other. The new approach was based on the premise that revolutionary tasks could be accomplished only by the peasant masses and the bedouin —the "inexhaustible reservoir of insurrectionary forces"—who bore the brunt of Zionist as well as Arab feudal exploitation.[15] The twin objective of the party was to wean the Arab masses away from the influence of the feudal *bourgeoisie* led by the Husaynis and the Nashashibis[16] and to promote close co-operation between

[14] Laqueur, n. 4, pp. 75-8.

[15] "J. B.", "The Class Character of Palestine Rising", *Labour Monthly*, vol. 12 (April 1930), pp. 248-9.

[16] Soon after the British took over the administration of Palestine, Al-Haj Muhammad Amin al-Husayni, a scion of the influential landowning clan of Palestine, was elevated to the offices of the Mufti of Jerusalem and President of the Supreme Muslim Council. This evoked the envy of the rival aristocratic clan of the Nashashibi headed by Raghib Bey al-Nashashibi. The two clans jockeyed for position and influence under the British.

Arab and Jewish workers. But even before the new line could be given a trial, an eruption of Arab-Jewish communal strife of unprecedented intensity, in August 1929, dimmed the prospect of class-oriented politics, at least for the time being. These events further underlined the isolation of the Communists from the mass movement.

A Party Congress was convened in 1930 to review the entire situation. The Congress examined at length[17] the causes of Arab-Jewish conflict and the agrarian situation in Palestine and suggested revolutionary methods of solving these problems. Quoting from the Comintern's open letter of 26 November 1930 the Congress decried Zionism as "the expression of the exploiting and great-power oppressive strivings of the Jewish *bourgeoisie,* which makes use of the persecution of the Jewish national minorities in Eastern Europe for the purpose of imperialistic policy to insure its domination". It thus became "a tool of British imperialism to suppress the national liberation movement of the Arab masses". On the economic plane, Zionism expropriated the Arab peasants and crowded out the Arab workers and artisans. In this task, the Zionists found an ally in the Arab landlords from whom they secured ninety per cent of the land bought up for Jewish settlements. Hence the situation in Palestine called for a unified struggle against the imperialists, the Zionists, and the Arab landlords. Secondly, the Congress advanced the thesis that the key to the Palestine question was the agrarian question. The uprising of August 1929 "focussed attention of the imperialist government, as well as that of all parties in the country, on the Arab *fellah".* With thirty per cent of the peasants possessing no land whatsoever and more than fifty per cent owning an inadequate area, the peasantry of Palestine constituted a potent revolutionary force. The CPP, therefore, set upon itself the task of directing the active peasant forces along the line of decisive revolutionary struggle. This was to be achieved by Arabizing the party, by creating "durable links" between the urban workers and the mass of landless peasants and by establishing a united front of Arab and Jewish workers against Zionist usurpation and exploitation.

Soon after the Congress, the party initiated a vigorous campaign to arabize its leadership and the lower cadres. Between 1930 and 1935 more than thirty Arabs were despatched to Moscow for

[17] Text of the Congress Resolution in Spector, n. 11, pp. 91, 104.

elaborate training in doctrine and tactics. In the meantime the emergence of the liberal, nationalist, and middle-class-based Istiqlal Party offered better prospects of Communist-nationalist co-operation than the conservative group led by Amin al-Husayni.[18] The Communists succeeded in establishing close working relations with the radical wing of the Istiqlal Party headed by Hamdi al-Husayni. This new-born alliance was consolidated in the course of the Arab uprising of 1933, which, unlike the events of 1929, was directed solely against the British.

About this time "Musa", a Palestinian Arab Communist, returned to the country after undergoing extended training in the Soviet Union, and was appointed Secretary-General of the CPP. This event synchronized with the rise of Hitler in Germany which lent a new dimension to the Jewish question. As a result of Nazi persecution, Jewish immigration into Palestine touched the peak figure of 61,000 in 1935 as compared to 30,000 in 1925.[19] With an Arab at the helm of party affairs and the Palestinian Arab inclined to desperation as a result of the surging tide of the Jewish influx, the situation in Palestine was never so propitious for the Communist Party to blot out the stigma of being a "Jewish party". The Communist Party's stout advocacy of repeal of the Balfour Declaration, cessation of Jewish immigration, and a democratic régime in Palestine at last began to fall on receptive Arab ears. A British intelligence report said that as a result of Communist propaganda "the *fellaheen* believe that a Bolshei revolution in Palestine will mean three cows for each man, £4 a month in cash and 20 donums of land piece. On top of that the Communist will expel the Jews and all the rich colonies will become the property of the Arab peasants".[20]

The outbreak of the civil war of 1936-39 found the CPP politically and psychologically prepared to throw its weight behind the Arab Higher Committee—a coalition of Arab political parties formed in April 1936 under the presidency of Mufti Amin al-Husayni. W. Z. Laqueur claims that according to an agreement

---

[18] The Istiqlal was founded in 1932. Headed by 'Awni Bey 'Abd al-Hadi, a Jerusalem lawyer, the party represented the modern educated Arab *élite* which was getting increasingly allergic to the conservative Arab politics symbolized by Mufti Amin al-Husayni.

[19] William Yale, *The Near East* (Ann Arbor, Mich., 1958), p. 389.

[20] William B. Ziff, *The Rape of Palestine* (London, 1948), p. 387.

reached between the CPP and the Arab Higher Committee, two Arab Communists, Nimr 'Uda and Fu'ad Nassar, "were attached to the general staff which was planning and coordinating the revolt".[21]

The party's involvement in the first round of the civil war (April-September 1936) was admittedly unconditional. But in a circular issued in November 1939 it denied having had anything to do with subsequent clashes because, in its view, the people were still "weak and disorganized" and there was a danger of the Fascists "stealthily" taking over the movement.[22] The unconcealed hostility of Fascist Powers towards the Soviet Union and the growing influence of the Fascist propaganda over large sections of Palestinian Arabs induced the Communists to restrain judiciously their enthusiasm for the civil war. Henceforth, the British ceased to be the chief target of Communist attacks. On the contrary, the CPP heartily welcomed the British White Paper of May 1939 as "an achievement of Arab liberation movement and . . . a first step towards full liberation of the country". But this shift in policy proved as fickle as the international situation that dictated it. With the signing of the Nazi-Soviet Non-aggression Pact in August 1939 the Communists again trained their guns on British imperialism and stuck to this policy until Hitler launched an attack on the Soviet Union.

It must, however, be noted that during the period under discussion the CPP was a relatively weak element in the politics of Palestine which was dominated by non-Communist Jewish and Arab organizations. In the circumstances, the party's place in the overall political spectrum of Palestine was strictly peripheral. Added to this was the serious handicap that it was forced almost since its inception to work underground. At the same time it enjoyed the distinction of being the only political party in Palestine which strove—even though unsuccessfully and from a doctrinaire motivation—for Arab-Jewish co-operation.

Syria and the Lebanon

Constancy, flexibility, and absence of factional bickerings were the distinctive features of the Communist movement in Syria and the Lebanon in the early years.

[21] Laqueur, n. 4, p. 97.
[22] Al-Hakm Darwaza, *Ash-Shiyu'iya al-Mahliya wa Ma'rkat al-'Arab al-Qawmiya* (Beirut, 1963), edn. 3, pp. 274-5.

The pioneers of the movement were romantic visionaries unini-
tiated into the intricacies of the Marxist-Leninist doctrine but
deeply fascinated by its humanistic and egalitarian appeal. In
the autumn of 1922 they started a journal called *As-Sahafi at-Ta'ih*
(The Wandering Journalist), which began to propagate their
views on equality of man, eradication of poverty, and abolition of
injustice to workers. The first issue of the journal was published
in Zahle (Lebanon) on 28 September, 1922 under the editorship of
Iskander al-Riyashi. It contained none of the blood-curdling
slogans against religion and privileges. On the contrary, Riyashi
persuaded his readers that socialism was close to "the basic principles of religion" and endorsed by the holy books revealed to
Jesus and Muhammad. It was not long before Riyashi was joined
by another intellectual, Yusuf Ibrahim Yazbak of Beirut, and the
two began to peddle socialist ideas of classless society, communal
ownership of land, and internationalism. On 1 May, 1923 the journal
sponsored the celebration of the first May Day in the history of
Syria and the Lebanon. About this time Riyashi set out to organize
the workers of Zahle and by the month of June a trade union was
registered, and a charter advocating the workers' right to (*i*) English
week (i.e. eight-hour day), (*ii*) share in profits, and (*iii*) pension
and social security issued. A unique feature of the *Sahafi* group
was that it was not wholly committed to Marxian ideology or
Soviet practice and criticized both if they clashed with its own
admittedly "moderate socialism".[23]

By 1924 the group was reinforced by Farid Tu'ma, Ilyas Qashi'ami,
Butrus Hashimi, and, above all, Fu'ad ash-Shimali, an Egyptian
trade union leader who had been expelled from his country for
alleged Bolshevik activities. At this juncture an emissary of the
Communist Party of Palestine, Joseph Berger, got in touch with
the group for the purpose of setting up a branch of the Palestinian
party in the Lebanon. Yazbak, however, insisted on forming an
independent Communist organization for the Lebanon; and his
views eventually prevailed. The organization was discreetly named
Hizb ash-Sh'ab al-Lubnani (People's Party of Lebanon).

In the meantime Fu'ad ash-Shimali made appreciable headway
in organizing the tobacco workers of Bikfiya, Biskanta, Antalyas,
and Zahle. Early in 1925 the party had acquired enough following

[23] S. Ayyub, *Al-Hizb al-Shiyu'i fi Suriya wa Lubnan, 1922-58* (Beirut,
1959), pp. 13-54.

to hold a public convention which pledged to fight for the rights of Lebanese workers. Following this, barbers' and carpenters', printers' and truck-drivers' unions in Beirut and power-plant workers' union in Damascus were formed. This was followed by the merger of the Armenian Communist organization, the "Spartacus Party", led by Artin Madoyan,[24] with the People's Party, which was then rechristened the Communist Party of Syria and the Lebanon (CPSL).

The French Mandatory authorities in Syria and the Lebanon viewed with disquiet the growing Communist influence on workers, for the bulk of the labour force in Syria and the Lebanon was employed by the French-owned public utilities. The Druze revolt of 1925, though not sponsored but openly hailed by the Communists, gave additional cause for concern. Soon after the party held its first Congress in December, the French struck. The party was banned, and Yazbak and Madoyan arrested. But this set back was not to last for long and the Communists were able to resume their activities after the Druze revolt petered out in 1926. In 1928 the party was affiliated to the Comintern.

In 1931, the CPSL attempted, in collaboration with the Communist Party of Palestine, to evolve an integral approach to the problems of the entire Arab world. This was spelled out in a resolution adopted by the two parties. It represented the first ever attempt by Arab Communists to view the national question in a pan-Arab framework. "The gist of the Arab national question", said the resolution, "consists in the fact that English, French, Italian and Spanish imperialists have dismembered the living body of the Arab peoples, hold the Arab countries in a state of feudal fragmentation, deprive each and every one of these countries of the prerequisites for an independent economic and political development, and block the national political unification of the Arab countries." The imperialists had achieved their ends with the support of reactionary monarchical cliques, feudal and semi-feudal landowners and shaykhs, native *bourgeois* compradores, and the

---

[24] The Armenian minority, numbering about 100,000 in Syria and 31,000 in Lebanon, were divided between the nationalist Tashnak Party which wished to see Armenia once more an independent nation-state and Communists who endorsed the incorporation of Armenia in the USSR and were eager to acquire Soviet citizenship. See A. H. Hourani, *Syria and Lebanon* (London, 1946), p. 121, 136.

higher clergy. Hence the striving of the Arab masses for national unification was inseparable from their endeavours to liberate themselves from the yoke of imperialism and its Arab collaborators. Secondly, the resolution dilated on the counter-revolutionary character of the Arab *bourgeoisie*. The *bourgeoisie* was incapable of leading the struggle against imperialism and tended to strike a deal with the latter "within the framework of limited pseudo-constitutional concessions". This was exemplified by the Syrian *Kutla* (National Bloc), which stoutly refused "to take part in any revolutionary activities, and in any real struggle". It was the task of the Communists to combat the national reformism of the *bourgeoisie*. Finally, the two Communist Parties stressed that any further development of the anti-imperialist struggle was "unthinkable" without a consistent and systematic effort on the part of the Communist Parties to carry out an agrarian peasant revolution leading to the establishment of a workers' and peasants' government. Towards that end, the resolution commended a united front of peasants, workers, and the small *bourgeoisie*, increased reliance on mass campaigns, and exchange of experience and co-ordination of work among the Arab Communist Parties.[25]

The 1931 resolution denoted an uneasy marriage between the *bourgeois* ideal of pan-Arabism and the stern thesis of the Sixth Comintern on the national *bourgeoisie*. In practice, however, the pan-Arab theme was not followed up; and the antagonistic attitude towards *bourgeois* nationalism was also abandoned at the outset of the Popular Front era.

The next decade was occupied by ideological education and organizational work. Fu'ad ash-Shimali, the trade union expert who led the party between 1928 and 1932, took keen interest in streamlining the party machine. Several new branches were opened. Tripoli, Beirut, and Damascus emerged as the chief centres of Communist activity. It was during this period that Khalid Bakdash, barely eighteen years old at that time, joined the party. The energetic, intelligent, and tenacious Kurd was soon to acquire a key position in the CPSL. The details of the inner party struggle for leadership during this period still remain obscure. But it is certain that in 1932 Bakdash took over from Fu'ad ash-Shimali the leadership of the party and rallied round him Rafiq Rida (a new

[25] Text of the Resolution in Spector, n. 11, pp. 75-82.

recruit), Artin Madoyan, Niqula Shawi,[26] and Farjallah Hilu.[27]

The early years of Bakdash's stewardship were somewhat un-eventful except for minor strikes of railwaymen and oil-refinery workers. In 1933 Bakdash published the first Arabic translation of the *Communist Manifesto*[28] and Stalin's thesis on the "Question of Nationalities". An ideological journal called *At-Tali'a* (The Vanguard) was started under the direction of a committee con-sisting of 'Umar Fakhuri, Yusuf Yazbak, and Qadri Qal'aji.[29] On the whole, however, the party's ideological bias for proletarian orientation had set strict limits to its appeal and political effective-ness. It held the leadership of the National Bloc (that bore the brunt of the struggle against the French rule) in contempt because it consisted of members of rich landowning families like Jamil Mardam Bey, Hashim al-Atasi, and Shukri al-Quwatli. Its anti-religious outbursts outraged the susceptibilities of the conservative sections of society.

Against this backdrop, the sudden ascendancy of the CPSL in the late thirties was nothing short of a miracle. This was made possible by significant political developments in France no less than by the resourcefulness and skill of the Communist leadership to seize the opportunities which offered themselves.

The advent to power of Léon Blum's Communist-backed Popular Front cabinet (with Yvon Delbos as Foreign Minister) in June 1936 brought about a marked improvement in the French attitude to the colonial question. The negotiation for a Franco-Syrian treaty, already under way in Paris, was spurred towards a fruitful consummation. The Communist Party of France gained official recognition and respectability which it quickly radiated to Com-munist organizations in French-administered territories.

Khalid Bakdash hailed the triumph of the Popular Front as "a victory of the Syrian people against imperialist assault and of the French people against Fascism". As the French administration in Syria and the Lebanon relaxed its hostility towards local Com-munists, the latter gave all-out support to the abortive Franco-

[26] Born in Tripoli in 1911, Niqula Shawi hailed from an affluent Greek orthodox family.

[27] Farjallah Hilu later became an important figure in the Communist Party of the Lebanon.

[28] It was reprinted in 1947 and 1955.

[29] Ayyub, n. 23, pp. 58-74.

2

Syrian Treaty. Bakdash declared that although the Treaty did not offer complete independence, it was destined to bring it nearer and that it inaugurated an epoch of freedom and created new opportunities for action and consolidation. He decried those who wanted "everything or nothing".[30]

The chief components of the party line in the Popular Front era were: maximum co-operation with France, mobilizing public opinion against the Fascist menace, and a broad national front resting on a moderate political and economic programme.

France was now projected by the CPSL as "the Democratic France", "the France of the Popular Front", "the France of 1879" and "the France of Liberty, Equality and Fraternity". To establish close liaison with the French Communist Party, Rafiq Rida, a member of the Central Committee, was dispatched to Paris, where he set up an office to promote joint endeavours by the two parties on matters of common interest to France on the one hand and to Syria and the Lebanon on the other.[31] At home, the CPSL created, in 1938, its first "front organization" called *Mu'tamar Mukafihat al-Fasistiya* (Anti-Fascist League) under the presidency of Antun Thabit.[32] The League was intended to rouse public opinion against the rising tide of Fascism in Europe and Fascist groups in the Arab East. Following the familiar methods of "front organizations", the League cast its net wide. Its first Congress held in Beirut in May 1939 was attended by some leading non-Communist personages. Shukri al-Quwatli and Nazim al-Qudsi sent messages of greetings.[33]

In the midst of these hectic activities the CPSL did not neglect the crucial task of expanding its base and influence in Syria and the Lebanon. Towards that end, the party put its revolutionary programme in cold storage and issued the catchy slogan: "Freedom and Bread"! The truce with the local authorities was utilized to carry the influence of the party to remote towns of Syria and the Lebanon. The party gained many sympathizers among the urban intelligentsia. On the trade union front too it acquired more

[30] Khalid Bakdash, *Fi-Sabil Hurriyat ash-Sha'b al-Wataniya wal Demoqratiya* (n. p. or d.), p. 32.

[31] Ayyub, n. 23, pp. 76-8.

[32] An engineer by profession, Antun Thabit soon became an important figure in the Communist Party.

[33] Laqueur, n. 4, p. 145.

followers. In May 1937, the party launched its own organ, *Sawt Ash-Sha'b* (Beirut), and even tried its hand, though unsuccessfully, at parliamentary elections. According to Laqueur the party membership rose, during 1936-39, from a bare 200 to the impressive figure of 2,000.[34]

Being the chief beneficiary of the "spirit" of the Popular Front, the Communists clung to it even when, after Blum's second fall in March 1938, it had all but faded out of existence. While nationalist opinion in Syria was deeply agitated over the non-ratification of the Treaty by the French Parliament and the surrender of the Syrian district of Alexandretta to Turkey, the Communists continued to harp on Franco-Arab amity and co-operation. It was not until after the outbreak of the war in Europe—when the French authorities eventually suppressed the *Sawt ash-Sha'b*[35] and rounded up Bakdash, Hilu, Rida and Mustafa al-'Aris—that the Communists buried the corpse of the Popular Front.

Iraq

Unlike the Arab lands of the Eastern Mediterranean, which were ceaselessly exposed to European political and intellectual influences, Iraq was relatively isolated, backward, and stagnant. When the British came to Iraq, first as a conquering power and later as a Mandatory, they saw political advantage in harnessing the collaboration of existing feudal and oligarchical elements which thus gained a fresh lease of life. Nor was there any urban middle class or intelligentsia to serve as a lever on the body politic. Hence, in the early years of the Mandate, Iraqi politics was confined to a small clique of notable personages whom the British manipulated according to their convenience.

These conditions were by no means conducive to the growth of modern party politics. Organized Communist activity in Iraq did not begin until 1934 when Yusuf Salman Yusuf, popularly known as "Fahd" (leopard), gathered together scattered Communist sympathizers and founded the Communist Party of Iraq. But no appreciable advance could be made until after the outbreak of the Second World War. It would, however, be pertinent to mention briefly the emergence of a parallel Leftist group in Iraq called Al-Ahali which formed the nucleus of the latter-day National

[34] Ibid., p. 142, 145.
[35] The last issue of *Sawt ash-Sha'b* having appeared on 25 September, 1939.

Democratic Party—the only non-Communist Leftist movement in the Arab East with which the Communists condescended to co-exist peacefully. The leading lights of the Ahali group were the Columbia-educated 'Abdul Fattah Ibrahim and the Laskiite Muhammad Hadid. They were soon joined by the India-born 'Abdul Qadir Isma'il, Kamil al-Chadirchi, and Ja'far Abu Timman. The ideology of the group converged on democratic socialism while allowing for a wide spectrum of individual preferences ranging from 'Abdul Qadir Isma'il's outspoken Marxism and Hadid's Fabianism to Abu Timman's radical liberalism. The group had a major hand in hatching the Bakr Sidqi *coup d'état* of 29 October, 1936, but the alliance fizzled out as soon as the army officers were securely established in power.[36]

---

[36] See Majid Khadduri, *Independent Iraq* (London, 1960), pp. 69-74.

CHAPTER TWO

EXPANSION AND CONSOLIDATION
1941-1945

THE interlude between the conclusion of the Nazi-Soviet Non-Aggression Pact and Hitler's assault on the Soviet Union in June 1941 was a time of excruciating embarrassment to Communist organizations in the Arab East. After the rise of Hitler in 1933 the Soviet Union had deemed it essential for its security to effect a *rapprochement* with the Western "*bourgeois* democracies". The new line, sanctified by the Seventh Congress of the Comintern held in August 1935, exhorted co-operation with anti-Fascist elements everywhere even though it might mean postponement of "the overthrow of capitalism" and of "the victory of the proletarian revolution". The Popular Front régimes in France and Spain were its immediate outcome. For the colonial world the counterpart of the Popular Front theme was the National Front which stipulated conciliation and co-operation with the national *bourgeoisie* and the local representatives of the metropolitan régimes. The adoption of this policy by the Arab Communists did not exactly enhance their prestige in the eyes of the so-called *bourgeois* nationalists who saw no reason to call a halt to the anti-colonial struggle. At the same time it helped the Communists to make common cause with those liberal elements which were genuinely perturbed by the growing influence of Fascist propaganda on the Arab masses. The new policy earned rich dividends for the Communists as long as it lasted. But the Communist *volte face*[1] following the Nazi-Soviet Pact, which Molotov defended in terms of power politics and national interests,[2] exposed them to the nationalist ridicule on the one hand and the wrath of the colonial administrations on the other. As a result, the Communists were sternly suppressed everywhere. Some of them carried on the resumed

---

[1] The Communist Party of Syria and the Lebanon was the sole exception to this. See below.

[2] See Molotov's speech before the Supreme Soviet on 31 August 1939. Text in Robert V. Daniels, ed., *A Documentary History of Communism* (New York, 1960), vol. 2, pp. 121-4.

anti-imperialist propaganda from their underground hide-outs. But, on the whole, they were relegated to the background until the march of Nazi divisions on Russia once again changed the perspective for the better.

Syria and the Lebanon

On the eve of the outbreak of the Second World War the Communist Party of Syria and the Lebanon was the strongest Communist organization in the Arab East. Its initial non-compliance with the Moscow line following the Nazi-Soviet Pact was perhaps indicative of the value attached by the party leadership to its own national position. Accordingly, the party organ, *Sawt ash-Sha'b*, continued its tirade against Fascism. The issue of 11 September, 1939 carried texts of telegrams from Khalid Bakdash, Rafiq Rida, Farjallah Hilu, and Niqula Shawi to the French High Commissioners pledging support to France and offering to join the French soldiers in the trenches. The French apparently had no use for these gratuitous offers and responded by banning the party as well as its journal.

Following the capitulation of France, in June 1940, Syria and the Lebanon came under the Vichy rule. After a period of uncertainty and confusion during which attempts were made by the Axis Powers to use the mandated territories as a stepping-stone to the conquest of West Asia, Allied and Free French troops crossed the frontiers of Syria and the Lebanon on 8 June, 1941. After a month-long campaign, the Vichy High Commissioner, General Dentz, surrendered. At the outset of the operations General Catroux, the Commander of the French contingent, proclaimed, with British concurrence, that the Allies intended to confer independence on Syria and the Lebanon. France's relations with the two states were, however, to be determined by a negotiated treaty. Accordingly, General Catroux proclaimed the independence of Syria and the Lebanon on 18 September and 26 November, 1941 respectively. But the nationalists in Syria and the Lebanon were disenchanted, if not thoroughly disillusioned, by the arbitrary appointment of the pro-French Shaykh Taj ad-Din al-Hasani as President of the Syrian Republic and Alfred Naccache as President of the Lebanese Republic. The French authorities evinced no desire yet to hold elections or to transfer power to Syrian and Lebanese Governments.

With the nationalists being sceptical of French intentions, Catroux saw in the CPSL the one political element which was willing to back the Allied war effort to the hilt. Besides General Charles de Gaulle had already arrived at an understanding with the French Communists to co-ordinate underground resistance in France. Russian involvement in the war removed whatever psychological obstacles still remained in the way of Franco-Communist co-operation in the Levant. Accordingly, Communist detenus were released and the party resumed its activities with renewed vigour without the usual governmental restrictions. The party organ, *Sawt ash-Sha'b*, resumed publication on 20 January, 1942. This was in addition to a new fortnightly called *At-Tariq* (Beirut), launched a month before, which soon grew into an influential ideological magazine.

But what really intrigued the nationalists was the Communist reticence on the pressing nationalist demand for transfer of power from the French Delegate-General (who also performed the functions of High Commissioner since the declaration of independence) to the elected representatives of Syria and the Lebanon. The Communists evaded facing the problem squarely but indirectly hinted that its solution should await the conclusion of the war. Bakdash wrote in the first issue of *Sawt ash-Sha'b* that "the greatest aim of mankind" was "to destroy the Nazis". Everything else, including the attainment of national independence, was ancillary to this supreme goal. It was, therefore, left to the nationalists to pressurize the French to concede the demand for representative rule.

But as soon as the French announced the decision, early in 1943, to hold elections in Syria and the Lebanon, the Communists girded up their loins to join the battle for parliamentary seats. The CPSL having decided to put up its own candidates in selected constituencies, Khalid Bakdash set out on an extensive tour to project the image of the party. Throughout the election campaign, Bakdash dwelt upon the need for national unity and liberal reforms. He pleaded that the party stood for national unity. "It is a national party in character, background and policies. It extends the hand of friendship to all sincere nationalists irrespective of their class, wealth, organization or affiliation." He urged that since there was no single party, in Syria or the Lebanon, representing all sections of the people, national unity could be forged only through co-operation between various political parties.[3]

The dissolution of the Comintern, "the directing centre of international working-class movement", in May 1943 came as a boon to the CPSL which lost no time in employing it to refute those who accused it of extra-territorial loyalties. But what really conferred the halo of respectability on the Communists was the victory of Soviet arms at Stalingrad rather than their own performance at home. Henceforth the influence of Axis propaganda registered a sharp decline in the Arab East and the Soviet image emerged burnished in the process. And Arab Communists were not lacking in initiative to reap the benefits of this favourable turn in the fortunes of war.

The party now revived, with added embellishment, the call for a broad-based national front. This was eloquently outlined by Khalid Bakdash in his May Day (1943) public speech:[4]

> The issue before us is not to establish socialism in Syria or Lebanon. All that we want, and for which our deputies in the Syrian and Lebanese parliaments will fight, is the introduction of certain democratic reforms of which everyone talks. All are agreed on the desirability of these reforms. We do not and will not demand, nor is it part of our programme, confiscation of national capital and industries. On the contrary, we want them to progress and prosper. All that we ask for is the amelioration of the conditions of workers and democratic labour legislation. ...We assure the landlords that we do not and will not ask for the confiscation of their estates and lands... On the contrary, we want to help them by proposing extensive irrigation plans, facilities for the import of fertilizers and introduction of modern implements. All that we ask for is leniency to the peasant, relief from poverty and ignorance, and spread of education and sanitation in the villages. We assure the traders that we will never ask for the confiscation of their business, however big it may be. We only demand facilities for mutual trade with the Arab and other neighbouring areas and restrictions on unlawful profits accruing

[3] S. Ayyub, *Al-Hizb ash-Shuyu'i fi Suriya wa Lubnan, 1922-1958* (Beirut, 1959), pp. 97-99.

[4] Khalid Bakdash, *Al-Hizb ash-Shuyu'i fi Suriya wa Lubnan. Siyasatihi al-Wataniya wa Barnamijihi al-Watani* (n. p. or d.), p. 30.

from atrocious monopolies or deprivation of the people. These are our economic and social aims and they are indeed very moderate and democratic. . . . Some people will shout that this is a trick ! But what trick? If it were a trick we would not talk about it openly before tens of thousands of witnesses!

What Bakdash offered was a mild programme of liberal reforms —a far cry from the Communist ideal of revolution!

All this, however, did not add up to electoral victories. The party had put up two candidates in Syria: Khalid Bakdash (Damascus) and ʻAbd al-Jalil Siris (Aleppo); and four in the Lebanon: Farjallah Hilu (Mount Lebanon), ʻUmar Fakhuri (Beirut), ʻAlamuddin (North Lebanon), and Mayar Masʻad (South Lebanon). All of them lost. But some of them mustered enough votes to show that the party's following was steadily on the increase.[5] The election also afforded it a priceless opportunity to approach the masses directly.

It was a measure of the buoyant, confident mood of the CPSL that it decided to hold the Second Party Congress[6] in the fall of 1943. The Congress met in Beirut from 31 December, 1943 to 2 January, 1944 and was attended by 180 delegates—representing 50 organizations and 7,000 members—from Homs, Aleppo, Marjaʻiyyun, Mount Lebanon, Beirut, Damascus, and Tripoli. Messages of greetings poured in from all and sundry. Several non-Communist writers, deputies and political leaders, including Deputy Premier Habib Abi Shahla, appeared at the Congress in person. In the words of *Swat ash-Shaʻb* this was the first public conference of the CPSL.

Historically, the Congress is noted for three major decisions: the bifurcation of the party into two autonomous units; adoption of a new charter; and framing of a new constitution governing the internal organization.

The decision to create autonomous party units for Syria and the Lebanon should be viewed against long-time controversy between the Arab nationalists in the two countries who emphasized

[5] Ayyub, n. 3, pp. 105-6. The elections were held in Syria in July and in the Lebanon in August 1943. Farjallah Hilu secured 9,060 votes, Bakdash and Fakhuri 1,050 and 2,046 respectively. In the second round, Bakdash polled 130 out of 830 votes.

[6] The First Congress was held in 1925.

the Lebanon's historical ties with Syria on the one side, and the Maronite Christians who stood for the continued existence of the Lebanon as an independent political entity on the other. The Communists had been on the side of the Arab nationalists in this debate which also explained the existence of a single Communist Party for both the countries. But this position had become manifestly untenable after the proclamation of Lebanese independence. Hence to avoid confusion and to facilitate smooth functioning of the organization the Second Party Congress decided to fraction the party into two. Bakdash publicly explained that the decision underlined the party's deference to national sentiment and was in line with the dissolution of the Comintern. The two parties set up their own central committees and adopted the flags and the national anthems of their respective states. It was, however, stipulated, that a joint committee of the two parties would continue to co-ordinate their work. Soon after, Bakdash was elected as chief of the Syrian unit and Farjallah Hilu that of the Lebanese unit.[7]

Next, the Congress adopted, almost in identical terms, a twenty-point national charter for Syria and a nineteen-point charter for the Lebanon comprising the respective party programmes. The two charters pledged, *inter alia*, (i) complete national independence and sovereignty; (ii) solidarity with the Arab countries; (iii) national control over alien financial, industrial, and commercial concerns; (iv) nationalization of schools and introduction of free and compulsory primary education; (v) free medical aid; (vi) eradication of poverty and illiteracy and raising of the status of women; (vii) protection of small producers; (viii) protection of workers and promotion of better relations between workers and employers on the basis of justice and national interest; (ix) emancipation of peasants from backwardness, poverty, and ignorance; and (x) equitable distribution of tax-burden and relief to small traders and producers.[8]

But for the new emphasis on national independence and the need to control foreign enterprises the charters only confirmed the early

[7] See Ayyub, n. 3, pp. 116-8; Walter Z. Laqueur, *Communism and Nationalism in the Middle East* (London, 1957), p. 148; and Muhammad 'Ali Zarqa and Ilyas Marqas, *Khiyana Khalid Bakdash l'il Qawmiya al-'Arabiya* (Damascus, 1959), pp. 53-54.

[8] Texts of the two charters in Ayyub, n. 3, pp. 118-20.

party line adopted in the course of the election campaign. Bakdash proudly claimed that it was not a party charter; it belonged to the entire nation. It did not even formally mention the word socialism. Bakdash's explanation was that the immediate task before Syria and the Lebanon was to attain full political and economic sove-reignty and to rid themselves of the vestiges of the Middle Ages. Only then could they look forward to "the next higher stages of development". Those who talked of attaining socialism at this stage were mere "left-sectarians", declared Bakdash.[9]

Thirdly, the Congress adopted a new constitution which laid down definite rules concerning the internal organization of the party. Rules governing recruitment were liberalized. Anyone who accepted the national charter, belonged to some organization of the party, and rendered it material help according to his capacity was entitled to membership. The principle of "democratic cen-tralism" was affirmed. Decisions taken by the high command would be binding on all members. At the top of the party hierarchy stood the *Lajnat al-Markaziya* (Central Committee), which directed the day-to-day work of the party with the help of its executive organ called *Maktab ar-Riyasa* (Presidium). The Central Committee itself was elected by the *Mu'tmar al-Hizb* (Party Congress) re-presenting all the regional committees of the party and to be convened, ordinarily, every two years. Party members belonging to a locality or village formed the *Firqa* (unit); and a grouping of several units in a certain area was called *Lajnat al-Mantiqa* (Regional Committee). Internal constitutional arrangements, like the charters, were identical for the two wings of the party.[10] Though outwardly the new constitution marked a step towards democratization of party life nothing much could be gained in actual practice. No party congress has been held since then, and Bakdash's opponents ascribe this to his autocratic temperament.

While the Communists tried to come closer to the nationalists on most of the political and economic issues they continued to strike a discordant note on the question of French presence in Syria and the Lebanon. The newly installed national governments in Damascus and Beirut appeared determined to take the French declaration of independence of the two countries at its face value

[9] Khaled Bakdache, *La Charte Nationale du Parti Communiste en Syrie et au Liban* (Beyrouth, 1944), pp. 16 and 43.

[10] Ayyub, n. 3, pp. 125-7.

and insisted upon actual transfer of power. The representatives of the *Comité Francais de la Libération Nationale* in the area, who claimed to have inherited the Mandate from the Third French Republic and who were keen to salvage French political and economic interests therein, argued, on the other hand, that this could be done only after the war and conclusion of a negotiated treaty.

The dispute over transfer of power came to a head in December 1943, when the French authorities arrested the Lebanese President Bishara al-Khuri and Premier Riad as-Sulh. The Communists held the view that it was impolitic on the part of the nationalists to have precipitated the crisis and that preservation of the link with France had its advantages. Farjallah Hilu wrote in the *Sawt ash-Sha'b* of 15 December:

> We believed and still believe that the Lebanese people do not want to weaken their links with the French people.... France will not be the same after war...and every far-sighted patriot can see that Lebanon's interest lies in going closer to France not away from it, in strengthening friendship with it not weakening it.

From the *Labour Monthly* came the rejoinder that by refusing to negotiate with the Free French the Lebanese leaders "have placed themselves in the position of being used as a lever against the representatives of the great traditional friend and ally of the Syrians and the Lebanese, the French people, now in the vanguard of the fight for national freedom".[11]

At the Second Party Congress Khalid Bakdash tried to rebut the charge that the Communists were taking a conciliatory position *vis-à-vis* the French but nevertheless emphasized the need for "an *entente* with the French people" in order to destroy Fascism and open the way for independence.[12] The mounting popular uproar against the French in the ensuing months, however, compelled the Communists to fall in line gradually with the nationalists. In July 1944, Khalid Bakdash demanded "purging" of the French administration in Syria and the Lebanon of "Fascist elements who ignore our rights and think that Syria and Lebanon must remain a market

---

[11] I. Rennap, "The Middle East", *Labour Monthly* (London), vol. 26 (January 1944), p. 27.

[12] Bakdache, n. 9, pp. 26-27.

of concessions, jobs, plunder and authoritarian rule". And after the French launched an armed offensive against the nationalists in Syria on 29 May, 1945, Farjallah Hilu wrote a cutting editorial in the *Sawt ash-Sha'b* captioned: "Down with Imperialist Barbarism". Thereafter the Communists unreservedly joined the campaign against the French and sustained it until French evacuation was achieved in April 1946. This change in Communist attitude coupled with Soviet diplomatic support to the cause of Syrian and Lebanese independence helped the party wipe off the stigma of collaboration with the colonial Power.

The war period was most propitious for the Communists in Syria and the Lebanon. Absence of restriction on party activity, benevolence of the French administration, the electrifying psychological impact of Soviet victories, and the sprouting of a talented party leadership—all these combined to enhance Communist power and influence. In July 1944 Farjallah Hilu claimed that the party was gaining 150 members a day.[13] Niqula Shawi informed the British Party Congress in November 1945 that the membership of the Syrian Communist Party had risen from 1,000 in 1941 to 10,000 in 1945 and that of the Lebanese Communist Party from 1,500 to 15,000 during the same period.[14] These claims were perhaps exaggerated but not far removed from the actual Communist gains.

Palestine

The war period in Palestine was marked by an uneasy truce between the Arabs and the Jews. The Arabs welcomed the respite afforded by the White Paper of 1939; the Jews caught between the devil of Fascism in Europe and the deep sea of Arab hostility nearer home had no option but to support the British war effort. The Palestinian Communists, though weak and ineffectual, adopted a different course. Considerations of loyalty to the Soviet Union, which had made peace with Hitler, demanded that the struggle against the British imperialists should not relax. As late as March 1941 the CPP's Hebrew organ *Kol Haam* (Voice of the People) wrote:[15]

[13] Farjallah Hilu, *Al-Islah ad-Dakhili wa Matalib ash-Sha'b* (Matabi' al-Kashshaf, n.p., 1944), p. 33.

[14] Text of Shawi's address in *Labour Monthly*, vol. 28 (February 1946), pp. 56-57.

[15] Al-Hakm Darwaza, *Ash-Shuyu'iya al-Mahliya wa Ma'arkat al-'Arab al-Qawmiya* (Beirut, 1963), pp. 279-80.

The workers ask us: "What should we do?" They ask for sincere advice. We tell them: "Well, it is true that the German and Italian armies are at the door-step. But it is also true that the armies of Churchill are already in our country. It is only proper that we fight the enemy within first."

It was not until the fall of 1941 that the CPP completely modified its attitude towards the British and called for an anti-Fascist front "from Tobrak to Leningrad". In return, the British released the party chief Musa, his Jewish deputy Samuel Mikunis, and other Communist leaders. Henceforth the party busied itself with what everyone else in Palestine was engaged in: to close the ranks to mobilize public support and to get ready for the final reckoning which the war had only served to postpone to a later date.

Communist efforts to bring together the Arabs and the Jews under a single organization having failed by and large, the only practical course open to the party was to admit failure and to separate the Arab and Jewish cadres into two distinct parties. This was at last effected in 1943, when the Arab Communists formed their own party called *Asbat al-Taharrur al-Watani* (League for National Liberation [LNL].) Emile Tuma, an Arab Christian, assumed the leadership of the LNL and Samuel Mikunis that of the CPP. While *Kol Haam* continued as the organ of the CPP, the LNL started its own Arabic journal called *Al-Ittihad*. As a Palestinian Arab Communist later put it, the separation was merely "a matter of tactics".[16] For the two parties continued joint consultations and planning. At the same time it is true that, henceforth, the leaders of the two parties irresistibly tended to cater to the mutually irreconcilable national sentiments of their respective communities. This process led the CPP to announce, in April 1945, that it would join the *Histadrut* to demand abrogation of the White Paper which restricted Jewish immigration and acquisition of agricultural lands.[17] The LNL, on the other hand, drew closer to the Arab Higher Committee in opposing Zionism tooth and nail though the two still differed on the issue of status of the existing Jewish community in Palestine. The Arab Communists

[16] Fathi Salim Sharab, *Ana w'ash Shuyu'iya* (Beirut, 1956), pp. 77-78.

[17] US Congress, House Committee on Foreign Affairs, *Strategy and Tactics of World Communism: Report of Sub-Committee No. 5* (Washington, D.C., 1949), p. 24.

were in favour of granting Palestinian citizenship to all the Jews
who had immigrated into the country, the Arab Higher Committee
insisted upon restricting it to only those Jews who were in Palestine
in 1918.[18]

The exigencies of the war-time British administration in Palestine
and the creation of the LNL cleared the way for the Communists
to acquire a foothold in the Arab community. The Communist
advance was most conspicuous on the trade union front. The
spurt of government-sponsored undertakings as a result of the
war and its concomitant emergency needs had swelled the size
of the Arab labour force to 35,000 by 1942. Mounting costs of
living and the deep undercurrent of political tension soon generated
labour unrest. As a precautionary measure the administration had
already sponsored the Right-wing *Jami'at al-'Ummal al-'Arabiya
al Falastiniya* (Palestine Arab Workers Society) headed by
Sami Taha, whom the Communists had dubbed as "a Right-wing
reactionary and an agent of the imperialists". The Jaffa and Jerusalem branches of the Palestine Arab Workers Society (PAWC),
however, fell under Communist influence. Towards the end of
1942 the Communists formed a rival Federation of Arab Trade
Union and Labour Societies which initially commanded the allegiance of some 31,000 workers mostly belonging to the oil industry,
naval workshops, and Haifa transport. Its influence increased
rapidly until the Gaza branch of the Federation, created in 1943,
alone acquired a following of 5,000 workers. In August 1945,
the Communist-dominated branches of the PAWC merged with the
Federation to form the *Mu'tamar al-'Ummal al-'Arab* (Arab Workers
Congress). The 30,000 strong Congress functioned as the labour
wing of the LNL and played an active rôle in the World Trade
Union Congress.[19] In the words of Laqueur, the LNL itself emerged
as "the only real Arab party in the modern sense, the others being
mere pressure groups of the leading families".[20]

Egypt

The war period saw the rebirth of the Communist movement in
Egypt. Lacouture has described the 1919-24 phase of Communist

[18] Laqueur, n. 7, p. 112.
[19] Sharab, n. 16, pp. 21-23; and J. C. Hurewitz, *The Struggle for Palestine*
(New York, 1950), pp. 121-2, 188-9, and 234.
[20] Laqueur, n. 7, p. 112.

activity in Egypt as "the pre-historic period" which had nothing in common with the next phase except the label.[21] The latter started in the wake of Hitler's invasion of Russia and gathered momentum after the Battle of Stalingrad.

Developments during the war proved disastrous for the prestige of all the three parties which together constituted Egypt's perennial power-triangle: the Wafd, the King, and the British. The Wafd lost its patriotic lustre because it seized power (in February 1942) with the backing of British bayonets; the King lost his face because he succumbed to British blackmail; and the British lost whatever little trust the Egyptian still reposed in them because their action demonstrated that the independence conferred by the Treaty of 1936 was mere sham. This all-round corrosion of the moral authority of the Egyptian Establishment was turned to account by extremist elements.

On the extreme right Hasan al-Banna's Muslim Brothers and Ahmad Husayn's Fascist-leaning *Misr al-Fatat* (Young Egypt)[22] considerably enhanced their influence. At the other end of the political spectrum a number of Marxist study circles sprang up in Cairo and Alexandria during 1941-42. Following this, the intrinsic non-conformism of the Egyptian Communists came into full play, and the study circles got split into a number of disjointed fragments. The more notable among these were (i) *Mouvement Egyptien de Libération Nationale* (MELN), established in 1942 by Henri Curiel, a bookseller and scion of a millionaire Jewish family; (ii) *Iskra*, also founded in 1942 by another Jew called Hillel Shwartz; (iii) *Tahrir ash-Sha'b* (People's Liberation), founded in 1943 by a dissident faction of the MELN; and *At-Tali'a* (The Vanguard), founded by a group of young Wafdist students and intellectuals. Three more groups appeared on the scene after 1943; the Marxist League, the *Citadelle* and *Al-Fajr al-Jadid* (The New Dawn).[23]

Barring MELN, none of these groups possessed any great following. But that did not deter them from quarrelling fiercely; and they got further divided over the question of the relative significance of the proletariat and the intelligentsia in Communist organizations. The preponderance of non-Arab minorities continued unabated. Curiel's MELN which stood for the "Egyptianiza-

[21] Jean and Simonne Lacouture, *Egypt in Transition* (London, 1958), pp. 257-8.
[22] The party changed its name to Islamic Nationalist Party in 1940.
[23] Laqueur, n. 7, pp. 42-43.

tion" of the party emerged as "the most dynamic branch of the left" and counted about a thousand trained followers.[24]

Unlike the Rightist detractors of the Wafd, the Communists hailed the installation of Mustafa Nahas into office by the British. A British Communist interpreted it as "a great victory for the progressive forces in Egypt and a defeat for the Axis Powers".[25] In the ensuing years the Communists were able to penetrate into government offices, newspaper bureaux, the Wafd, and, above all, the trade unions. In 1942 the Wafdist Government passed a Trade Union Law which gave trade unionism a legal basis. The new law, however, contained certain reservations which were frowned upon by the Communists. It did not allow peasants to form trade unions nor was an individual union permitted to join others in a common federation. The Communists concentrated on textile workers in the industrial centres of Mahalla al-Kubra, Shubra al-Khayma and Alexandria. According to one Communist writer the number of trade unions rose, by 1944, to 210 with a membership of 104,000.[26]

Iraq

Fahd's return to Iraq, after having spent, reportedly, two years in the Soviet Union, set the stage for the reorganization of the Communist Party of Iraq (CPI). He took over from Zaki Khayri and Sharif ash-Shaykh and set up a regular central committee consisting mostly of newcomers such as Zaki Basim, Husayn Muhammad ash-Shabibi, 'Abid T'amir, Malik Sayf, Mulla Sharif, Krikor Badrossian, and Sami Nadir. The organization, which had remained secret ever since its inception, started a clandestine newspaper called *Ash-Sharara*. The appearance of the domineering Fahd at the helm of party affairs, however, induced disgruntled members of the oldguard to sponsor rival Communist groups. Abdullah Mas'ud and Da'ud as-Sayigh formed the Iraqi Communist League. Another anti-Fahd splinter was headed by Zaki Khayri and Sharif ash-Shaykh.

It is significant that the Charter adopted by the first Party Congress convened by Fahd in 1945, evinced unmixed hostility

[24] Jean and Simonne Lacouture, n. 21, p. 259.

[25] I. Rennap in *World News and Views* (London), 21 February 1942, p. 123.

[26] Shuhdi 'Atiya ash-Shafi'i, *Tatawwur al-Harkah al-Wataniya al-Misriya, 1882-1956* (Cairo, 1957), p. 86.

3

towards the *bourgeois* nationalists and lauded the virtue of proletarian orientation.[27] Its political extremism was perhaps not entirely
unrelated to the conditions of extreme repression under which it
functioned. Even the Sidqi-Sulayman régime, which had initially
enjoyed the backing of the radical Ahali group, shared the hostility
of its predecessors towards the Communists. In 1938 the Iraqi
Parliament had passed legislation outlawing Communism and
prescribing stringent penalties for its votaries. Article 89A of the
Penal Code read as follows:[28]

(*i*) Whoever expresses approval of or disseminates by any of
the means of publication mentioned in Article 78 of this
law, any of the Doctrines of Bolshevik Socialism (Communism), anarchy or the like, which aim at a change in
the system of government and the fundamental principles
and status of society that are guaranteed by the Organic
Law, shall be punished with penal servitude or with imprisonment not exceeding seven years or with fine or with both.

(*ii*) If the expression of approval or the dissemination of the
said doctrines mentioned in paragraph (i) is carried out with
violence or by threat to use violence or by any other illegal
means, the penalty shall be penal servitude for life or imprisonment not exceeding fifteen years.

(*iii*) If the aforesaid expression of approval or dissemination
of the said doctrines takes place before more than one member
of the armed forces or the police, the offenders shall be
punished with death or with penal servitude for life or with
imprisonment not exceeding fifteen years.

This extraordinary law was patently out of all proportion to
the strength or influence of the Iraqi Communists. But it undoubtedly
armed the government to deal with all its opponents whether
Communist, nationalist, or democratic.

However, the real contest in Iraq at that time was not between
the Communists and non-Communists. Rather Iraq was deeply
divided between Pan-Arab nationalists who wanted to disentangle
Iraq from British influence, and moderates who wanted to work
with Britain within the limits of the Anglo-Iraqi Treaty of 1930.

[27] Laqueur, n. 7, pp. 183-8.
[28] US Congress, House Committee on Foreign Affairs, n. 17, p. 14.

After the outbreak of the war the Pan-Arabists, headed by Rashid 'Ali al-Gaylani, pleaded to the utter discomfiture of the British, for Iraqi neutrality *vis-à-vis* the belligerent Powers. Early in April 1941 Gaylani seized power with the help of the Army. The British denounced him as an agent of the Nazis and after a month-long war brought about his downfall.

It must be noted that Gaylani and his group saw in the Axis Powers a welcome counterweight to British and French presence in the Arab East and were keen to take advantage of it. At the same time Gaylani was no more a Nazi agent than Nasser is a Soviet agent.

The Communists were in full sympathy with Gaylani's revolt. This was in full accord with the Comintern line. Besides, the Soviet Union was one of the few foreign states which accorded diplomatic recognition to the new régime. Gaylani's downfall was quickly followed by Russia's involvement in the war which induced the Communists to offer full co-operation to the British. This gave the Iraqi Communists one of their rare respites from relentless repression. And they utilized this opportunity to cultivate their influence among students, workers, and intellectuals. As the influence of Fascist propaganda on the Iraqi youth began to wear thin in the wake of Soviet victories, the Communists made a big thrust on the student front. The CPI also stepped up its trade union activities and acquired considerable influence on Basra dock workers, Baghdad tobacco workers, and Kirkuk oil workers and railroad workers. The new cadres, trained and indoctrinated during the war period, proved to be of immense value to the party in the course of the stormy decade that lay before it.

CHAPTER THREE

COMMUNISTS AND THE PARTITION OF PALESTINE

THE closing of the war in Europe once again brought the Palestine question to the fore. The basic issues in Palestine had remained unchanged; but not so the international situation. Hitler's abominable crimes against the Jews in Europe had outraged the conscience of the civilized world. Such Jews as had survived the nightmare were eager to leave the continent so that they might start life afresh in less inhospitable lands. One of the alternatives was Palestine. But as President Harry S. Truman's special envoy, Earl Harrison, discovered it after an on-the-spot investigation, most of the Jewish refugees opted for Palestine because the "opportunity to be admitted into the United States or into other countries in the Western Hemisphere is limited".[1] Another significant change was that, in the course of the war, the centre of the international Zionist movement had shifted from England to the United States which housed the largest—and financially and politically the most influential —concentration of Jewish population in the world.[2] Add to this the new international balance of power in which the United States outweighed all other Western Powers and it becomes evident that the power of final decision on Palestine had shifted from London to Washington. The US Government was determined to exercise this power in a manner satisfactory to the American Jews. The American drive was greatly reinforced by the last-minute shift in Soviet policy favouring the creation of Israel. After the tortuous motions of investigation by the Anglo-American Committee and the United Nations and an acrimonious debate in the General Assembly, Palestine was eventually partitioned and the Zionist dream of a Jewish state realized.

This new situation confronted the Communists in Palestine and the neighbouring Arab countries with a most formidable challenge. How did they respond to it?

[1] See M. S. Agwani, *The United States and the Arab World, 1945-1952* (Aligarh, 1955), p. 63.
[2] About 5 million.

Prelude to Partition

As the drama in Palestine drew close to the last scene the Communists encountered increasing internal squabbles. The splitting of Arab and Jewish Communists into autonomous parties has already been noted. In addition, there emerged a Jewish Marxist group called the Palestine Communist Union (PCU). An older radical Left-wing group known as *Hashomer Hatzair* (Young Guard) also gained considerable strength mostly at the expense of the orthodox CPP. This last group which came closest to subscribing to the basic Zionist demand for a Jewish state claimed a following of 10,000.[3] It functioned independently and openly defied the Comintern line on Zionism and other international problems. The PCU stood for a bi-national solution of the Palestine problem. It commanded a membership of 900 and many more sympathizers.[4] As for the two principal Communist organizations, the CPP and the LNL, although the original parting of the ways had been interpreted as a tactical move, the two parties tended to drift apart in actual practice. Outwardly they still subscribed to Arab-Jewish co-operation, unity of Palestine, and emancipation from the British. But underneath the surface, the LNL moved closer to the Arab standpoint on the future of Palestine, and CPP became distinctly assertive on Jewish rights. This ambivalence, though ideologically untenable, helped the Arab and Jewish Communists keep their respective communities in a tolerant frame of mind and even gain in strength. By 1946 the CPP and LNL wielded considerably more influence than their hard core membership (1,500 and 1,000 respectively) would suggest. In particular, the LNL had succeeded in entering more areas. It formed a new organization called the Arab Writers Circle (*Ar-Rabita al-Muthaqqafin*) with headquarters in Jerusalem. It started a literary journal called *Al-Ghad* (Tomorrow). This together with the Arab Workers Congress became the principal front organizations of the LNL.[5]

The growing difference of opinion among the Communists on

[3] US Congress, House Committee on Foreign Affairs, *Strategy and Tactics of World Communism: Report of Sub-Committee No. 5* (Washington, D. C., 1949), p. 27.

[4] United Nations General Assembly, *Official Records*, (*GAOR*), session 2, supplement 11, vol. 3, Annex A, *Oral Evidence Presented at Public Meetings to the UNSCOP*, p. 239.

[5] Ibid., p. 39.

the Arab-Jewish problem was reflected in their varying attitudes towards the United Nations Special Committee on Palestine (UNSCOP). Whereas the CPP and the PCU, the two Jewish Communist groups, appeared before the UNSCOP to present their respective views, the League of National Liberation refused to do so in deference to the Arab Higher Committee's decision on a policy of non-co-operation.[6] Deposing on behalf of the CPP, the Party Secretary, Samuel Mikunis, confined himself to generalities:[7]

> Put an end to the Mandate, evacuate the British troops, proclaim the independence of Palestine and the two peoples of our country will unite and work together for the realization of a prosperous Arab-Jewish democratic state.

His co-deposer, Meir Vilner, underlined the party's position of equidistance between the Arab Higher Committee and the Jewish Agency. He assailed the Jewish Agency for its demand for a Jewish state and the Arab Higher Committee for its clamour for an exclusively Arab Palestine. It was, however, in the course of cross-examination that Mikunis revealed his party's position on the crucial issue of continued Jewish immigration into Palestine. He took the line that the Jewish refugees abroad should be helped by the United Nations to emigrate to Palestine and other countries "on the basis of relatives, because there are many Jews who have relatives in Palestine".[8]

Preminger, who appeared on behalf of the Palestine Communist Union, advanced a proposal which was even more accommodating to the Zionists. He contended that the need of the hour was "a political settlement that would safeguard both peoples against the danger of domination and will solve the problem of majority and minority—and will certainly also guarantee the right of the Jews to immigrate". Towards that end he proposed recognition of (i) the existence of two nations in Palestine; (ii) the right of both peoples to national self-determination "up to secession"; (iii) political equality between the two nations on the basis of parity in matters of representation, etc.; and (iv) the Jewish right to

[6] J. C. Hurewitz, *The Struggle for Palestine* (New York, 1950), p. 293.
[7] *GAOR*, n. 4, pp. 149-50.
[8] Ibid., pp. 156 and 160.

immigration provided it did not "strike at the right of the existing population of Palestine".[9]

Partition and After

In short, whereas the Jewish Communists were prepared to offer varying degrees of concessions to the Zionists and the Arab Communists to the Higher Committee, none subscribed to the principle of partition. The precipitous decision of the Soviet Union to back up partition, therefore, had a stunning effect on the Palestinian Communists, particularly the CPP and the League.

The first indication of change in Soviet policy was made by A. Gromyko before the Special Session of the UN General Assembly on 14 May, 1947, when he proclaimed that it would be "unjust" not to take the sufferings of the European Jews into consideration and deny them the right to realize their aspiration to establish "their own state". He then qualified the statement by adding that an independent Arab-Jewish state with equal rights for the Jews and the Arabs would be the best solution; but if that proved impossible "it would be necessary to consider" partition. These proposals were further circumscribed by Gromyko's initial observation that it was "apparently difficult to take any definite and, still more, any final decision on the substance of the problem at that preliminary stage".[10] Even so, the drastic change in Soviet attitude —from denouncing Zionism as an "imperialist conspiracy" to conceding its basic claim—gave a severe jolt not only to the Palestinian Communists but to all the Arabs. That the Communists still toed the "independent, democratic, Arab-Jewish state" line was perhaps due to ignorance of the fact that the Soviet Union had taken a definite and final decision. This was at last confirmed on 13 October, 1947, when the Soviet spokesman, Tsarapkin, unequivocally endorsed the partition plan which "under the present circumstances . . . could be better put into practice" than the minority scheme.[11] On 26 November, Gromyko went a step further and decried Arab criticism of the Soviet stand as being inadmissible:[12]

[9] Ibid., pp. 234-7.
[10] GAOR, special session 1, vol. 1, pp. 128, 132 and 134.
[11] Quoted in Hurewitz, n. 6, p. 305.
[12] GAOR, session 2, plen. mtg. 125, vol. 2, p. 1360.

The representatives of the Arab States claim that the partition of Palestine would be an historic injustice. But this view of the case is unacceptable, if only because, after all, the Jewish people have been closely linked with Palestine for a considerable period in history.

Whatever the reasons for the Soviet somersault, it was no easy task even for the most ingenious among the Communists to sustain it ideologically. But once the Soviet Union had stated its position in unmistakable terms, the Communists had no option but to make readjustments. The Jewish Communists accomplished it adroitly. Samuel Mikunis declared that the Soviet stand in the UN "inspired" the peoples of Palestine in their struggle and strengthened their confidence in victory. He also came forward with a new thesis which viewed Arab politics in Palestine in terms of a struggle between the "feudal-*bourgeois* circles" allied to the Anglo-American imperialists and the "industrial *bourgeoisie*" who wanted Arab Palestine's merger with Transjordan. Either side went counter to the interests of an independent Arab state in Palestine.[13] But the Arab Communists had an immensely difficult time explaining to their followers the reasons underlying the Soviet posture. Among the arguments advanced were that the provision for economic links between the proposed Arab and Jewish states would heal the effects of political division and that Israel was bound to be a "socialist paradise" which would inevitably influence its Arab partner.[14] But these idle visions carried little conviction to a people drawn into the vortex of large-scale hostilities which commenced immediately after the UN decision on partition.

The Communists emerged from this final act of the Palestinian tragedy severely bruised and battered, morally as well as politically. There was acute confusion in the Communist ranks. The Jewish Communists hastened to expiate for their past hostility to Zionism by joining up in the Israeli "defensive war".[15] On the Arab side, there was a rift in the LNL leadership. Those who rejected the

[13] S. Mikunis, "The Peoples of Palestine Struggle for National Independence", *For a Lasting Peace, For a People's Democracy* (Bucharest), 15 April 1947.

[14] Fathi Salim Sharab, *Ana w'ash Shuyu'iya* (Beirut, 1956), pp. 81-82.

[15] Walter Z. Laqueur, *Communism and Nationalism in the Middle East* (London, 1957), p. 113.

Soviet line on Palestine—among them Emile Tuma and Musa Dajani—plunged into the Arab "preventive war" against Israel. But most of the Arab Communist leaders who had quietly swallowed the Soviet line on partition stayed on in Israel and joined the CPP which was renamed the Communist Party of Israel. These leaders included Emile Habibi, Hasan Abu 'Isha, and' Awdat al-Ashhab.

Communism, Arab Nationalism, and Zionism

The Soviet support for partition and its mechanical endorsement by the Communists produced reactions which were not confined to Palestine. In fact, the Palestine question had, from its very beginning, been a live issue in the politics of almost all the Arab Eastern countries—an issue on which any political party could ill afford to take a non-commital attitude. This presented no serious difficulty to the Communists. For as early as 1920 the Second Congress of the Comintern had written off Zionism as a retrograde idea inspired by reactionaries and imperialists. To the extent this posture brought the Arab Communists in direct conflict with Jewish nationalism it served to conciliate Arab nationalism. But Communist somersaults consequent upon the shift in Soviet policy in the fall of 1947—and again in 1955—could not but evoke deep distrust of their motives in the Arab world.

The reactions of the non-Palestinian Arab Communists to the Arab-Jewish problem followed a fixed pattern. In the period preceding the UN decision on partition they adopted a sophisticated anti-Zionist line which clearly distinguished between the Jews who had been living in the Arab world for long without posing any problem and Zionists who were merely a "tool" in the hands of world capitalism and deserved to be firmly fought against. Partly because of this and partly because of the disproportionately high ratio of Jews in the Arab Eastern Communist parties the anti-Zionism of the Arab Communists did not deviate into anti-Judaism. The Communists also tried to activize local Jews against Zionism though without any spectacular results. The Iraqi Communist Party even organized an anti-Zionist League in 1946. These postures also helped the Communists generally to keep on the right side of the anti-Zionist Arab forces.

Having elaborately and advantageously developed this line over some decades, the shift in Soviet policy in 1947 spelled an unparalleled set-back for the Arab Communists. That the Soviet

Union had not thought it worth while to confide its intention to the Arab Communists made the latter's position preposterous as well. As a result, the Communists failed to realize the import of hints dropped by Gromyko in the UN General Assembly about partition being one of the likely solutions of the Palestine problem. Almost on the eve of UN decision a joint statement of the Communist Parties of Syria and the Lebanon made the fanciful claim that "all forces of freedom in the world today, led by the great Soviet Union, stand on our side on the issue of Palestine".[16] When the Soviet Union cast its vote for the creation of Israel, violent anti-Communist demonstrations occurred in various parts of the Arab East. In Aleppo and Damascus the Communist Party offices were ransacked by frenzied mobs. In some places, Soviet diplomatic missions were also attacked. In the Lebanon, the authorities closed down the *Sawt ash-Sha'b*. Iraq perhaps offered the only example of a Communist-organized demonstration in favour of the partition resolution.

The Communists did not play any significant role in the pandemonium that accompanied the birth of Israel in May 1948. Arab armies marched into Palestine to forestall the implementation of the UN resolution and an Arab-Jewish war ensued. While fighting was going on, the Communists confined themselves to denouncing it through posters, handbills, and clandestine publications. The Communist Party of Iraq announced that it was the duty of every "Arab democrat" to oppose the "dirty war" in Palestine and to co-operate with "the democratic forces" in Israel to prevent it. The Communist Parties of Syria and the Lebanon blamed the imperialists for plotting the Arab-Israeli war in order to prevent the creation of an independent Arab state in the Arab sector of Palestine and to facilitate its annexation to 'Abdullah's Trans-Jordan. The Egyptian *Mouvement Démocratique du Libération Nationale* (MDLN) maintained that the war was being waged by the "imperialists" and their "sordid agents" and that it could not "but harm the interests of the people and their liberation movements".[17] These propaganda gimmiks made little difference

---

[16] S. Ayyub, *Al-Hizb ash-Shuyu'i fi Suriya wa Lubnan, 1922-58* (Beirut, 1959), p. 162.

[17] The MDLN was formed in 1947 by merging the MELN and *Iskra*. Some of the non-Jewish members of the new party, however, openly defied the Soviet support for partition.

to the outcome of the Palestine war. But the rich evidence left behind by the Arab Communists on this subject offered plenty of ammunition to their adversaries who have turned it to account.[18]

The Arab Communists persisted in upholding the validity of the Soviet stand on Palestine until expediency and self-interest compelled the Soviet Union itself to abandon that claim. This came about in 1955 in the wake of the Baghdad Pact which induced the Soviet Union to write off Israel and draw closer to the Arab neutralists. The Arab Communists, then, quickly switched to the new Soviet line.

---

[18] See Al-Hakm Darwaza *Ash-Shuyu'iya al-Mahliya wa Ma'arkat al-'Arab al-Qawmiya* (Beirut, 1963), pp. 317-30.

CHAPTER FOUR

STRUGGLE FOR POWER IN EGYPT
1945-56

NOTWITHSTANDING its endemic factionalism the Communist movement profited greatly from the post-war conditions in Egypt. In the course of the war the labour force in Egypt had expanded considerably. The Anglo-American armed forces alone employed some 300,000 workers.[1] The termination of hostilities presented them with the grim prospect of unemployment. It also brought to the fore the subdued tensions and frustrations generated by the socio-economic disruptions and political abrasions of the war period. In short, Egypt was seething with political unrest bordering on hysteria. The situation in Egypt was reminiscent of 1919. But there was one important difference. In 1919 the leadership was in the hands of a small upper middle class of professional groups and the newly awakened *bourgeoisie*. By 1945 the initiative had passed to the progeny of the 1919 Revolution—the pauperized lower middle class and the rootless industrial proletariat. The battle-cry of the new leadership was the total evacuation of British forces from Egyptian soil and the unification of the Nile valley.

The 1946 Clash

The Egyptian Communists entered the fray with great vigour and soon entrenched themselves on the trade union and students' front. On the eve of the first conference of the World Federation of Trade Unions held in Paris in September 1945, the MELN and *Iskra* together formed a Congress of Workers' Unions. It claimed to represent the bulk of the Egyptian labour organized in 465 unions with a membership of 115,000.[2] On their return from Paris the Egyptian trade union leaders established contacts with students and formed a National Committee of Workers and Students headed by Mustafa Musa, who later entered the Egyptian

[1] US Congress, House Committee on Foreign Affairs, *Strategy and Tactics of World Communism: Report of Sub-Committee No. 5* (Washington, D.C., 1949), pp. 20-21.
[2] Ibid.

Parliament as a Left-wing Wafdist deputy.[3] The stage was thus set for a headlong clash between the Communists and the authorities. It started with a series of strikes in the textile industry and ended up in a direct confrontation with the Isma'il Sidqi Government on the evacuation issue. The Abbas Bridge incident of 9 February, 1946, in which reckless police action resulted in the death of over 20 students by drowning, paved the way for a general strike on 21 February in which another 3 demonstrators were shot dead and 120 wounded. The February incidents, in which students and workers played a key rôle, shook the Sidqi régime and gave the Egyptian Communists a feeling of being in the centre of Egyptian politics, a factor to be reckoned with.

The Government retaliated by rounding up over 200 Communists in July 1946. This was the beginning of a vigorous anti-Communist drive which culminated in the proclamation of martial law in May 1948. But what the Communists lost in terms of freedom of action was offset by some measure of inner cohesion induced by stringent police repression. In May 1947 the MELN and *Iskra* sank their differences and merged into a single organization called the *Mouvement Démocratique du Libération Nationale* (MDLN).[4] With its 1,500 members the MDLN emerged as the largest Communist group in Egypt—a factor which contributed to the eclipse of smaller factions. But inside the MDLN itself factional differences continued. These centered on the desirability of a united front with non-communist organizations and the Soviet line on Palestine. Besides, the Arab-Jewish friction inside the party continued unabated. Sa'id Sulayman ar-Rifa'i, who stood for the complete "Egyptianization" of the party pressed for the expulsion of Henri Curiel and Hillel Shwartz.

Despite police repression and inner dissensions the Communist influence continued to increase. In September 1947 the Communists organized a strike of 27,000 workers in an industrial suburb of Cairo. In January 1948 strikes were organized in the University of Cairo on the Sudan question. The striking students trampled on the portraits of King Faruq and shouted anti-Faruq slogans, following which the University was closed down for an indefinite period. In April, Communist students came out in support of

---

[3] G. E. Kirk, *Survey of International Affairs: The Middle East, 1945-1950* (London, 1954), p. 118.

[4] Its Arabic abbreviation was HADETU.

striking policemen who demanded a raise in salary and an eight-hour working day. Massive demonstrations were organized in Cairo and Alexandria leading to clashes with the Army. The Communists used this opportunity to raise the wider demand for bread and work.[5] Besides, a large number of new Communist cells were established in educational institutions, workers' unions, and the armed forces. In the prison camps of Hukstep and Abukir the Communist detenus were able to influence the minds of several Muslim Brothers and radical Wafdists whom the Egyptian Government had rounded up at the time of the Palestine war.

The Second Round

The defeat of Egyptian arms in Palestine, widespread charges of Faruq's complicity in the arms scandal, and the continued deadlock with Britain compelled the King to patch up with the Wafd by the middle of 1949. The Wafd scored a thumping victory in the January 1950 elections. It started its new tenure with the lifting of the Martial Law. Political detenus, including the Communists, had already been set free in the fall of 1949. Once again, conditions were ripe for intense political activity. And the Communists readily availed themselves of the new opportunities that lay before them.

The Communists employed the relative freedom of action permitted by the Nahas régime to organize a broad-based Peace Movement. In February 1950, a National Committee for the Defence of Peace was formed. The Committee's campaign for signatures to the Stockholm Peace Appeal was not a spectacular success. But the movement itself attracted a galaxy of well-known figures including Muhammad Kamil Bindari Pasha. former Ambassador to Moscow; Doria Shafiq, the feminist leader; 'Abdul Razzaq Sanhuri, an eminent jurist; Fathi Ridwan, Secretary of the Watani Party; and several Left-wing Wafdists.[6] The key positions in the organization were, however, occupied by Sa'd Kamil and Yusuf Hilmi of the MDLN.[7]

The experience gathered in the course of the Peace Movement and earlier contacts with the Moslem Brothers and other groups

---

[5] *At-Tariq* (Beirut), vol. 7 (April 1948), pp. 106-7.

[6] *At-Tariq*, vol. 10 (January 1951), pp. 39-43.

[7] Walter Z. Laqueur, *Communism and Nationalism in the Middle East* (London, 1957), pp. 57-58.

inside the prison camps paved the way for the new Communist tactics of united front which the Communists put to test during the crucial period between October 1951 and the July 1952 military *coup d'état*. On 8 October 1951 Premier Nahas proclaimed the unilateral abrogation of the Anglo-Egyptian Treaty of 1936. The Anglo-American response to this move was the proposal for an Allied Middle East Command which would replace the British garrison in the Canal Zone by the combined forces of the participating nations. Most Egyptians thought that the remedy suggested was worse than the original malady. The Egyptian Government rejected the proposal to the accompaniment of popular applause. In the meantime British forces remained entrenched in the Canal Zone, and the Egyptian Government seemed to possess neither the will nor the means to translate its proclamation into concrete reality.

It was against this backdrop that the initiative in the matter was seized by the extremist elements of the Left and the Right. While the Government evinced utter helplessness in controlling the consequences of its own precipitate policy-decision the Communists put themselves at the head of the tide of anti-British feeling that swept the entire country. The Communists forged a united front in collaboration with the Muslim Brothers and Ahmad Husayn's semi-Fascist Socialist Party.[8] Together they organized resistance to the British in the Canal Zone and commanded the streets of Cairo, Isma'ilia, and Port Sa'id. The Communists took the line that the Nahas Government was not prepared to go beyond "diplomatic protest and damagoguery" and that it was even "trying to arrive at an understanding with the British" in order to "save its own face".[9] They called upon the people to take direct action to rid the country of "elements of treachery and defeat" and to encircle the British from all sides "from the Sudan, from Iraq, from Syria, from the east, from the west", and to accomplish their extermination.[10]

The period 1951-52 stands out as a distinct watershed in the history of Egyptian Communism. The MDLN not only emerged as the largest Marxist group in the country but also succeeded in "Egyptianizing" the movement. Henri Curiel having disap-

---

[8] Before 1950 it was known as *Misr al-Fatat* (Young Egypt).

[9] K. Habib in *At-Tariq*, vol. 11 (January 1952), pp. 56-62.

[10] Muhammad Jalal, *Al-Jabha ash-Sha'biya* (Cairo, 1951), pp. 34-35.

peared from the scene following his arrest and deportation to
Italy in 1950, the party leadership passed into the hands of Sa'id
Sulayman ar-Rifa'i. On the ideological plane, the MDLN abandoned the doctrinaire pretension to being a purely proletarian
organization and openly advocated the need for a national democratic front of workers, peasants, students, intellectuals, professional
groups, and the army.[11] With this change in outlook the MDLN
was able to seduce radical elements from the rival political parties.
Its supporters in the army even made their way into the clandenstine
Free Officers' movement which was to topple the monarchy in
July 1952. On the eve of the military *coup d'état* the Communist
strength in Egypt was estimated at 5,000 card-carrying members
—over three times its following in 1947.

In the meantime Egypt's slide into chaos continued unabated.
On 26 January, 1952 the pent-up nationalist feelings of the masses,
fed on empty slogans month after month, burst into an orgy of
violence and arson directed at the vast foreign property in Cairo.
The Communists disowned responsibility for these incidents and
ascribed them to "political intriguers" and *agents provocateurs*.[12]
But the burning of Cairo marked the collapse of civil authority.
In the event, the Communists and the Muslim Brothers appeared
to be the natural heir to political power in Egypt. Both were well-
organized and possessed considerable popular appeal. The Communists had even succeeded in harnessing the nationalist upsurge
into anti-imperialist revolutionary channels. And yet, in this most
decisive moment of Egyptian history, the initiative was seized by
the Free Officers' movement which cautiously disclaimed commitment to any political ideology. And the military *coup d'état* it
carried out on 23 July, 1952 gradually transformed the entire setting
of Egyptian politics.

That the Egyptian Communists drew a blank in this critical
hour of decision was perhaps not entirely due to the vast gap
between their influence and actual strength. The Communist
failure also owed a great deal to the existence of the Muslim Brothers
as a formidable rival and to the unredeemed factionalism in their

[11] Anwar 'Abd al-Malik, "Problems of Socialism in the Arab World", *Nuovi
Argomenti* (Rome), March 1963 - February 1964. English translation in US
Department of Commerce, *Translations of International Communist Developments*
(Washington, D.C.) no. 572, 17 March 1964, p. 53.

[12] Habib, n. 9, pp. 56-62.

own ranks. Lacouture enumerates at least ten groups contending for recognition as the sole Communist organization of Egypt at that time.[13]

Clash with the Junta

The Communists were caught napping by the July *coup d'état*. But the MDLN at least had the consolation that it had two ardent supporters—Lieutenant Colonel Yusuf Sadiq and Major Khalid Muhi ad-Din—in the now all-powerful Revolutionary Command Council (RCC). At the same time, the Communists viewed with suspicion the junta's refusal to define its position in regard to the Western proposal for a Middle East Command.[14] All in all, in the initial weeks the Communists rejoiced over the destruction of Faruq's rule and hoped to achieve legal status, respectability and influence. But all these hopes were soon shattered to pieces and with a stunning impact.

The Communists perhaps were not entirely responsible for the accident which marred their relations with the junta. The euphoria generated by the RCC's revolutionary verbiage enthused the cotton-mill workers of Kafr Dawr—a town close to Alexandria— to demand higher wages from their employers. When the armed police was called upon to disperse the demonstrators, the latter set fire to two buildings and took possession of a factory. This was followed by a pitched battle between the workers and the police resulting in 9 killed, 30 wounded and 200 arrested. The RCC reacted brutally. A court martial, appointed to try the ring-leaders of the workers, found Mustafa Khamis and Ahmad al-Bakri guilty of "a grave crime against the State" and condemned them to death. The hangings were carried out on the factory premises.[15]

In the Communist folklore the Kafr Dawr incident ranks beside the Dinshwai tragedy.[16] Some non-Communist Leftists later

[13] Jean and Simonne Lacouture, *Egypt in Transition* (London, 1958), pp. 262-3.
[14] Wasfi al-Bani, "What after the Egyptian *Coup*", *At-Tariq*, vol. 11 (August 1952), pp. 16-19.
[15] *For a Lasting Peace, For a People's Democracy* (Bucharest), 12 September 1952.
[16] In 1906 some British Army officers hunting pigeons at Dinshwai village accidentally set a farm on fire which provoked the villagers to a fight killing one officer. The British retaliated by hanging six villagers. This incident created a nation-wide stir.

explained that Naguib, not Nasser, was responsible for Kafr Dawr hangings and that this stern measure was intended to strike terror in the hearts of the Communists. The RCC also took this opportunity to round up several Communists and ban the Peace Partisan's organ *Al-Katib* (The Writer) and the Communist newspaper Al-Mu'arda (The Opposition). The Communists, in turn, wailed that "after sparing Faruq, the feudal lords, traitors, and swindlers", the military dictators "spilled only the workers' blood".[17]

The Communists now waited for an opportune moment to hit back. In the meantime, they made common cause with the disbanded Wafdists whom the junta feared and abhorred most because of its political past and mass following. In January 1954 the Muslim Brothers, too, were banned. The Communists immediately came out with a pamphlet offering to join hands with the Brothers against "the fascist dictatorship" of Nasser and his "Anglo-American props".[18] The tactical alliance between the Communists and the Muslim Brothers, explained in terms of the latter's "mass character" and "anti-imperialist programme and propaganda",[19] fully exploited the opportunities offered by the Naguib-Nasser tug-of-war during February-March 1954 and the Anglo-Egyptian Agreement on Suez concluded later in the year. On the one hand, they backed Naguib who promised restoration of parliamentary democracy and, on the other, assailed Nasser and the junta for the Suez Agreement which was caricatured as "a deal with the imperialists".

Nasser eventually routed Naguib and his supporters in the internal tussle; and he did so with the help of trade unions—the Cairo transport workers in particular—which had been systematically purged of Communist elements ever since the Kafr Dawr incident. That also sealed the fate of Lieutenant Colonel Yusuf Sadiq and Major Khalid Muhi ad-Din, the Communist members of the RCC.[20] The Communists interpreted this as yet another proof of the junta's "complicity with the imperialists".

[17] Lacouture, n. 13, p. 166.

[18] Richard P. Mitchell, The Society of Muslim Brothers, unpublished doctoral dissertation, Princeton University, Princeton, N. J., 1959, p. 159.

[19] See A. M. Goldobin's "The Dissolution of the Muslim Brotherhood in Egypt in 1954" in *Mizan Newsletter* (London), vol. 4 (September 1962), pp. 17-19.

[20] Sadiq's dismissal followed an article by him in a Cairo daily, *Al-Misri* (24 March 1954), calling upon President Naguib to form a coalition govern-

It was, however, not long before new developments forced the Egyptian Communists to reassess completely the character and potentialities of the military régime. By the end of 1954 the Communist apprehension that following the Suez Agreement Nasser would fall for some Western-sponsored military alliance was completely dispelled by the latter's vehement opposition to such moves. In April 1955, at Bandung, Nasser made his début on the Afro-Asian scene as leader of an emergent non-aligned nation. In September, the same year, he smashed the Western embargo on supply of arms by entering into a deal with Czechoslovakia. The next year, he nationalized the Suez Canal. All these steps were greatly lauded by the Soviet bloc countries. L. N. Vatolina, a leading Soviet specialist in Arab affairs, wrote that "the national liberation movement is widest in scope in Egypt" and lauded "the positive element in the foreign policy of Nasser's government".[21] The Egyptian Communists, too, hurriedly revised their line attributing past attitudes to "left-sectarian errors".[22] This, however, did not in any way improve the Communists' prospects at home; and for many reasons. First, there was a clear time-lag between Moscow's reappraisal of the rôle of the national *bourgeoisie* in the newly independent nations and the Egyptian Communists' follow-up in the same direction. Secondly, Nasser's daring initiative had generated a national euphoria which greatly strengthened his position *vis-à-vis* all other domestic political elements. In the event, Nasser decided to combine a pro-Soviet posture abroad with an anti-Communist line at home. Even after the Czech arms deal the drive against domestic Communism was kept up. Less than a month before nationalization of the Suez Canal the Supreme Military Court of Egypt sentenced forty Communists to various terms of hard labour ranging from two to seven years.

---

ment of the Wafd, the Communists and the Muslim Brothers. Khalid Muhi ad-Din also fell out with Nasser and paid the price for it.

[21] L. N. Vatolina, "The Growth of National Consciousness Among the Arab Peoples" in Walter Z. Laqueur, ed., *The Middle East in Transition* (New York, 1958), p. 492.

[22] See Manfred Halpern, "Middle East and North Africa", in *Communism and Revolution* (Princeton, N.J., 1964), pp. 323-4; and Goldobin, n. 19.

CHAPTER FIVE

UPS AND DOWNS IN SYRIA AND THE LEBANON
1946-1956

Early Years of Independence

Having survived the stigma of collaboration with France, the Communists entered the post-Independence era with studied prudence. Khalid Bakdash fully endorsed the national aims out lined by President Shukri al-Quwatli in his inaugural address. Avoiding any reference to partisan demands Bakdash emphasized the need to emancipate Syria from the remnants of colonialism, to foster national unity, to eradicate poverty and ignorance, and to establish a truly democratic régime. He advocated solidarity with the Arabs and subservience to none. "I mean, our policy should not follow Washington, London or Moscow. It must be a Syrian and Arab policy".[1]

The Communists also gave up the habitual negative approach to religion. A Communist writer went so far as to present the early Islamic upsurge and the Russian Revolution as links in a single chain of human progress. The great revolution which Islam brought about, he contended, by abolishing idolatry, prohibiting the burial of girls, and eradicating feudalism was not an isolated phenomenon but part of a continuous process in the history of mankind.[2]

In short, the Communist approach, in the early years of Independence, conformed to the general policy subscribed to by the nationalists who had inherited power in Damascus and Beirut. However, as the domestic and international situation after the war began to crystallize, the Communists evolved their own emphasis and angularities.

On the domestic front the Communists stepped up trade union work and took up cudgels against two potential rivals the *Parti Populaire Syrien* (PPS) and the Muslim Brothers. On the external front, they set out to organize public opinion against the Western

[1] *At-Tariq*, vol. 5, nos. 7-8 (1961), p. 32.

[2] Ra'if Khuri, "The Progressive Character of the Early Arab Renaissance", *At-Tariq*, vol. 5, nos. 23-24 (1946), pp. 3-4.

moves in the area following the outbreak of the Cold War. The
Peace Movement served as a means to co-ordinate the domestic
and international policies of the Syro-Lebanese Communists.

The exit of the French and the active part taken by workers
in the popular agitation that preceded it created a favourable
climate for the liberalization of trade union laws. In June 1946,
the Syrian Chamber of Deputies enacted a new labour code which
placed matters concerning organization of trade unions, arbitra-
tion, hours of work, and labour welfare on a modern footing.[3]
But trade unionism flourished more rapidly in the Lebanon than
in Syria. In 1946, Mustafa al-'Aris, member of the WFTU executive,
was elected Chairman of the Lebanese Syndicate of Labour Unions,
which covered most of the workmen's association and guilds
in the Lebanon.

While observing correct relationship with the nationalist parties
the Communists mounted a tirade against the PPS and the Muslim
Brothers. The *Sawt ash-Sha'b* decried the PPS as "Fascist",
"traitorous", and "agent of Hitler" and started a systematic
campaign demanding a ban on the party. A concerted attack on
the Muslim Brothers was launched in July-August 1947. A colum-
nist of the *Sawt ash-Sha'b* accused it of being subservient to the
British.[4]

In foreign affairs, the Communists took the line that Britain
was out to take the place of France in Syria and the Lebanon
and that its aim was to bring the entire Arab East under its direct
or indirect control. It was trying to achieve this end through varied
means including the Arab League, bilateral alliances and the
"Greater-Syria" project. The Communists also played on the
theme of the emergence of the United States as a force in the area,
its growing accord with Britain, and the ambition of the two powers
to draw the Arabs into an anti-Soviet alliance.[5] To counter this,

---

[3] A. Aziz Alluni, "The Labour Movement in Syria", *Middle East Journal*
(Washington), vol. 13 (Winter 1959), pp. 67-68.

[4] S. Ayyub, *Al-Hizb ash-Shuyu'i fi Suriya wa Lubnan, 1922-1958* (Beirut,
1959), pp. 163-64, 167. The PPS was founded in 1932 by Antun Sa'ada, a
Lebanese Christian brought up in Brazil. The party believed in the existence
of a Syrian nation derived from a common social consciousness developed
over a long period of history and comprising the entire Fertile Crescent.
It was organized on fascist lines and was opposed to Arab nationalism.

[5] Khalid Bakdash in *At-Tariq*, vol. 6 (January 1947) pp. 28-37; and of March
1947, pp. 83-105.

the Communists organized a broad-based "Peace Movement" which also helped them to spread their influence among writers, artists, and even religious divines.

The Communists, however, suffered two set-backs during this period: Soviet support to the partition of Palestine and the migration of several Armenians to Soviet Armenia in 1947 in response to Russian overtures. While the former produced anti-Communist sentiment in Syria and the Lebanon, the latter deprived the Communists of several active members and sympathizers belonging to the Armenian minority.[6]

Disenchantment with Bourgeois Nationalists: 1949-1953

The Communist Parties of Syria and the Lebanon were banned following the Soviet vote in favour of creation of Israel. This was the price they were made to pay for their last-minute *volte face*. But the nationalist régimes in Damascus and Beirut also could not escape unharmed from the national outrage created by the defeat of Arab arms in the Palestine war. In March 1949 Colonel Husni Za'im carried out a *coup d'état* against the National Bloc Government headed by Khalid al-'Azm. A counter-*coup* by Colonel Sami Hinnawi in August spelled the end of Za'im's short-lived régime. Hinnawi was, in turn, toppled by Lieutenant-Colonel Adib Shishakli in December the same year. In the Lebanon a loose coalition of disgruntled Leftist and reformist groups brought about the fall of Bishara al-Khuri's presidency in a bloodless *inqilab* (overthrow) in September 1952. These changes marked the temporary eclipse of that group of conservative nationalists who had led the struggle against the French, but having come to power conspicuously failed to measure up to popular expectations.

The Syrian Communists had no hand in the political convulsions of 1949. On the contrary, successive military dictators took more stringent measures against the Communists than ever contemplated by the ousted constitutional régime. Husni Za'im rounded up a large number of Communists which drove the party underground.

---

[6] The Armenian community of Syria and Lebanon, numbering about 150,000 formed a distinct minority imbued with a strong sense of national solidarity. The bulk of the 70,000 Armenians in the Lebanon were those who had fled from Turkish persecution during and after the First World War. Most of them took to crafts, trade and other urban occupations. See A. H. Hourani, *Minorities in the Arab World* (London, 1947), pp. 66-67, 83-84.

Under Hinnawi there was some relaxation and Khalid Bakdash even contested election though unsuccessfully, to the Constituent Assembly in November 1949.[7] This brief respite was followed by Shishakli's ruthlessly anti-Communist rule.

These set-backs, however, did not hinder the broad-based Peace Movement which indeed became the principal medium of Communist operation during the period. Among the diverse elements which supported the Stockholm Peace Appeal were some religious dignitaries such as Habib A. Ibrahim, Mufti of Ba'lbak and Buqa' and the Shi'i Mujtahid, Shaykh 'Abd al-Husayn Sharafuddin. Peace Congresses were held in Syria and the Lebanon in 1950, their object being to attract all sections of the people by carefully restricting the slogans to the banning of the atom bomb, disarmament, and strengthening of world peace.[8]

According to Communist analysis the 1949 *coups d'états* were the result of acute Anglo-American rivalry in the Arab East. Whereas Britain wanted to consolidate its position in the area through creating "Greater Syria" or a Syro-Iraqi alliance, the United States was eager to unite its "stooges" in Eygpt, Saudi Arabia, Syria, and the Lebanon under a "collective security pact".[9] Accordingly, the Za'im's *coup d'état* was master-minded by the United States, in collaboration with the French, in order to forestall British attempts to usher in "Greater Syria" (comprising Syria, the Lebanon and Jordan) with the help of "Anglophile elements in Syria's Parliament and Government". The British countered by backing Hinnawi who not only favoured "Greater Syria" but abrogated his predecessor's deal with the American oil companies for laying oil-pipelines across Syrian soil. In the third round the United States again gained the upper hand; and the Shishakli régime put the "Greater Syria" and the Syro-Iraqi federation projects into cold storage.[10] A Lebanese Communist, on the other hand, saw in the ascendancy of the army in Syria and Egypt a concerted effort by the "imperialists" to "purge" the Arab countries of "constitutions and remnants of democratic life".[11]

---

[7] The Communist Party of Syria set up a "National Democratic Front" which nominated ten candidates, four of them Communists.

[8] See *At-Tariq*, vol. 9 (November 1950), pp. 68-81.

[9] Sabit in *For a Lasting Peace, For a People's Democracy*, 13 April 1951.

[10] Butrus, "What is Taking Place in Syria", ibid., 13 January 1950.

[11] Wasfi al-Bani in *At-Tariq*, vol. 12 (February 1953), pp. 9, 15.

Though not wholly unfounded, these explanations could not cover up the fact that contrary to popular belief the Communists still remained on the periphery of the Syrian body politic as revealed by the events of 1949—a revelation as dejecting to the rank and file as it was embarrassing to the party leadership. Bakdash's report to the secret session of the Central Command of the Communist Parties of Syria and the Lebanon held in January 1951 must be examined in this context. Bakdash started with the blunt admission that the general milieu in which the party had hitherto functioned was petty *bourgeois*, not proletarian, and that 75 per cent of its activity was confined to that class. He, then, hastened to explain that in the early stages such an approach was necessitated by the weakness of the class struggle in Syrian society as well as the need to create the "greatest possible noise" in order to acquaint the public with Communist ideas. But having achieved that, the party ought to have prepared for the next phase of the struggle which demanded greater reliance on the working class and the peasants. In a scathing criticism of the national *bourgeoisie*, Bakdash observed that it was "not a revolutionary class and cannot play a basic, decisive, or guiding role in the struggle against imperialism". He contended that Syria and the Lebanon had become independent "only in a legal sense". "For the truth is that our country is not independent as long as the American, British and French imperialists dominate our most important utilities by means of their companies and as long as they also direct the régime in our country through their agents in the régime." He also debunked the Ba'th and Junblat's Progressive Socialist Party, which, according to him, were merely trying to exploit the increasing popularity of socialist ideas by raising slogans such as land-to-the-tiller and "buying out of foreign companies", which they call "nationalization". Bakdash, then, pleaded that the immediate goal of the party should be to bring about a National Democratic Revolution which would (*a*) abolish imperialist political and economic domination; (*b*) liquidate the remnants of feudalism; and (*c*) establish a popular democratic régime. These measures, he said, would pave the way for a socialist revolution in the not-too-distant future. To achieve all this, collaboration with non-Communist elements was still necessary and desirable. But the concept of united front needed re-definition. As Stalin had put it, "the united front can have a revolutionary significance only under the circumstances and conditions in which the Communist Party enjoys complete freedom to carry out its political and organizing activity". Bakdash added that this principle should govern Communist conduct even in regard to the Peace Movement.[12]

The report, unanimously adopted by the Central Command, represented a sharp turn in the approach of the Syro-Lebanese Communists to broad political and economic issues. It must, however, be added that Bakdash did not allow this patently dogmatic posture to stand in the way of joining a broad alliance with other political parties designed to oust Shishakli from power. This came about in 1953. In the Lebanon, too, there was no tangible shift towards sectarianism, in actual practice.[13]

Back to United Front: 1954-1956

The marked shift in the Communist attitude towards the national *bourgeoisie* in the fall of 1953 was primarily the result of Soviet reassessment, after Stalin's death, of the so-called national reformist movements in the Asian-African world. But Khalid Bakdash was perhaps the only Communist leader in the Arab East who instantly perceived the potentialities of the new Soviet approach and set out to make the best of it. The Communist call for a "National Front", however, made no immediate impact whether on the Left-leaning Ba'th or on other anti-Western elements. But conditions became eminently favourable to the Communists following the conclusion of the Baghdad Pact.

Earlier, the Communists joined the election battle with fanfare, particularly in Damascus, where Bakdash himself was a candidate. In a major election speech on 10 September, 1954, Bakdash took pains to explain that although scientific socialism as practised in Russia remained the ultimate goal of his party any talk of realizing it in Syria, in the circumstances prevailing there, was "meaningless". Syria's immediate requirement was a national democratic government supported by peasants. workers, the middle classes and the national *bourgeoisie* and wedded to agrarian reforms, protection of workers, and world peace. He also made a frontal attack on Egyptian dictatorship and praised the Wafd and the Muslim

[12] Text of the report in *Middle East Journal*, vol. 7 (Spring 1953), pp. 206-21.

[13] Antun Thabit continued to urge upon the Partisans of Peace to enrol the support of all sections of people irrespective of their political affiliations. See *At-Tariq*, vol. 11 (January 1952), pp. 10-13.

Brothers for fighting against it. This was indicative of the nature of alliance he was contemplating in Syria.[14]

The Communist Party being still formally illegal its candidates fought under the guise of a "National Union". Besides, the party also solicited support for independent candidates willing to co-operate with it. Bakdash won the election with a thumping majority and thus became the first Communist legislator in the Arab East. Ma'ruf ad-Dawalibi and Khalid al-'Azm won with Communist backing. The Communist success in the elections, which, by their own admission, were held "in an atmosphere of comparative freedom, never before known either in Syria or in any other Arab country", was, however, more symbolic than real.[15] But it offered an excellent opportunity for probing the prospects of tactical alliances which were of immense value to the party in the immediate future.

At this juncture a realignment of rival forces in the Syrian body politic set in motion by Shishakli's overthrow began to take a distinct form. All Leftist elements other than the Communists converged on the Ba'th Socialist Party which was anti-Soviet but neutralist in foreign policy and had won sixteen seats in the Parliament. On the extreme Right stood the small but well-knit, fanatical and pro-Western PPS. The two larger parties—the *Hizb ash-Sha'b* and *Hizb al-Watani*—though strong in Parliament, were either vague or divided on domestic and foreign issues. In the circumstances, the youthful Ba'thists, immensely popular with the student community and intellectuals and proficient in secret manoeuvres and mass agitations, worked their way to the centre of the Syrian political scene. Concomitantly, tensions generated by international rivalries in the region touched a new high following the conclusion of the Turko-Iraqi Pact in February 1954. Western pressure on Syria to fall in line with the Pact followed by the Soviet counter-move to offer it aid and protection[16] made both Russia and Communism respectable in the eyes of most Syrians. It also brought the Ba'th closer to the Communists. The Communists, in turn, renounced their antipathy towards Arab neutralism and its most ardent exponent, Gamal 'Abd al-Nasser of Egypt.

[14] Khalid Bakdash, *Khitab Khalid Bakdash* (Matba' an-Najah, n.d.).

[15] Khalid Bakdash, "The October Revolution and the Arab East", in *For a Lasting Peace, For a People's Democracy*, 18 November, 1955.

[16] See Patrick Seale, *The Struggle for Syria* (London, 1965), pp. 233-4

The Communist Party of Syria seized this opportunity to refurbish its own public image. It had been long associated in public mind with atheism, class conflict, violence, and the like. Communist propaganda now emphasized that the CPS was wedded to nationalism, democracy, and progress and was anxious to co-operate with all those who subscribed to these ideals. Khalid Bakdash summed up his party's position in the Syrian Parliament in 1955 in the following words:

> We Communists have always said—and we repeat it today—that our policy is, essentially, to search for points of agreement, not points of difference, with all sincere nationalists. Our programme in the current stage of national liberation and democracy is crystal clear. It comprises independence and sovereignty; strengthening of independence and sovereignty; exercise of independence and sovereignty to the widest possible extent; co-operation in the task of strengthening world peace; defeating imperialist plots and countering the conspiracies and machinations of its agents; strengthening of democracy; emancipation and development of the economy, agrarian reforms and raising of the standard of living of the masses—workers, peasants and all the toilers—so that they live with dignity.

And to allay apprehensions about Communist methods, Bakdash declared that "the path of each people towards socialism (which he described as the next stage in the process of social evolution) is determined by its circumstances, historical evolution, economic conditions and other national characteristics".[17]

If a good many Syrians were inclined to listen to Bakdash in 1955, it was not because Syria was on the verge of a far-reaching revolution. Nor was the country passing through serious economic difficulties. On the contrary, Syrian agriculture—the mainstay of its economy—had made spectacular advance since Independence. And yet the soul of Syria was ailing. Its malady sprang from a profound sense of lack of political fulfilment, from the shocking contrast between the pre-Independence vision and the post-Independence reality. In despair, the impulsive Syrian began to grope for new sources of inspiration and new objects of loyalty. And

[17] Ayyub, n. 4, pp. 182-3.

for the time being he found all these in the glittering chimera conjured up by dexterous Leftist propaganda.

The increasing radicalization of Syrian politics from 1955 onwards, it must be noted, was not the exclusive doing of the Syrian Communists. In fact, the Communists constituted one of the many forces that were simultaneously exerting in the same direction and with a variety of motives. The Ba'th Party with its elaborate socialist programme, deftly articulated by Akram al-Hawrani, had caught the fancy of certain sections of Syrian peasantry. Another factor was the ingenious Colonel 'Abdul Hamid Sarraj, head of the Army Intelligence Bureau, who worked hand-in-glove with the Ba'th on the one hand and the Egyptian Envoy Mahmud Riyad on the other, and was steadily preparing himself for the rôle of a Syrian Nasser. Then there was Khalid al-'Azm, the "progressive millionaire", who having failed to achieve high political office by other means joined the Leftist bandwagon along with the thirty independent deputies who supported him in the Parliament.[18]

Nevertheless, the fact remains that the Communists now came to wield influence and prestige far in excess of their size and resources. And they owed it as much to their tactical ingenuity as to the international crisis brewing in the region.

On the home front, the Communists successfully exploited the rivalry between different political groups. The Ba'th and the 'Azm groups were determined to destroy the conservative Sha'b and the PPS, the two remaining stumbling blocks in the pathway to power. The Communists fervently joined hands with them to bring this about. A concerted offensive by the emerging Leftist alliance brought about the fall of the Faris al-Khuri Cabinet in February 1955. In the new Cabinet headed by Sabri al-'Asali, Khalid al-'Azm secured the key portfolios of defence and foreign affairs. For the first time since the restoration of constitutional rule, the Sha'b Party was completely excluded from the Cabinet even though it constituted the largest single group in the Parliament.

The Communists also joined the fierce anti-PPS campaign launched by the Ba'th and its supporters in the army following the murder of Colonel 'Adnan al-Maliki—a Ba'thist sympathizer—by an alleged supporter of the PPS. This came as a handy pretext

[18] This group of Independents precariously held together by 'Azm adopted the label of Democratic Bloc.

for the Left to liquidate the PPS whose pan-Syrian ideology and pro-Western postures had been anathema to Arab nationalists as well as Communists. The PPS had a small but well-knit organization complete with a cell in the army headed by Major Ghassan Jadid[19] which Maliki had been trying to root out. The Ba'th Party and its supporters in the army, therefore, cried for revenge. The Communists rushed in to support the Ba'th and in the process gave a calculated anti-Western twist to the Maliki affair. The Communists alleged that the PPS was in league with the United States and that both had plotted to subvert the Syrian régime by means of an army *coup d'état*. Partly because of the Syrian's habitual distrust of the West and partly because of the unconcealed solicitude for the PPS exhibited by a section of the Western Press, the Communist propaganda produced the desired effect of creating an anti-Western hysteria in Syria. The Leftists seized this opportunity to purge the PPS sympathizers from the army and the administration. The trials of the leading members of the party continued until June 1956, by which time the organization was practically crippled.

The Maliki affair revealed to the Leftists the potentialities of concerted action against the conservatives. A by-election in Homs, in the fall of 1955, proved its efficacy in the electoral sphere as well. In the course of the election campaign an electoral alliance was forged between the Communists, the Ba'th, and a section of the Watani Party. In the event, its joint candidate, Hajj Yunus, trounced the Sha'b Party's nominee by a margin of 4,000 votes. The CPS viewed this as a momentous event. A hurriedly convened meeting of the Central Committee noted that the experiment had

> strengthened the conviction of the people that a national alliance is the only effective means of mobilizing the masses for struggle against the imperialist pacts. It also showed that such an alliance, effected within a single region and in no way preventing any of the parties belonging to the front from preserving its own programme, principles and independent policy, could be effected on the same conditions on a country-wide scale.[20]

[19] Ghassan Jadid had been eased out of the Army only a fortnight before Maliki's murder.

[20] *For a Lasting Peace, For a People's Democracy*, 6 January 1956, p. 4.

Concomitantly, the Communists made tactical adjustments to take full advantage of the intense regional and international rivalries that erupted in the Middle East in the wake of the Anglo-Egyptian Agreement[21] on the evacuation of British forces from the Suez Canal Zone. At this point, the Western-sponsored move to group the Middle Eastern states into an anti-Soviet military arrangement brought about a tactical alliance between the Egyptian neutralists and the security-conscious Russians. The consummation of the Baghdad Pact early in 1955 further strengthened the Cairo-Moscow accord. From now onwards both Egypt and the Soviet Union looked around in the area for support against the Baghdad Pact. And their choice fell on Syria where Leftist groups engaged in a struggle for hegemony against pro-Western conservative elements were already disposed to embrace Egyptian neutralism and to welcome Soviet diplomatic support. The unwritten tripartite accord was sealed in February-March 1955 when, in quick succession, the wavering Faris al-Khuri Cabinet was replaced by a blatantly neutralist one headed by Sabri al-'Asali (13 February) and Molotov promised (23 March) Soviet aid in any form whatsoever to ward off Turko-Iraqi pressures on Syria.[22] Whether the accord was a *marriage de covenance* or a full-fledged Soviet-led alliance was not clear at this stage. Yet there was no doubt that Soviet influence in Damascus was soaring rapidly. In Novmeber, the Soviet diplomatic mission in Damascus was raised to the status of an Embassy. The Egyptian arms deal with Czechoslovakia in September was followed by a surreptitious supply of Soviet arms to Syria later in the year. The Syrians were believed to have received MIG-15 aircraft, tanks, self-propelled guns, field and anti-aircraft artillery, light weapons, and other military hardware worth £20 million before the outbreak of the Suez war.[23] Trade between the two countries initiated under an agreement in November 1955 was extended to other Soviet bloc countries in 1956. Exchange of cultural, trade union, and student delegations went hand in hand with expanding commercial and political ties. In June 1956 Foreign Minister Shepilov visited Damascus to reassure Syrians of continuing Soviet support. On 3 July Syria reciprocated by recognizing the People's Republic of China.

[21] The Agreement was concluded on 19 October, 1954.
[22] Seale, n. 16, pp. 233-4.
[23] *The Times* (London), 3 October, 1957.

The Soviet overtures to neutralize Syria were accompanied by a corresponding endorsement of neutralism by the Communist Party of Syria. In March 1956, an all-party committee, including the CPS, approved a National Charter which underscored "positive neutralism" as the basis of Syrian foreign policy.

In sum, Soviet and Syrian Communist policies in the pre-Suez era were mutually complementary. The latter's tactical alliance with the non-Communist Left involving adjustments on domestic and foreign issues greatly weakened Syrian inhibitions about Communism and the Soviet Union. Soviet backing to Syria, on the other hand, enhanced the prestige and influence of the Syrian Communists. It was this ominous aspect of the Syrian situation which evoked a hysterical "red scare" in some Middle Eastern and Western capitals comparable only to the alarms raised by the Syrian Communists earlier about imminent threats of a Western-sponsored *coup d'état*. Later events were to reveal that fears on either side, though not wholly unfounded, were greatly exaggerated.

CHAPTER SIX

IRAQ: FRUITS OF REPRESSION

THE war period in Iraq left behind a legacy of contradictions. After Gaylani's overthrow, political power passed into the hands of a coterie of oligarchs,[1] who proceeded to monopolize it with the help of British patronage on the one hand and ruthless suppression of political dissidence on the other. At the same time, wartime propaganda as well as relaxation of restrictions hitherto imposed on liberal and radical elements served to create a widespread clamour for democracy and socio-economic change. The story of Iraq during the decade following the war centres on the theme of ceaseless conflict between these irreconcilable trends. As Bazzaz later put it, "everyone who was discontented or wanted change, every opponent of the existing régime was either accused of being Communist or was liable to such accusation" by the authorities. Hence the official coinage of such labels as "Communist Muslim Brothers" and "Fascist Democrats".[2]

Struggle Against the Treaty: 1945-1949

The question of internal liberalization and reform in Iraq was closely tied to that country's relationship with Britain as defined by the Anglo-Iraqi Treaty of 1930. The British had invoked this treaty to intervene in Iraq in 1941 and had ever since exercised veiled but decisive influence on Iraq's foreign and domestic policies. Hence the future of the treaty became the focus of attention for all nationalist and radical groups in Iraq.

Under mounting public pressure the Suwaydi Cabinet granted permission, in February 1946, for the formation of political parties. Of the five political parties which were formed immediately after this, four were clearly in favour of terminating Iraq's dependence on Britain. The Right-wing nationalist Istiqlal Party shared this

---

[1] Prominent among them were Nuri as-Sa'id, Arshad al-'Umari, Hamdi al-Pachachi, Jamil Midfa'i and Fadhil al-Jamali. Premiership changed hands between them in an endless game of musical choirs.

[2] 'Abd ar-Rahman al-Bazzaz, *Safhat min al-Ams al-Qarib* (Beirut, 1960), pp. 20, 118-9.

view with the Leftist National Democratic Party (*Hizb ad-Dimuqrati al-Watani*), the National Union (*Ittihad al-Watani*), and the People's (*Sha'b*) Party.[3]

Fahd's Communist Party of Iraq was not permitted to come out in the open. Doubtless the People's Party came very close to it except for the rather personal differences between Fahd and 'Aziz Sharif[4] which divided the two groups. Also Kamil Chadirchi's National Democratic Party, which stood for democratic socialism, was not particularly hostile to Communism, and its Left-wing splinter, the National Union, led by Ibrahim 'Abd al-Fattah, was much less so. But the Fahd group's request for official permission to form the *Taharrur al-Watani* (National Liberation) Party was rejected by the authorities which prompted the former to set up a front organization under the deceptive label of the Anti-Zionist League.

Suwaydi's experiment in liberalization, which had permitted Communist and other Leftist elements a certain measure of freedom, was frowned upon by the old-guard politicians who brought about his fall in May 1946. His successor, Arshad al-'Umari, who had no use for political parties and free Press, reverted to old methods. Indicative of this was the suppression of the Anti-Zionist League in June following a peaceful demonstration organized by it in Baghdad in support of the Palestine people. 'Umari, then, imposed restrictions on the Press. These measures were decried by all the recognized political parties.[5]

Close on the heels of the Baghdad demonstration came the strike of oil workers in Kirkuk who demanded an increase in wages and the right to form a union. Police firings on workers resulted in eight killed and many times that number wounded. Towards the end of the year the railwaymen and postal workers also struck. Though largely caused by hard economic conditions, the Communists had a big hand in organizing these strikes.

Seriously upset by these incidents, the Government initiated close watch on underground Communist activities. In a surprise raid

[3] The fifth one was Suwaydi's own *Ahrar* (Liberal) Party which subscribed to moderate social reform and revision of the Treaty.

[4] 'Aziz Sharif enjoyed the patronage of the CPS chief Khalid Bakdash and his articles appeared in the latter's organ, *Sawt ash-Sha'b* (Beriut). See *Al-Ayyam* (Damascus), 27 May 1959.

[5] See Majid Khadduri, *Independent Iraq* (London, 1960), p. 256.

5

on 19 January, 1947, the police arrested most of the prominent Communists, including Fahd, Ibrahim Najib Shumail, and Zaki Basim. They were immediately tried and convicted for "propagating Communism among civilians and members of the armed forces and for being in contact with foreign Communist parties". Fahd, Shumail and Basim were awarded life sentences, later commuted by the Iraqi High Court to life imprisonment, and twenty-seven other Communists to prison terms varying from 1 to 15 years.[6]

These repressive measures were directed not only at the Communists but all the Leftist elements. In September 1947 the Salih Jabr Cabinet disbanded the Sha'b and the National Union Parties. Even Kamil Chadirchi of the moderate National Democratic Party was put on trial. Ironically, this line of action produced the not wholly unexpected result of uniting the hitherto warring Leftist factions. By the end of 1947, the Fahd group, 'Aziz Sharif's Sha'b, Kamil Qazanji's Left-wing splinter of the National Democratic Party, the Haqiqat group of Zaki Khayri and Sharif ash-Shaykh, and the Kurdish faction of the CPI composed their differences. A Jewish youth, Sason Dalal, became the leader of the enlarged party.[7]

Early in 1948 the Communists got an excellent opportunity to retaliate against their oppressors. After protracted secret negotiations with the British Foreign Office, Premier Salih Jabr concluded the Portsmouth Treaty with Great Britain on 15 January 1948. Although the new agreement was an improvement upon the 1930 treaty which it sought to replace, the fact that it had been arrived at behind the back of the Iraqi political parties and that it placed such a vital matter as defence under an Anglo-Iraqi Joint Defence Board deeply outraged Iraqi public opinion. The official release of the text of the treaty set off a wave of angry demonstrations lasting for ten days. Violent clashes between the authorities and the demonstrators claimed several lives. The old guard eventually yielded to the popular demand and gave up the treaty as well as its chief architect, Salih Jabr.

The Communists openly claimed credit for the repudiation of the Portsmouth Treaty. It is true that the student community which was conspicuously active throughout the January demonstrations

[6] *New York Times*, 25 June and 15 July, 1947.

[7] Walter Z. Laqueur, *Communism and Nationalism in the Middle East* (London, 1957), pp. 189-91.

was largely under Communist influence. But the treaty was equally frowned upon by moderate nationalists of the Istiqlal and the social-democrats of the National Democratic Party. The Communists fervently collaborated with them and thereby acquired first-hand experience of the strength and potentialities of the nationalist sentiment in Iraq. No doubt the Communists were made to pay heavily for the adventure. Hundreds of them were arrested and consigned to Naqrat as-Salman prison camp. Fahd and his three associates, Zaki Muhammad Basim, Muhammad Shabibi, and Ibrahim Siddiq, were tried again and sent to the gallows in February 1949.

Towards a National Front

The Iraqi Communists would have ordinarily taken a long time to recover from this telling blow. But the old guard's contemptuous disregard for all political dissent, whether radical or moderate, succeeded in creating many more foes besides the Communists. Its allergy to seemingly popular clamour for democratic rule and remodelling of Anglo-Iraqi relationship on a basis consistent with national aspirations drove even moderate elements to desperation. This enabled the remnants of the Communist Party of Iraq to repair the party machine and resume organizational and propaganda work, though with greater secrecy and caution than before. They turned prison camps into centres of political education and recruitment. Outside the prisons, they intensified work among students and workers. The Partisans of Peace Movement, started in 1949, served as a convenient front organization to mobilize writers, intellectuals and even religious personages.[8] It carried on the campaign against the 1930 Treaty and the Western proposal for a Middle Eastern military alliance.[9]

By 1952 the Iraqi opposition parties, including the Communists, were ready for the next round with the ruling clique. In October they demanded a revision of the Electoral Law in order to provide

[8] The leading lights of the Peace Movement in early years were poet Muhammad Madhi at Jawahiri, Tawfiq Munir, Muhammad Salih Bahr al-'Ulum, and Dr Khalil Jamil. In July 1954 the Partisans held the first National Congress which elected a Council comprising, inter alia, 'Allama Shaykh 'Abd al-Karim al-Mashta, Shaykh Muhammad al-Shabibi, Dr Faruq Partaw and Dr Nasiha Dulaymi. For a short history of the movement see Iraq Times (Baghdad), 19 April, 1959. Special Supplement.

[9] At Tariq, vol. 13 (August 1954), p. 33.

for direct election to Parliament. As political passions were being stirred on this issue a strike by the students of the College of Pharmacy against a certain regulation of the College suddenly developed into a violent mass upsurge directed against Mustafa al-'Umari's Government and Western interests in Iraq. This time the demonstrations spread to other towns including Basra, Karbala, Najaf, Kut, and Amara; and order could not be restored until after martial law was proclaimed (23 November), all political parties disbanded, and about 300 leaders arrested.[10] The martial law régime of General Nur ad-Din promulgated a new Electoral Law providing for direct election; but what was conceded in form was nullified in practice by official manipulation of the electoral process in the subsequent elections.

Unrelieved frustration eventually drove the incongruous opposition elements into an alliance. By 1954 the National Democratic Party, the Istiqlal, the Communists and their various front organizations, and the relatively young Ba'th Socialist Party (founded secretly in 1952) formed what came to be known as the National Front with the apparent purpose of overthrowing the combined alliance of the pro-Western Royal Diwan and the illiberal oligarchs who had been ruling Iraq since Independence.

Kurds and Communists

The political alliance between the Iraqi Communists and an influential section of the Kurds had been based more on mutual convenience than doctrinal conviction. Caught between the conflicting interests of rival Middle Eastern nations and foreign Powers, Kurdish nationalism was scuttled by the territorial arrangements following the First World War. The four million Kurds were sucked, though not assimilated, into Turkey (2,000,000), Iran (750,000), Iraq (700,000), Syria (250,000), and Soviet Armenia and Azerbaijan (100,000).[11] What made the relatively small grouping of Iraqi Kurds more articulate than Kurds in the neighbouring countries was that they comprised one-fifth of Iraq's total population. There were sporadic Kurdish uprisings in Iraq during the twenties and thirties which, however, failed to achieve any significant results. It was the creation, with Soviet support, of the Kurdish Republic

[10] Khadduri, n. 5, pp. 278-85.
[11] Robert F. Zeidner, "Kurdish Nationalism and the New Iraqi Government", Middle East Journal, vol. 10 (January 1959), p. 26.

at Mahabad soon after the end of the Second World War that gave Kurdish nationalism a new dimension. A relatively spirited section of the Iraqi Kurds, led by the Barazanis,[12] saw in this development a new hope for Kurdish nationalism. Their youthful leader, Mulla Mustafa Barazani, was actively associated with the Mahabad Republic until its fall in 1946, whereupon he fled to Iraq and thence, in 1947, to the Soviet Union.

It was also at Mahabad that a national organization called the Kurdish Democratic Party (KDP) was set up in November 1945. Though actively supported by some Kurdish leaders from Turkey and Iraq, the programme of the KDP was primarily concerned with the Kurdish region of Iran. In less than a year a parallel organization emerged in Iraq. The Iraqi KDP was the result of the merger of sundry Kurdish groups including the relatively influential Hiwa (Hope) Party. It is important to note that over years the Hiwa Party had acquired a distinctly Leftist complexion and its propaganda organ frankly advocated a united front against reaction, feudalism, and imperialism.[13] The more radical elements in the Hiwa Party, therefore, resisted the call for merger and eventually joined the Communist Party of Iraq.

Notwithstanding the initial alienation of some Kurdish Communists, the KDP soon emerged as a broad-based organization which attracted diverse elements such as liberals, Marxists, and conservatives to its fold. As in the case of its predecessor, the KDP's programme retained a socialist bias. This was apparently a concession to the party's radical youth which was neutralized by the election of Mulla Mustafa Barazani—whose conservatism on socio-economic matters was sharply juxtaposed by his relentless fervour for Kurdish national rights—as the party chairman.

Barely two years after its formation the KDP was split into two rival groups. Hamza 'Abdullah, who was leader of the Marxist faction in the party, defected and formed a rival organization called the Progressive KDP. But 'Abdullah's overtures were effectively countered by Ibrahim Ahmad, a shrewd politician and a learned ideologue who had emerged as an important KDP leader during Mulla Mustafa's prolonged sojourn in the Soviet

[12] The Barazanis broke away from the more orthodox Naqshbandis in the late nineteenth century.

[13] Hasan Arfa, *The Kurds: A Historical and Political Study* (London, 1966), p. 123.

Union.[14] Ibrahim Ahmad's judicious manipulation of Communist shibboleths helped him stop the Communist drain upon his following. The Communist propagandists ascribed this trend to the growing influence of the *bourgeois* class on the KDP.

[14] Ahmed was elected Secretary-General of the KDP in 1952.

CHAPTER SEVEN

JORDAN: YEARS OF FERMENT

COMMUNISM became an appreciable factor in the politics of Jordan only after the annexation of the West Bank of the Jordan River to the erstwhile Kingdom of Transjordan following the partition of Palestine in May 1948.[1] Before that, attempts had been made in the thirties by Subhi Abu Ghanimah of the Istiqlal Party of Palestine and Qasim Milhim to organize workers' unions in Transjordan. Their pioneering zeal did produce a few militant trade unionists without, however, making any spectacular impact on the country's political life.

The annexation of the West Bank added about 800,000 Palestinians, half of them refugees, to Transjordan's original population of 400,000. Preponderance of the urbanized and politically articulate Palestinians in the new state injected an element of turmoil into King 'Abdullah's paternalistic polity. Henceforth, the Palestinians, who cherished no loyalty to the King and even held him and the Western Powers responsible for the creation of Israel, set the pace of political life in Jordan. With them came political parties, trade unions, modern professional groups and, what is even more potent, the indignation, frustration, and mistrust characteristic of a lost people.

Soon after the partition of Palestine the League for National Liberation (LNL)[2] set out to reorganize its followers on the West Bank. In the murky conditions of Jordan the LNL, now led by Fu'ad Nassar,[3] Rushdi Shahin, and Ridwan al-Hilu, found a fertile ground for political work. Yet, in the early years its progress was somewhat unimpressive. The hostility of the authorities was one of the obstacles; but that applied to other political organizations as well. What arrested its growth in the early period was the party's

[1] The enlarged State was renamed Kingdom of Jordan in March 1949.

[2] Started in 1943 the LNL was the Arab Communist Party of undivided Palestine. See above, Chapter 2.

[3] Born in 1910 Nassar hailed from an Arab Christian family. He participated in the Arab uprisings of 1936-39 and subsequently fled to Iraq. He returned to Palestine in 1943 and became Secretary-General of the LNL in the late forties.

own doctrinal rigidity. It stubbornly refused to accept the annexation of Palestine by King 'Abdullah, already an accomplished
reality. It was, of course, dead opposed to monarchy. Above all,
the party could not live down the stigma of having endorsed the
partition resolution of the United Nations. The LNL's subsequent
attempts—through its clandestine organ, *Al-Muqawima ash-Sha'biya*
(People's Resistance)—to combine this stand with a denunciation
of Zionism and the "Anglo-Hashimite rulers" scarcely improved
the party's tarnished image. The party kept aloof from the first
parliamentary election since merger held in April 1950.

These dogmatic postures having been proved infructuous, the
Communists began to take a more practical view of politics in the
early fifties. The shift in Communist tactics was caused by the
marked success of the Partisans of Peace movement. In a country
where the large majority of the people attributed their sufferings
and deprivations to the omissions and commissions of the Western
Powers and where almost all articulate political groups resented
the continued British presence, the Stockholm Peace Appeal came
in handy as a battle-cry against Western imperialism. Herein lay
the germs of a broad-based movement which could undermine
the position of Britain and thereby clear the way for internal
revolution. And the LNL plunged into it with singular zeal. In
the process, the party shed much of its misconstrued extremism
and relaxed its bristling intolerance towards other political
groups.

The Partisans of Peace attracted a large number of non-
Communist politicians, lawyers, doctors, and men of religion,
including public figures such as Sulayman Nabulsi and Sulayman
Haj Faruqi. The success of the experiment revealed to the Communists the immense potentialities of the new tactics and prepared
the ground for a united front with the nationalists.

In the meantime, the Central Committee of the LNL decided
(June 1951) to change the party's name to the Communist Party
of Jordan (CPJ). The change of name was symbolic of the party's
resolve to function more openly than before. Accordingly, on the
eve of the August 1951 parliamentary election,[4] the Communists
sponsored the *Kutla al-Wataniya* (National Bloc)—a loose conglomeration of Communist sympathizers, fellow travellers, and

---

[4] Fresh elections were necessitated by the Parliament's refusal, in early 1951,
to vote the official budget.

non-Communists. Although the National Bloc lost in all the three constituencies where it had put up candidates—Rushdi Shahin and 'Abd al-Majid Abu Hajla (Nablus) and Mahmud Mutlaq (Amman)—it had the satisfaction of having polled 37,902 votes out of the total electorate of 342,714.[5]

This spurt of Communist activity inevitably aroused the wrath of the Jordanian officialdom. Fu'ad Nassar, the Secretary-General of the party, was arrested in December 1951. He was later tried and sentenced to ten years' rigorous imprisonment. Towards the end of 1953, the Anti-Communist Law of May 1948 was amended to proscribe under pain of severe punishment any kind of association with Communist activities.[6]

The Anti-British Campaign

Undeterred by the Government's persistent hostility, the CPJ forged ahead with the plan to form a united front with other opposition groups. This was the time when Britain, in an attempt to shore up its tottering political prestige in the Middle East, came forward with the proposal to form a regional military alliance. Since Jordan, already a recipient of British subsidy, was regarded as a natural candidate for the proposed alliance, the opposition promptly went into action to forestall this move.

A formidable agitation against the foreign-sponsored military alliance soon got under way. The CPJ placed itself in the forefront of the movement though it was by no means its sole champion. The pan-Arab Ba'th Party figured prominently in it. So did the newly formed National Socialist Party (NSP)[7] led by Sulayman Nabulsi. The informal alliance between these three parties determined the course of events in the next few years.

Reassured by their increasing popularity the Communists entered the campaign for the October 1954 elections. At that time the party's basic cadres numbered about 700.[8] Nablus, Jerusalem,

[5] See Walter Z. Laqueur, "Communism in Jordan", *World Today* (London), vol. 12 (March 1956), pp. 112-13; and A. H. H. Abidi, *Jordan: A Political Study* (Bombay, 1965), p. 209.

[6] Munib al-Madi and Sulayman Musa, *Tarikh al-Urdun fi'l Qarn al-'Ishrin* (n.p., 1959), p. 664.

[7] Started in July 1954 the NSP at first advocated Jordan's union with Iraq. But after the conclusion of the Baghdad Pact it progressively turned to Egypt and non-alignment.

[8] Laqueur, n. 5, p. 114.

Ramallah, and Amman were its strongholds.[9] Earlier in May, the party had unsuccessfully applied for permission to form a front organization called *Al-Jabha al-Wataniya* (National Front). The National Front, nevertheless, started functioning publicly. It enjoyed the support of Qadri Tuqan and 'Abd al-Qadir Salih, both members of Parliament, and several other public figures.[10] The party started a weekly called *Al-Jabha* (The Front), which was, however, closed down in August 1954. The National Front's candidates fought the elections as independents; and two of them, 'Abd al-Qadir Salih and Rashad Maswadi, were returned from the Nablus and Hebron constituencies respectively. Even those who lost did not do too badly at the polls. Considering the severe restrictions imposed on Communist publications two months before the elections, not to speak of the alleged tampering of the ballot-boxes by the officials, the Front's performance manifested its political strength.

However, for the realization of their immediate objective, namely the elimination of British influence from Jordan, the Communists and the rest of the opposition did not look upon the Parliament as the main battle-ground. In the initial phase, the opposition concentrated fire on the person of Glubb Pasha, the British commander of the 35,000-strong Arab Legion, and on the proposed military alliance. Earlier, in October 1953, it had seized upon the Qibya incident in which Israeli troops had massacred 66 Jordanians, including women and children, to organize mammoth demonstrations against Glubb Pasha and the British. Two years later, whispers about secret negotiations between the Jordanian authorities and the Baghdad Pact Powers to pave the way for Jordan's accession to the Pact touched off a series of riots and wild demonstrations resutting in the fall of Hazza' Majali's cabinet. In December 1955 the crowd in Amman chanted: "No more imperialism after today" and "No more monarchy after today". It was in face of this mighty upsurge that the King decided to beat a tactical retreat. The first

[9] Ilyas Marqas, *Tarikh al-Ahzab ash-Shuyu'iya fi'l Watan al-'Arabi* (Beirut, 1964), p. 293.

[10] Their names were: Yahya Hamudah, Rashad Maswadi, 'Abd ar-Rahman Shuqayr, Jabra al-Anqar, Ibrahim Bakr, 'Abd al-Majid Abu Hajla, Nabih Arshidat, Muhammad al-Yahya, Salih 'Awn al-Allah, Sulayman al-Sawdi, Turki al-Kayid, Ahmad al-Hamud, Fa'iq Warrad, Fazal al-Tahir, Nimr Hasan al-'Izza, Mahmud al-Qadi, Jawda Shahwan, Juris Hamarneh, Fakhri Marqa, and Mahmud al-'Abd Khayr ad-Din. See Madi and Musa, n. 6, p. 599.

step in that direction was the dissolution of the Parliament and replacement of Hazza' Majali by Ibrahim Hashim with the limited mandate of holding fresh elections. Hashim released all those who had been arrested in the course of recent disturbances and reassured the opposition that his government did "not intend to join any pacts".[11]

Soon after the December-January upsurge the Communists predicted Glubb's fall within three months.[12] Glubb was actually dismissed by the King on 2 March, 1956. With him also went his two top British aides, Colonel Sir Patrick Coghill, head of the Army Intelligence Department, and Brigadier William Hutton, Chief of Staff. The dismissal of Glubb, who was regarded by the Communists as "British imperialism's overseer in the Middle East", put an end to direct British control on the Arab Legion and enhanced the manoeuvring capability of the opposition parties. The Communists, who had always decried the Arab Legion as an instrument of repression against "the politically more advanced sections of the Arab population" and a "defender" of British oil interests in the entire Arab East, hailed the event as a significant milestone in the struggle for national liberation.[13]

Thus on the eve of the Suez war the Jordanian Leftists had manifestly scored a vital point against the régime. There were, however, many more hurdles to overcome. First, the dismissal of Glubb was by no means an unmixed blessing. For it enhanced the popularity of the youthful monarch who then assumed the rôle of a patriotic King. At the same time, the King was discreetly vague on the future of Anglo-Jordanian relations. The bedouin Arab Legion, though freed from British control, still remained loyal to the King. These were the issues to which the emerging united front of the opposition groups addressed itself in the coming months.

[11] For a Lasting Peace, For a People's Democracy, 23 December 1955, p. 6.
[12] Glubb attributes the accuracy of Communist prediction to mere "coincidence". See Sir John Bagot Glubb, A Soldier with the Arabs (London, 1957), p. 411.
[13] See Jan Marek, "General Glubb Gets the Sack", For a Lasting Peace, For a People's Democracy, 9 March, 1956, p. 4.

PART TWO
THE POST-SUEZ ERA

CHAPTER EIGHT

EGYPT: PRECARIOUS PARTNERSHIP

THE Czech arms deal marks a watershed in the history of the modern Arab East. It destroyed many a time-honoured assumption and illusion about the pattern of politics in the area and created new ones. Among the illusions destroyed was the belief, common to Western circles, that nationalism in the area could be propitiated by marginal concessions within a paternalistic framework designed to protect foreign strategic and economic interests. On the other hand, the Soviet bloc was not a little taken aback by the unsuspected potentialities of the so-called *bourgeois* Arab nationalism. The most confounded lot of all, however, were the Arab Communists whose copy-book maxims about the chronic ailments of the national *bourgeoisie*—vacillation and betrayal being the most notorious among them—stood utterly exposed. Among the new illusions fostered by the fateful events of 1955-56 were the widely shared belief in the Western capitals that any reverse suffered by them could not but mean a gain for the Soviet bloc; the high hopes entertained by Moscow that the West had been at last cornered in an area since long considered its special preserve; and the wild notions cherished by the Arab Communists that the era of the national liberation struggle of the Marxist-Leninist text-books was round the corner. These old and new illusions and the hopes and fears generated by them conditioned the events of the next decade.

Communists and the Suez Crisis

Nasser's daring initiatives in the field of foreign affairs stirred the Egyptian Communist detenus in the Abu Z'abal camp to re-examine their attitude towards the military régime. It was ultimately decided to give "all-out support" to the Government. Restoration of democracy was also to be stressed but not as a condition for co-operation.[1] This conciliatory gesture could evoke only minor

[1] Anwar 'Abd al-Malik, "Problems of Socialism in the Arab World", *Nuovi Argomenti* (Rome), March 1963-February 1964, Eng. trans. in US Department of Commerce, *Translations on International Communist Developments* (Washington, D. C.), no. 572, 17 March, 1964, p. 67.

concessions. Following the announcement of the January 1956
Constitution, Communist prisoners held without trial were released;
some of these were also rehabilitated in cultural and educational
institutions. But the junta's hostility to Communist "activists"
persisted. In fact, it was not until the nationalization of the Suez
Canal and the menacing protests it evoked in London and Paris
that the junta began to see more use for the support proffered by
the domestic Left.

In a statement issued by the Communists in July 1956 the nationalization of the Canal was described as the culmination of a series
of steps—namely Egypt's adherence to the Bandung declarations,
evacuation of British forces from the Canal Zone, strengthening of
the Egyptian Army, recognition of the People's Republic of China,
and establishment of economic and cultural relations with socialist
states.[2] The Communists now placed Egypt in the category of
nations whose national *bourgeoisie* had moved out of the imperialist
orbit and elevated the national struggle to a higher plane. This,
they contended, was rendered possible by the economic and
political support which the re-invigorated socialist camp offered.[3]

The tripartite attack on Egypt in October 1956 ended, at least
for the time being, whatever reservations still lingered on either
side. For the Communists it was a heaven-sent opportunity to
wipe out the remaining vestiges of British influence in Egypt. It
suited Nasser, too. Fighting against heavy odds and for his very
existence, Nasser appealed to the patriotic sentiments of all Egyptians including his opponents. A large number of MDLN detenus
were released. Later they claimed credit for having organized,
together with the Left-wing Wafdists, an effective civilian resistance
at Port Sa'id. They fanned out into the entire Western Canal Zone
equipped with arms liberally distributed by the authorities. At
Port Sa'id they led the heroic resistance against the British occupation forces. Drawing a balance sheet of the Suez War, Salama Musa
wrote that the Soviet threat to fling rockets at the aggressors deterred
the latter and enabled Egypt to emerge victorious. Another major
cause of Egyptian victory, he added, "was the solidarity of the
people and the army in Port Sa'id which prevented quick penetra-

---

[2] *At-Tariq* (Bierut), vol. 15 (September-October 1956), pp. 15-16.

[3] Other nations included in this category were India and Indonesia. See
Mahmud Amin al-'Alam, "For a Comprehensive Arab National Congress",
At-Tariq, vol. 15 (October-November 1959), pp. 17-18.

tion of the enemy in the Canal Zone as was originally planned".[4]

The Suez War and its aftermath elevated the Egyptian Communists to a position of unprecedented respectability. But the Communists owed this more to Bulganin's stern warnings to Britain, France, and Israel, the Soviet and Chinese offers of volunteers, and Egypt's greater dependence on the Soviet bloc for arms, economic aid, and trade, than to their own strength or influence in the country. In any case, the result was a large-scale influx of Marxists in journalistic, educational, and cultural organizations. A pro-Soviet daily newspaper called *Al-Masa'* was started under the direction of Khalid Muhi ad-Din, who had been in eclipse ever since his abortive attempt in 1954 to mobilize army support for General Naguib.

The Communists now enjoyed a measure of freedom they had not known since the inception of the movement. But they were still on the outer periphery of the citadel of power firmly held by the Revolutionary Command Council. What course the latter would adopt in the future was a moot question. At this juncture an attempt was made by the two major Communist factions, namely the MDLN and the Communist Party of Egypt, to close their ranks. The two factions indeed merged into a single organization in February 1958 but only to drift apart by the following autumn. The differences centred on the question of Arab unity and evaluation of the Egyptian revolution. One group endorsed President Nasser's pan-Arab policy and pleaded for cautious support of his "*bourgeois*-nationalist reformist" movement; the other one, on the contrary, upheld the separatist posture of the Iraqi Communist Party and warned that in the final analysis Nasser's revolution was a tool of the monopolists. On the question of foreign policy both factions were equally suspicious of Nasser's discreet neutrality between Washington and Moscow. Both factions styled themselves the Egyptian Communist Party.

Second Rift with the Régime

Towards the end of 1958 the uneasy co-existence between the Egyptian Communists and the Nasser Government abruptly came to an end. The real cause of the rift was, of course, mutual suspicion and distrust. The Communists felt that co-existence with Nasser and pan-Arabism was increasingly working against their own interests. In Egypt itself, the authorities had kept them at arm's

[4] Salama Musa, *Tarbiya Salama Musa* (Cairo, n.d.), p. 262.

6

length. The merger of Syria and Egypt meant extension of Nasser's policies to Syria where Communism had registered spectacular successes in recent years. The Egyptian and Syrian Communists, therefore, looked upon the Iraqi Revolution of 14 July 1958, in which local Communists had played no mean part, as an appropriate occasion to be quits with Nasser. On the other side, Nasser was deeply perturbed by the unconcealed enthusiasm of the Egyptian and Syrian Communists for the Iraqi Revolution, which had been steadily emerging as a rallying point of Arab Communist loyalties against the rising tide of Nasserism.

Nasser's initial attack was directed against the Syrian Communists whom he accused of having opposed the merger of Syria and Egypt and of having betrayed Arab nationalism by joining the ranks of the "stooges of imperialism and Zionism".[5] Following this declaration at Port Sa'id on 23 December 1958, about a hundred Communists comprising teachers, writers, trade unionists, and the editor of the Syrian Communist daily An-Nur,[6] were rounded up in a lightning operation. In Egypt, however, large-scale arrests were carried out in the wake of the Mosul Revolt. Early in March 1959, as Kassem proceeded to crush the Cairo-inspired abortive coup d'état in Mosul, Khalid Muhi ad-Din's Al-Masa' (Cairo) came out with a front-page leader captioned: "The Iraqi people suppress the Shawwaf revolt".[7] This provoked the Government to swoop down on Egyptian Communists of all hues including those who had been afforded cushy jobs in newspaper offices and propaganda organs of the Government since the Suez War.[8] After the defection of some leading Syrian Communists from their party the UAR police got clues leading to the arrest of several underground Communist leaders in the Egyptian region. Abu Sayf Yusuf, the First Secretary of the Egyptian Communist Party, was arrested in December 1961.[9]

It is important to note that the defiance of Nasser by the Egyptian and Syrian Communists coincided with a corresponding shift in Soviet tactics in the area. By supporting Nasser on Suez and

---

[5] President Gamal Abdel-Nasser's Speeches and Press-Interviews, 1958 (Cairo, n.d.), pp. 353-4.

[6] An-Nur (Damascus) was edited by 'Abdul-Baqi Jamali.

[7] Colonel 'Abdul Wahab ash-Shawwaf was the leader of the ill-fated armed insurrection.

[8] Al-Hayat (Beirut), 21 February and 21 May, 1959.

[9] Ibid., 25 January, 1961.

Arab neutralists in general Moscow had secured a niche for itself in Arab Eastern politics. Its next objective was to reduce dependence on Nasser. Having been checkmated by Nasser in Syria at the beginning of 1958, Moscow appeared determined to build up Kassem's Iraq as a counterweight to Nasser in order to seek maximum concessions from both. Hence the angry public exchanges between the UAR and the Soviet Union in 1959 and again in 1961.

In sharp contrast to the warm cordiality which prevailed between Cairo and Moscow since 1955, Khrushchev now derided Nasser as a "hot-headed young man" who spoke about Communism in "the language of the imperialists" and was "taking on things which are more than his stature permits".[10] Nasser retorted that "had it not been for this hot-headedness we would not have been able to achieve the great miracles which we have realized.... Had it not been for this passion Egypt would have been turned into rocket bases against the Soviet Union and the whole Communist world".[11] In the next round, Fikri Abaza, a leading Egyptian journalist, published an open letter to Khrushchev in the Cairo weekly, *Al-Musawwar*, saying that the Soviet Union had received back in full measure all that it had given in the form of loans, aid, and moral support: the UAR had paid a "high price" through its "policy of neutrality and non-participation in military blocs". This evoked an angry rejoinder from *Pravda* (Moscow) reproaching "the journalistic huckster" for attempting "to turn the blood of the martyrs of Port Sa'id into an object of commonplace barter".[12]

The Communists' explanation for the showdown with Nasser was that the latter had been taken in by American overtures to divide the liberated Arab peoples of Iraq and the United Arab Republic (UAR). The UAR officials were also accused of having raised the slogan that the struggle against imperialism was over.[13]

Unresolved Dilemma

In 1959, Arab Communism and Nasserism had staked rival claims to inherit the Arab East. By the middle of 1963 exuberant

---

[10] *Mid-East Mirror* (Beirut), vol. 11 (22 March 1959), pp. 2, 20.

[11] Ibid., 29 March, 1959, p. 3.

[12] *Mizan Newsletter* (London), vol. 3 (June 1961), pp. 5-8.

[13] "Ibn Khaldun", "Arab Solidarity: A Basic Condition of National Liberation and Progress". *Ath-Thaqafa al-Wataniya* (Beirut), vol. 8 (May-June 1959), pp. 24, 31.

optimism on either side yielded to sobering realism bordering on frustration. The Kirkuk massacre (July 1959) and its repercussions all but extinguished the hopes of Iraq developing into an Arab Soviet. On the other side, Nasser's faith in the invincibility of Arab nationalism and his own infallibility was shaken by the unceremonious secession of Syria in September 1961.

Syria's separation from the UAR and Nasser's open conflict with the Ba'th Socialist Party on that issue proved immensely beneficial to the Egyptian Communists. In the course of his battle with the Ba'th, Nasser gradually neutralized the Egyptian Communists. This tactical readjustment also fitted into Nasser's domestic programme envisaged in the 1962 Charter.[14] The fact that the Charter adopted much of what the Communists had been promising all along stirred many an Egyptian Leftist into taking a fresh look at the military régime. The July 1961 legislation which envisaged state control over a wide range of commercial and industrial enterprises convinced the Communists that Nasser wanted— whether from conviction or from necessity was immaterial—to develop the Egyptian economy on non-capitalist lines and that he meant business. The Charter and the July Laws formed the subject of heated discussion among the several hundred Communist detenus huddled up in concentration camps. There were those who argued that these documents were merely a blueprint of bureaucratic State capitalism and those who discerned progressive elements in them. At any rate, most of the Communists tended to concede that Nasser's practice was far more eloquent than his theory, particularly in respect of resisting colonialism and reorganizing the national economy on non-capitalist lines.

The Charter and the July Laws also evoked considerable interest in Communist circles outside Egypt. The Soviet experts, while conceding that these measures signified "the end of the anti-imperialist revolution and the beginning of a socialist revolution", blandly underscored the un-Marxian features of the Charter such as its solicitude for religion, belief in non-exploiting private property, and rejection of the concepts of class conflict and dictatorship of the proletariat.[15] It was also pointed out that Nasser's socialism was being "decreed from above", without enlisting support of wide

[14] Government of the UAR, Information Department, *The Charter* (Draft) (Cairo, 1962).

[15] B. Abasov quoted in *Mizan Newsletter*, vol. 4 (July-August 1962), pp. 8-9.

sections of the workers, and without unleashing the creative initiative of the masses, and that its leadership was confined to "a narrow circle of participants".[16] The view of the Communist Parties of Syria, the Lebanon, Iraq and Jordan on the Egyptian developments were expressed in a symposium held in the autumn of 1964. A working paper prepared for the occasion by the "Lebanese comrades" described Nasser's socialism as "a conglomeration of scientific and Utopian socialism, petty-bourgeois ideas, narrow nationalism, religious prejudices, and subjective idealism". But in the course of the discussion that followed a more positive approach to Nasserism seemed to emerge. It stressed the need for understanding "the dynamics of Nasserism", for "completely dispelling the mistrust and suspicion between the Communist movement and Nasserism", and for tackling the "negative features" of Nasserism such as its dictatorial nature in "a friendly and constructive way".[17]

But the Charter having blunted the edge of Communist propaganda, Nasser was not in a hurry to enlist Communist support. Only a few Communists were released in 1962 and early 1963. They were those who had promised to work with the régime as individuals. In July 1963, however, Nasser abruptly announced the decision of his Government to release all political prisoners, most of them being Communists, by the end of the year and invited them to join the Arab Socialist Union and "to actively participate in the construction of socialism".[18] Whether the measure was dictated by the need to countervail the mounting hostility of the propertied classes towards the July Laws or by the necessity to propitiate Khrushchev, who was due to visit the UAR early in 1964, or by both, remains a moot question. Haykal explained the momentous decision in terms of the vigour of the Egyptian body politic to withstand the Communist doctrine. The time was gone, he contended, when the Egyptian society had no means of fighting Communism and the Communists except through police and prisons. It could now safely permit them to have their say and let the people pronounce on it.[19] In any case, the promise was carried out and by

[16] R. M. Avakov and G. I. Mirskiy quoted in ibid. (September 1962), pp. 2-6.

[17] "Problem of National Liberation Movement of the Arab People: A Symposium" in *Peace, Freedom and Socialism* (Prague), vol. 7 (September 1964), pp. 52-59. The participants included Khalid Bakdash (Syria), 'Aziz al-Haj (Iraq), and Fu'ad Nassar (Jordan).

[18] *Le Monde* (Paris), Sélection Hebdomadair, 4-10 July 1963.

[19] Muhammad Hasanayn Haykal in *Al-Ahram* (Cairo), 29 January, 1965.

the end of 1963 all Communists other than those convicted for criminal offence were set free. The Communists reciprocated by offering to co-operate with the régime as individuals. On 25 April, 1965, *Al-Ahram* announced a rare development in the history of Communism: the organization known as the Communist Party of Egypt *disbanded* itself. The decision was taken at a prolonged meeting of the party's Central Committee after much "self-criticism" interspersed with unreserved admiration for the far-reaching social changes being carried out in Egypt under Nasser's leadership. In view of the above the Communists were advised to enrol in the Government-sponsored Arab Socialist Union (ASU) which "alone was competent to carry out the tasks of the revolution".

With the Communist Party having been "voluntarily dissolved" and the so-called "reformed Communists" explicitly committed to function within the framework of the Charter, what of the future of Communism in Egypt? The atomization of Egyptian Communism was perhaps the logical outcome of a movement which had been the most faction-ridden in the entire Arab East. But it brought in its train some compensating rewards. The Communist organizations ceased to exist, but not so the Communists. On the contrary, quite a few of them were assigned responsible rôles in the sprawling public enterprises, in the Press and in cultural institutions. Above all, the Communists secured some key positions in the ASU: Khalid Muhi ad-Din was at one time appointed as Secretary to the ASU's Press Committee;[20] Lutfi al-Khuli edits *At-Tali'a*, the ideological organ of the ASU; and Ibrahim Sa'd ad-Din heads the Arab Socialist Institute, which trains cadres for the ASU. But beyond that, the Communists have no option but to work under Nasser's leadership until the time when conditions become favourable for independent action. As Anwar 'Abd al-Malik put it soon after the 1963 thaw: "The socialist revolution will not be on the agenda until a later phase, by which time the actual development of Egyptian society will provide the means to solve the basic problems."[21]

---

[20] He is in addition General Secretary of the National Peace Council of the UAR and a member of the Presidium of the World Peace Council.

[21] Anwar 'Abd al-Malik, n. 1, pp. 66-67.

CHAPTER NINE

SYRIA: FAILURE OF FRONT TACTICS

THE outbreak of the Suez War found Syria in a state of violent emotional convulsion. There was a spontaneous outburst of sympathy for embattled Egypt, Syria's sole trusted mentor in the Arab East. As a mark of Syria's deep sympathy for Egypt, Colonel Sarraj's men blew up the British oil pipelines connecting the Iraqi oilfields to the Mediterranean. Martial law was promulgated in the whole country to ward off any mischief by the régime's internal foes. Then came Moscow's stringent warnings to London, Paris, and Tel-Aviv only to confirm most Syrians in the belief that the Soviet Union was their dependable protector in an area infested by colonial sharks.

The Iraqi Plot

In the meantime, Colonel Sarraj had been poring over the reports on the suspicious movements of hostile elements within Syria and abroad. According to evidence later produced in the course of Syrian and Iraqi trials,[1] the plot against the Leftist-neutralist Syrian régime was contrived on Iraqi initiative reinforced by Anglo-American backing and active participation of Syrian political malcontents—the PPS exiles in the Lebanon; supporters of ex-dictator Adib Shishakli; 'Adnan al-Atasi and Faydi al-Atasi (Sha'b Party); the pro-Hashimite don, Munir al-'Ajlani; Mikail Ilyan (Watani Party); and tribal chiefs Shaykh Hail as-Surur and Amir Hasan al-Atrash. The immediate objectives of the Iraqi plot were: overthrow of the régime; assassination of Colonel Sarraj, Akram Hawrani, and Khalid Bakdash; purging the Ba'thists, Communists, and their sympathizers from the army and the administration; and abrogation of the Constitution. On the wider objective of uniting Syria and Iraq in fulfilment of the elusive Fertile Crescent Scheme, however, there was no perfect agreement among the plotters.

[1] The evidence adduced by the Syrian authorities was largely corroborated by that revealed in the Baghdad trials following the July 1958 *coup d'état*. For a detailed exposition of the subject, see Patrick Seale, *The Struggle for Syria* (London, 1965), ch. 20.

Sarraj's radio broadcast on 23 November 1956 announcing the discovery of the plot produced more convulsions in a country already rocked by the Suez crisis. A further swing to the Left followed. Khalid Bakdash and Akram Hawrani made a concerted effort to deal a fresh blow to their political opponents. The leading authors of the plot were either arrested or made to flee from the country. Early in December a National Front consisting of Leftist and the Watani deputies was formed. Towards the end of the month it succeeded in installing a more homogeneous cabinet pledged to "forgo partisan or selfish interests".[2] A significant development was Khalid al-'Azm's re-entry into the cabinet after a year-long absence. The Sha'b was once again excluded.

The Communist Party of Syria gained indirectly from these developments. But it was not in a position yet to press for a share in authority. All that it was able to secure was the appointment of Communist-leaning Colonel 'Afif Bizri as president of the military court which was to try the accused in the Iraqi plot. And this was of no small value. For Bizri's unconcealed bias in the handling of the court proceedings and the wild chorus of public denunciation of the accused and their foreign accomplices served to undermine the prestige which America had acquired by its disapproval of the tripartite attack on Egypt. Following this, Syrian-American relations worsened rapidly.

East-West Confrontation in Syria

The 1957 crisis that brought the Communist Party of Syria into unprecedented limelight marked the culmination of the Right-Left tussle in Syria and of the wider rivalry between the super powers for influence and hegemony in the Middle Eastern area.

The facts of the new development in Syria, which brought the crisis to a head, were simple enough. On 13 August the Syrian Government announced the discovery of yet another plot allegedly designed to overthrow the régime. This was quickly followed by an army purge and replacement of the conservative Chief of Staff, General Nizam ad-Din, by the Communist-leaning Colonel 'Afif Bizri, who was then promoted to the rank of Major-General. This development was interpreted in the Western camp as a Communist-led *coup d'état* designed to eliminate anti-Soviet officers from the

[2] Gordon S. Torrey, *Syrian Politics and the Military* (Ohio, 1964), p. 326.

Syrian army. Its apprehensions were summed up by *The Times* correspondent as follows:

> Of the men behind the *coup*...it can be fairly assumed that the Communist Chief, Khaled Baqdash, is a leading though little publicized actor. Certainly Baqdash is the most dominant personality in Syrian politics in spite of his lack of office.[3]

The international features of the crisis were, however, immensely more intricate. Some weeks after the exposure of the Iraqi plot, the US Government had announced the Eisenhower Doctrine, its first fumbling step in the direction of an independent Middle Eastern policy unencumbered by Anglo-French idiosyncrasies. Its broad purpose was to extend American aid and protection to such states in the area as were keen to combat domestic and world Communism. The American initiative, however, got into rough weather from the very beginning. Its assumption that the Anglo-French débâcle at Suez had left behind a "vacuum"—military, political, and economic—which the United States must fill before the Soviet bloc rushed into it was patently outrageous to Arab nationalist susceptibilities. Besides, the fact that the immediate objective of American policy was to pressurize Egypt and Syria, already drawn into the orbit of Soviet bloc policies, provoked loud protests in Cairo and Damascus.

Within hours of the announcement of the Doctrine (5 January, 1957) Damascus Radio repudiated the thesis that there was a Communist danger in the area. The Doctrine itself was officially rejected on 10 January. With the United States determined to pressurize Syria to rectify its Leftward drift and the Soviet Union resolved to reinforce its position there, a breakneck race between the two Powers ensued.

The Soviet Union started a programme of massive military and economic aid to Syria. Following President Quwatli's visit to Moscow in the fall of 1956 a second instalment of Soviet military hardware began to flow into Syria.[4] In March 1957 Czechoslovak Techno-Export Company secured the prestigious contract to set up Syria's first oil refinery at Homs. To top it all, the Soviet Union

---

[3] *The Times* (London), 21 August, 1957.
[4] *The Times* of 3 October, 1957 valued these arms at £50 million.

announced, on 6 August, massive economic aid to Syria. The deal, negotiated by Defence Minister Khalid al-'Azam, who had already earned the reputation of being the most ardent champion of Syro-Soviet friendship, envisaged a variety of projects ranging from construction of railways, dams, and hydro-electric stations to geological surveys and nitrogen-fertilizer plants. These were to be accomplished through Soviet credits worth £130 million at $2\frac{1}{2}$ per cent interest repayable in 12 years.[5]

The Syro-Soviet communiqué announcing the agreement stressed that Soviet economic aid and technical co-operation would be carried out "without any political or other strings being attached to it" and with "respect for the national sovereignty of the Syrian Republic".[6] Mustafa Amin, Secretary of the Syrian Peace Committee, lauded the agreement as "one of the biggest victories gained [by Syria] in her struggle for sovereignty and liberty".[7]

The American response to Soviet advances in Syria evolved on two mutually complementary levels. In a first-hand report on the post-Suez Middle East, Paul Johnson of the *New Statesman*[8] wrote on 6 July:

> Sooner or later, if their system is to work, the Americans must dispose of the Syrian régime. They are already hard at work using as their allies the Lebanese Government and the neo-Fascist parties which flourish in the tropical political atmosphere of Beirut and which maintain clandestine contacts with the opposition in Damascus.

On another level, the United States alerted Syria's pro-Western neighbours against the dangers implicit in the massive inflow of Soviet arms into their backyard. Even before the announcement of the Eisenhower Doctrine the State Department had declared, on 29 November, 1956, that the United States would view with "utmost gravity" any threat to the territorial integrity or political independence of Turkey, Pakistan, Iraq, and Iran and would support

---

[5] A final agreement to that effect was concluded on 28 October, 1957. Details in *Soviet News* (London), 1 November, 1957, p. 66. Also see *The Economist* (London), 31 August, 1957.

[6] *Soviet News*, 7 August, 1957, p. 93.

[7] Mustafa Amin, "A Voice from Syria", *Labour Monthly* (London), vol. 39 (October 1957), p. 466.

[8] *New Statesman* (London), 6 July, 1957, p. 21.

the "collective efforts of these nations to maintain their independence".[9]

The first line of approach was apparently rendered ineffective after the Syrian Government's disclosure, on 13 August, of a plot to subvert the régime. The Syrian charge that the conspiracy was masterminded by Howard E. Stone, an American diplomat in Damascus,[10] in collaboration with Adib Shishakli, Colonel Ibrahim Husayni, the Syrian Military Attaché in Rome, and the PPS, was flatly denied by the United States. President Eisenhower decried it as "a smoke-screen behind which people that have leftist leanings are trying to build up their power".[11] Patrick Seale, a shrewd observer of the Middle Eastern scene during those stormy years, however, believes that it is hard to dismiss the Syrian charges as fabrications.[12]

Whether the Syrian charges were well founded or not the United States, henceforth, took expeditious measures to exert extraneous pressures on Syria. Having realized that the intricate Syrian situation did not warrant direct intervention under the Eisenhower Doctrine, it resolved to communicate "assurances" to pro-Western states in the region that "if Syria's Muslim neighbours felt it necessary to take action against aggression by the Syrian Government, the United States would undertake to expedite shipment of arms already committed to the Middle Eastern countries and, further, would replace losses as quickly as possible". In the meantime American aircraft were sent from Western Europe to the US base at Adna and the Sixth Fleet was ordered to the eastern end of the Mediterranean.[13] Later in the same month Eisenhower dispatched Loy W. Henderson to the Middle East on a crucial mission to probe the prospects of collective action by Syria's neighbours against it. This was closely followed by concentration of Turkish troops along Syria's northern border.

American counter-moves having unnerved the Syrian régime,

[9] *Department of State Bulletin* (Washington, D. C.), vol. 35 (10 December 1956), p. 918.

[10] The Syrian authorities described Stone as "number one" expert on *coups d'états* who had earlier organized similar plots in Sudan, Iran and Guatemala. *New York Times*, 14 August, 1957.

[11] Ibid., 22 August, 1957.

[12] Seale, n. 1, pp. 293-5.

[13] Dwight D. Eisenhower, *The White House Years*: *Waging Peace* (London, 1966), pp. 198-9.

it was now Moscow's turn to reassure its Arab ally. On 11 September,
N. A. Bulganin formally warned the Turkish Premier, Adnan
Menderes, how the Turks would feel "if foreign troops were concentrated on their borders" and added that military action against
Syria could not remain "localized".[14] Later in the month when a
Soviet naval squadron called at Latakia the event was widely
acclaimed in Syria as proof of the Soviet undertaking to defend
Syria. Welcoming Vice-Admiral V. F. Kotov, commander of the
squadron, Defence Minister Khalid al-'Azm said: "Latakia is
not a Soviet base. However, the Soviet Union has a good base in
the heart of every Arab."[15] On 8 October, Khrushchev told James
Reston of the *New York Times* that Henderson having failed in
his mission to obtain co-operation of the Arab states against Syria,
the United States was now engaged in an effort to get Turkey to
launch an attack,[16] and dramatically added: "If rifles fire, the
rockets will start flying."[17]

The Anti-Climax

At this critical juncture Colonel Sarraj and the Ba'thists turned
the tables on both Washington and Moscow by inviting Egyptian
intervention in Syria. At the invitation of the Syrian Government
Egyptian troops landed at Latakia on 13 October, 1957. The step
was taken under the Syro-Egyptian Mutual Defence Pact of 20
October, 1955,[18] which stipulated immediate "preventive and
defensive measure" in the event of "an imminent threat of war
or a sudden international emergency of a menacing nature". On
the face of it, Egyptian action amounted to meeting its treaty
obligations to Syria, which feared an attack from its Turkish
neighbour. But Egypt's real purpose was, as corroborated by
later developments, to contain Soviet influence which had suddenly
shot up as a result of East-West confrontation.

With the Ba'th Socialists, Arab nationalist and others, except
the Communists, looking to Cairo for rescue, the tempers of the
contending super giants rapidly cooled down. On 29 October,

[14] *Soviet News*, 16 September, 1957, pp. 189-90.

[15] Ibid., 1 October, 1957, p. 3.

[16] The Tass later published a long statement giving the details of Henderson's
alleged plot. See ibid. 21 October, 1957, pp. 45-48.

[17] *New York Times*, 10 October, 1957.

[18] Text in *Middle East Journal* (Washington, D. C.), vol. 10 (Winter 1956),
pp. 77-79.

Khrushchev put in a surprise appearance at a Turkish Embassy reception in Moscow and proposed a toast to peace: "Let him be damned who wants war! Let him fight alone!" Referring to Syria specifically, he added: "The more talk there is of war the less likely war becomes."[19] Away in New York, where the UN General Assembly had been discussing the Syrian complaint against Turkey, the US Ambassador, Henry Cabot Lodge, quickly reciprocated by playing down the "red menace" and strongly supporting King Sa'ud's offer to mediate between Turkey and Syria. Earlier, the semi-official Egyptian daily, *Al-Jamhuriya*,[20] had advised restraint on the part of Syria notwithstanding "serious" incidents along the Syro-Turkish border and added:

> At this juncture it is judicious to observe absolute restraint. In fact, it is our bounden duty not to allow such provocations to prompt us to hasty retaliation.

On 30 October, a spokesman of the Syrian Foreign Ministry declared that tension on the border had "eased".

In the meantime the Syrian leaders started a vigorous campaign for immediate union with Egypt. On 18 November, a joint parliamentary session of Syria and Egypt (with a 35-member Egyptian parliamentary delegation present) voted for a federal union of the two states. The union was proclaimed on 1 February, 1958.

The Syrian Communists and the 1957 Crisis

Was the crisis of 1957 precipitated by the Syrian Communists? Was the Soviet Union working for a take-over by the Syrian Communists? And was the union of Egypt and Syria rushed in order to prevent that from happening? Definitive answers to these questions are hard to seek in the absence of archival material. But circumstantial evidence now available enables us to reach some tentative conclusions.

First, the seeming ascendancy of the Communists in 1956-57 rested on their own compromises and adjustments with the remaining constituents of the National Front. Whether in discharging political broadsides against the Rightists or in uncovering plots against the régime, the initiative always lay in the

[19] *The Times*, 30 October, 1957.
[20] *Al-Jamhuriya* (Cairo), 26 October, 1957.

hands of the Ba'th-Sarraj coterie. The Communists doubtless put these opportunities to maximum use but seldom created them. However, in the process the Communists acquired more strength and influence. They exacerbated Syria's differences with its pro-Western neighbours and throve on the tensions thus generated. They gained a foothold in the Popular Resistance Force, a para-military organization consisting of thousands of civilians and headed by Salah al-Bizri. In the process, their strength rose to 18,000.[21] In 1957, the party organ *An-Nur* claimed a circulation of 7,000.[22] A more spectacular gain was Colonel 'Afif al-Bizri's appointment as the Syrian Chief of Staff.

Born at Sidon in the Lebanon, Bizri had joined the Syrian army in 1937. He is said to have come under Marxian influence[23] during his student days in Paris. But unlike other Arab Communists he had fought in the war against Israel in 1948 and earned a reputation for gallantry. In the mid-fifties he joined an influential group of army officers—consisting of Colonel Sarraj, Captain Mustafa Hamdun, Amin al-Nafuri, Tu'mih al-'Awadatallah, and others —which together with the Ba'th was largely instrumental in giving a radical orientation to Syrian policies. According to Haykal, he had also gathered a group of about twenty Communist-leaning officers of the Syrian army around him.[24] But in the opinion of the infinitely more knowledgeable Colonel Sarraj, the choice fell on Bizri because he had "no personal following in the army and was connected with none of the major factions then feuding inside the general staff".[25]

On balance, some of the victories ascribed to the Communists were more apparent than real. As for the rest, if the Communists improved their position in Syria, so did their other Leftist partners. And the one cancelled out the other. It is clear that unlike the Communists in some East European countries, the Communists

[21] Torrey, n. 2, p. 295.

[22] Henry Loomis, "The Soviet Propaganda Campaign in the Middle East", in *New Look at the Middle East*, William Sands, ed.,(Washington, D.C., 1957) p. 20.

[23] After taking over as Chief of Staff Bizri repeatedly asserted that he had never been a Communist and "I am not one now." *Daily Star* (Beirut), 29 August and 17 November, 1957.

[24] Hasanayn Haykal, "What Happened in Syria?", *Al-Ahram*, 10 November 1961.

[25] Seale, n. 1, p. 295.

in Syria, though not lacking in political ambition, constituted a relatively weak link in an alliance dominated by the Ba'th and aspiring army officers.

Secondly, the thesis propagated by some Western Governments and Press that the Soviet Union was heading for a Communist take-over in Syria does not bear scrutiny. For Moscow's main objective at the time was to meet the challenge posed by the Eisenhower Doctrine. That the Doctrine infringed Soviet as well as Arab neutralists' interests automatically brought them closer to each other. Moscow must have also realized—and all evidence suggests that it did—that to turn Syria into an Arab Soviet would defeat the immediate purpose of its new Arab policy. And this thesis is further corroborated by the kind of instruments chosen by the Soviet Union to achieve its objectives. The mainstay of Soviet policy, it must be noted, was neither the Syrian Communists nor the Ba'th, but Khalid al-'Azm, the millionaire whom political ambition had driven into Leftist company but whom no one could seriously accuse of being a Communist. Besides, there were indications of lack of consistency between Soviet and Syrian Communist objectives. While the Communist Party of Syria (CPS) evinced a keen desire, particularly after the August 1957 events, to press forward its claims for share in political power, Moscow evidently was not in a mood to disturb its good relations with the dominant elements in Syria for the sake of local Communist gains of dubious value.[26]

In short, Soviet aid and comfort to Syria was in direct response to the West's forward policy in the Middle East. The West now apprehended that the Soviet initiative might as well be the prelude to a Khrushchev Doctrine for the Middle East. The crisis created by this confrontation was, in plain terms, the outcome of conventional power rivalries between the US and the USSR and not of a Soviet desire to acquire a Communist bastion in the Arab world.

Finally, Egyptian and Syrian motivations in bringing about a hasty merger of the two countries. Nasser is on record as having asserted that it was indeed to liquidate a plot of the Syrian Communists "to turn Syria into a Communist Soviet" that the union of Egypt and Syria "was rushed through" at the behest of Syrian

[26] For a searching analysis of Soviet motivations see *The Economist* (London), 24 August, 1957, p. 624.

patriots[27]—a claim which cannot be fully substantiated. Doubtless the Syrian Communists as well as the Soviet Union were not truly enthusiastic about merger,[28] for they saw greater opportunities for themselves in a neutralist Syria increasingly dependent on Moscow for defence and economic development. But they could not afford to oppose openly the clamour for union either: the Communists because they were not strong enough to survive an open rift with their Leftist allies, and the Soviet Union for fear of alienating the pan-Arabists whose support was crucial for the success of Soviet Middle Eastern policy. Hence political exigency persuaded Bizri to lead the Syrian team, in January 1958, to negotiate union with Egypt. He might have also hoped that Egypt would not accept the proposal immediately.[29] But contrary to Communist expectations Nasser endorsed the proposal for union. As a result the CPS inadvertently became party to an agreement which it in fact abhorred.

In the final analysis, it was the Ba'th, backed by some powerful factions in the army, which took the initiative in the matter. Not being powerful enough to rule Syria single-handed, the Ba'th decided to cash in on the widespread fear of a Communist take-over which they had themselves contributed so much to create. This stratagem stampeded non-Communist Syrian politicians as well as Nasser into a premature union.

Headlong Clash with Nasser

The birth of the United Arab Republic in the midst of surging Arab enthusiasm was greeted by the Syrian Communists with sullen calm. Nasser had agreed to merger only after securing compliance to his basic condition that all Syrian political parties should be dissolved. The Ba'th had readily accepted this proposition in the hope that it was intended only to get rid of the Communists and the reactionary Right-wing parties. The Communists, on their part, had no illusion about what was in store for them.

Even before the proclamation of the union the Communists

[27] President Nasser's interview to R. K. Karanjia, 17 April, 1959. Text in *President Gamal Abdel-Nasser's Speeches and Press-Interviews, 1959* (Cairo, n.d.), pp. 532-48.

[28] The Communist organ began to publicly ventilate its fears about the impact of the proposed union on the CPS and demanded that union should be based on "sound democratic bases". *An-Nur* (Damascus), 14 January, 1958.

[29] Haykal, n. 24.

began to ventilate their criticism of what was coming. On 22 January, the party organ, *An-Nur*, frankly questioned Cairo's demand for the "freezing" of party activity and observed that the Syrian people had fought hard for democratic freedoms and could not now surrender them.[30] At Homs, Badruddin as-Siba'i, a local Communist leader, attacked the Ba'thist leaders and their conception of unity which he claimed was inspired by greed for power. And on 5 February, as the Syrian Parliament assembled to vote on merger, Khalid Bakdash left for Moscow along with his wife and eight members of the Central Committee. Earlier the Committee had decided to destroy all party documents, membership lists, and records of front organizations.

While estrangement grew between the Government and the Communists, both sides discreetly tried to avoid open conflict. The party organ *An-Nur* switched from local politics to safer topics such as the Tashkent Conference and François Sagan. Cairo, in turn, appointed General 'Afif al-Bizri as Commander of the Syrian wing of the UAR army now called the First Army. But when Bizri resented Cairo's overriding control on postings and transfers and resigned in protest, Nasser tried to console him by giving him an assignment connected with economic planning carrying a minister's salary. Bizri accepted it.[31]

Bizri's exit from the army increased Communist resentment. But the Government's action, on the eve of May Day, prohibiting public demonstrations turned resentment into angry defiance. The authorities reacted by arresting thirty people. *An-Nur* sharply criticized the arrests and demanded redress.[32] On 23 June Khalid Bakdash candidly set forth the party's differences with the UAR régime:

> An attempt has been made to talk us into disbanding the party—at least formally and for a time—and voting for the new constitution, still far removed as it is from democratic principles. We declared that we were for Arab unity and that we would never vote for anti-democratic principles and would never agree to disband our party. By the way, the Communist Party has no authority which could disband it.... We shall

[30] *Ad-Difa'* (Jerusalem), 27 January, 1958.
[31] Haykal, n. 24.
[32] *Az-Zaman* (Baghdad), 11 May, 1958.

7

never give up our Communist Party. We know that its rôle
is growing and will grow still more in future.[33]

After the Iraqi *coup d'état* of 14 July, 1958, in which the Communist Party of Iraq also played a supporting rôle, the Syrian
Communists were convinced that the balance of political forces in
the Arab East had been tipped in their favour and that it was no
longer expedient for them to play second fiddle to the pan-Arabists.
With Baghdad emerging as an alternative rallying point for Arab
radicals, the Communists were naturally tempted to confront
Nasser with heavy demands. To that end the new programme of
the CPS, adopted in November, laid down thirteen points:

1 Free parliaments and executives for Syrian and Egyptian
   regions along with a central parliament and government
   dealing with national defence, foreign policy, and other
   general matters. All these bodies to be constituted on the
   basis of universal franchise and free elections.

2 Democratic liberties: freedom of the Press, assembly,
   demonstrations, and the right to strike; freedom of trade
   unions and the right of all the people and patriotic forces
   to free political association.

3 Fraternal relations and co-operation with the Republic
   of Iraq.

4 Fraternal relations and co-operation with the Soviet
   Union, the People's Republic of China, and other socialist
   countries.

5 Vigorous action against American imperialism.

6 To safeguard Syrian economy and to ensure markets for
   cotton and grain.

7 To put trade and economic relations between Syria and
   Egypt on a sound footing in order to ensure industrial
   development in both the regions.

8 To resist penetration of imperialist capital—American,
   British, Japanese, and West German.

9 Comprehensive agrarian reforms to provide all landless
   peasants with land, irrigation facilities, seeds, and imple-
   ments.

[33] Khaled Bagdash, "The Crisis and the Problems of the Middle East", *World
Marxist Review* (Prague), vol. 1 (September, 1958), pp. 68-70.

10 To protect the workers' wages and rights as envisaged in the Syrian Labour Code.

11 To expand and improve trade relations with Iraq, the Lebanon, and other Arab countries and with the socialist camp.

12 To raise the general material, cultural, and social level of the people.

13 To raise the general level of education and to respect the cultural and democratic rights of the Syrian students.[34]

The Communist programme was clearly a frontal attack on Nasser's concept of unity and his internal and external policies. The fact that it synchronized with similar trades from Baghdad prompted Nasser to hit back with bluster. On 23 December, at a Port Sa'id rally he denounced the Syrian Communists as "stooges of imperialism and Zionism". Immediately after, about a hundred Communists were rounded up and the semi-legal privileges enjoyed by the CPS and its organs abrogated. Among the Communist leaders arrested were: Nasuh al-Ghufri, Muhammad Amin, Ahmad Mahfil, Muhammad al-Hakim, Bishar al-Mawsali, Samih al-Jamali, and Wasfi al-Bani. The party went underground for the fourth time in its chequered history.

The conflict between Nasser and the CPS became even more intense after the abortive pro-Nasser uprising in Mosul in March 1959, which the Communists ascribed to Cairo's design to dominate the Arab world. A new wave of arrests followed. On 22 April, Khalid Bakdash retaliated by debunking the Egyptian revolution and its architect, Nasser:

So far the greatest victories of the Arab national liberation movement have been the liberation of Iraq and the establishment of the Iraqi Republic. Nasser is marching on the road of world reaction which aims at annihilating the Iraqi Republic. Nasser is now using Syria as a base of aggression against the Iraqi Republic. In so doing, he absolutely contradicts the will and interests of the Egyptian and Syrian peoples and also the very principles of positive neutrality.[35]

[34] Text of the Programme in *World Marxist Review*, vol. 2 (February, 1959), pp. 61-63.

[35] Bakdash's interview to *Nepszabadsag* (Budapest). Quoted in *Problems of Communism* (Washington, D. C.), vol. 8 (May-June 1959), p. 45.

Later in the year, Bakdash wrote about the crystallization of two trends in the Arab national movement: the *bourgeois*-democratic trend, headed by "the ruling circles of the UAR", comprising half-hearted reforms, pampering of the national- *bourgeoisie*, and compromise with the imperialists; and the national-liberation trend envisaging a united national front of anti-imperialist forces as being evolved in Iraq. To substantiate his indictment of Nasser, he contended that the Anglo-Egyptian financial deal,[36] the IBRD loans, and the influx of West German capital into the UAR were clear enough signs that Cairo was "inclining more and more towards a compromise with the imperialists". Secondly, the Arab unity movement spearheaded by Nasser was only a cover for the operations of the *Misr* Bank—the "stronghold" of the Egyptian big *bourgeoisie* commended by Nasser as a "people's institution in which all the sons of the country participate", and lauded by *Al-Ahram* as the "fourth Pyramid". Thirdly, Egyptian land reforms did not go "beyond the bounds of capitalist production relationship; nor did they go beyond the limit of *bourgeois*-democratic revolution". They did not signify "the transition to socialism" either.[37]

Impact of Defections

Suppression of the Communist Party in the Syrian region seriously undermined its political effectiveness but not its prestige. In the preceding years the party had successfully built up the reputation of being an ardent champion of independence, unity, and progress. This image was impaired not so much by Nasser's stinging attacks as by the large-scale defections from the party and various front organizations in July-August 1959. The deserters profusely exposed various aspects of party life affording fresh insights into its inner policies and mechanism. It should, however, be noted that the renegades had changed their minds while in prison and presumably under pressure. While making allowance for exaggeration on this count most of the charges seem only to corroborate the well-known propensities of the Communist movement.

[36] A financial agreement between Egypt and the United Kingdom was concluded in February, 1959.

[37] Khaled Bagdache, "Two Trends in the Arab National Movement", *World Marxist Review*, vol. 2 (November 1959), pp. 26-32.

The first batch of the renegades announced its renunciation of the party at a Press conference held in Damascus on 13 July, 1959. It consisted of Rafiq Rida, a member of the Central Committee;[38] Ilyan Dayrani, Chairman of the Writers' Association; 'Adnan Maroni, chief of the party unit in Hama; Munir Fara', chief of the party unit in Qasa' (Damascus); George Abu Sha'r, peasant leader in the district of Damascus; Mahmud Hakim, chief of the party unit in Latakia; Ratib Jabnah (Homs); 'Abdul Hakim Muhlami (Teachers' Association, Damascus); Hasib Kayyali (writer); Rifah Qaswat (writer); and Midhat Abu Khatir (Homs).[39] Another batch of fifteen Communists headed by 'Abdul Baqi Jamali, editor of the proscribed Communist daily, *An-Nur*, denounced the party on 10 August.

The charges broadly referred to Communist designs in Syria before merger, their hostility to pan-Arabism, absence of democracy in the party, reliance on alien support, and exploitation of front organizations. Rafiq Rida disclosed that the Syrian Communists had penetrated the Popular Resistance Force in 1957 with a view to exploiting it for their own ends. After the merger they contacted Egyptian Communist leaders, Khalid Muhi ad-Din and 'Abd al-'Azim Anis, with a view to setting up a single Communist Party for the UAR excluding all pro-Nasser elements.[40] Secondly, the Communist hostility to Arab unity was underlined by all the renegades. But Rida and 'Abdul Baqi Jamali made two specific points. Jamali stated that on the eve of his departure from Syria in February 1958 Khalid Bakdash had confided to him that his hurried exit was contrived to express his "wrath at the unfortunate union". "Even if I had issued a million statements proclaiming my hostility to the union, it would not produce the same effect as my exit and abstention from the historic meeting of the Parliament."[41] To this, Rafiq Rida added that addressing a meeting of the Central Committee on the eve of Nasser's Port Sa'id speech (23 December, 1958) Bakdash had posed the question whether Syria, with its 100,000 Armenians, 50,000 Assyrians, 100,000 Kurds, and 700,000 'Alawis, was Arab.[42]

[38] Originally a Lebanese, Rafiq Rida joined the party in 1931 and held many responsible positions in the organization.

[39] *Al-Hayat* (Beirut), 15 July, 1959.

[40] Full text of Rida's statement in *As-Sahafa* (Beirut), 14 July, 1959.

[41] *Al-Ayyam* (Damascus), 11 August, 1959.

[42] See Rafiq Rida's "Open Letter to the Arab People", in *Al-Ahram*, 4 October, 1959.

Thirdly, the renegades deplored the absence of democracy and freedom of expression and prevalence of autocracy and favouritism inside the party. Rafiq Rida alleged that "anybody who dared to raise a finger at Khalid Bakdash, Artin Madoyan, Niqula Shawi, and Farjallah Hilu, was sure to be expelled or slandered". He also referred to the arbitrary removal of Rashad 'Isa from the Central Committee because he was opposed to the partition of Palestine; to Ra'if Khuri's sudden elevation to the status of a "great writer" followed by denunciation as a "great spy" and ending up as editor of the Communist organ, Al-Akhbar;[43] and to the removal of Wasfi al-Bani from the Central Committee because Bakdash did not like his book on the Soviet Union. He further deprecated Bakdash's refusal to call a party congress over the past fifteen years for fear of challenge to his leadership.[44]

The party was also assailed for its subservience to alien interests. 'Abdul Baqi Jamali specifically charged that the printing press acquired for An-Nur was a gift from abroad. For the first six months the journal was distributed free, the party having subsidized it to the tune of L (S) 150,000 a year from its own hidden resources.[45]

Finally, the tactics of front organizations were exposed. Fida Hilal (also known as "Um Sulayman") and Asma' Saleh of the Women's Organization referred to such false pretences as peace, neutralism, and nationalism which the Communists liberally employed in order to attract people to the various front organizations.[46] Ilyan Dayrani, Chairman of the Writers' Association of Syria, reviewed the career of this organization since its formation in 1951 and concluded that its Communist and non-Communist clients had been used for party ends.[47] Khalid Zaqiq, the leader of the Peasants' Organization, referred to the unscrupulous exploitation by party workers of the sectarian loyalties of the peasantry as a means of raising followers: they posed as Naqshbandis among Naqshbandis and as Rifa'is among Rifa'is.[48]

The Communists on their part denounced the whole affair as

[43] Published from Beirut.

[44] Al-Ayyam, 7 and 9 August, 1959.

[45] An-Nur was started in 1955. See Al-Ayyam, 11 August, 1959.

[46] Al-Hayat, 6 August 1959 and Al-Ayyam, 7 August, 1959.

[47] Al-Ayyam, 4 September, 1959.

[48] Ibid; 16 August, 1959. Naqshbandis represent a Muslim sect founded by a fourteenth century saint, Muhammad al-Bukhari; and the Rifa'is represent another sect named after a twelfth century saint, Ahmad ar-Rifa'i al-Husayni.

an elaborate fraud designed to defame the CPS. The renegades were decried as "traitors, spies and dogs". On policy level, the party's attitude towards Nasser and the union hardened. Now it openly demanded secession. Late in 1959, Bakdash bluntly stated his immediate objective at the Hungarian Party Congress: "It has become necessary to start a united front in Syria in order to restore democracy and to review the bases of union between Egypt and Syria."[49]

Secession and Communist Revival

The secession of Syria from the UAR in September 1961 found the Syrian Communists, whether in exile or underground, in a jubilant mood. The fact that the rebels who broke the union were a motley coalition of disgruntled army officers and conservative political elements who had hated Nasser more for his radical socio-economic measures than for his authoritarianism was of little consequence to the Communists, who now hoped to regain freedom of action.

The CPS hurriedly issued a statement supporting the secessionist régime. It hailed the *coup d'état* as a "historic victory achieved by the Syrian people in collaboration with the army" and an expression of the Syrian people's contempt for "imperialism and Pharaonic domination". As for the immediate future it proposed that "the best means to preserve the victory achieved by the Syrian people is to establish a national democratic rule hostile to imperialism and based on free parliamentary elections".[50]

On 7 October Khalid Bakdash cabled the new Syrian Premier, Mamun al-Kuzbari, requesting him to permit him and his comrades to return to Damascus. The same day, Moscow formally recognized the rebel régime. Kuzbari, however, showed little enthusiasm. On the contrary, he told a Viennese journalist that Sarraj's head had been spared in recognition of his anti-Communist activities.[51] But oblivious of these antipathetic gestures Bakdash made an unfructuous attempt to enter Syria on 19 November. He was refused permission by the Syrian authorities to disembark at the

[49] *Al-Hayat*, 5 December, 1959.
[50] *An-Nida* (Beirut), 4 October, 1961.
[51] Colonel Sarraj was Cairo's mainstay in Syria during the period of union. See *Al-Ahram*, 11 October, 1961 and *Mid-East Mirror* (Beirut), vol. 13 (14 October, 1961), p. 6.

Damascus airport and was forced to return by the same plane.[52]

The next change of régime in Syria was scarcely more favourable to the Communists. The secessionist régime was overthrown by a Ba'thist *coup d'état* in March 1963. Coming as it did within a month after the Ba'thist *coup d'état* against Kassem and the Iraqi Communists it could not afford to be soft to the local Communists. Besides, it was clear that the Ba'th having itself seized power could not share its fruits with an ideological rival.

Early in 1965 Bakdash made a fervent plea to the Syrian President Lieutenant-General Amin al-Hafiz for a national front of all "progressive elements" in Syria. He lauded the Ba'thist régime's nationalization measures and offered his party's support for "preservation and protection of socialism in Syria".[53] But there was no favourable response from the Government which appeared to be more interested in cultivating a Beirut-based pro-Peking Communist faction which also claimed some following in Syria. This group was headed by Nasib Nimr, a former member of the Central Committee of the Communist Party of the Lebanon. The common ground between the two was their intense antipathy towards Nasser.

The Syrian régime's overtures to pro-Peking Communists had hardly crystallized when it was overthrown by Left-wing Ba'thists in February 1966. Smarting under the impact of a violent rift in the Ba'th Party and seething unrest in the country the Syrian leaders thought it expedient to patch up with Cairo and Moscow. The *rapprochement* with Moscow was facilitated by Soviet anxiety to checkmate Chinese penetration and to counteract the growing aggressiveness of pro-Western forces in the area now masquerading as pan-Islamists.[54] Simultaneously, Damascus and Cairo were drawn closer by the relentless crusade launched against their policies by the Teheran-Riyad-Amman axis in the name of defending Islam.

This was an opportune moment for the CPS to seek restitution in Syrian political life. Accordingly, a new party line emphasizing

---

[52] *L'Orient* (Beirut), 21 November, 1961.

[53] Text of Bakdash's message in *An-Nida*, 20 January, 1965.

[54] The Soviet offer of £60 million worth of credits towards the construction of the first stage of the Euphrates Dam enhanced the Russian prestige in Syria. Early in 1967 the co-operation between the two countries was extended to the field of ideology. A delegation of the Ba'th Party visited Moscow to hold talks with the Communist Party of the Soviet Union and recorded agreement on several regional and international issues. Text of the joint communiqué in *Al-Hayat*, 13 February, 1967.

"co-operation" between Syria and the Soviet Union and "cordiality" between Damascus and Cairo was evolved. In addition, the Communists acknowledged the progressive character of the Ba'th's domestic and foreign policies.[55] The ground was thus cleared for a Ba'thist-Communist alliance. Its follow-up was somewhat reminiscent of the 1955-57 period. Early in April Khalid Bakdash and other Communist exiles were permitted to return home. Soon after, the Syrian Premier, Yusuf Huzayyin, was invited to Moscow to discuss aid and trade. The Communist Party, though formally still banned, regained the status of semi-legitimacy it had enjoyed in the period immediately preceding the merger.

[55] See speech by the Syrian Communist delegate, Zahir, 'Abd as-Samad, at the 23rd Party Congress of the CPSU, briefly reported in *Daily Star* (Beirut), 7 April, 1966.

CHAPTER TEN

LEBANON: THE EMERGING TRIBUNE

FOR several reasons the Communist Party of the Lebanon (CPL) has evolved, in the post-war era, more as a tribune of Arab Communism specializing in the propagation of Marxian ideas and attitudes than as a serious contestant for local power. Having remained the traditional retreat of dissidents and non-conformists for centuries, the Lebanon has learnt to be more tolerant of new-fangled ideas and creeds than its neighbours. At the same time, the rigid sectarian orientation of the Lebanese body politic offers little scope for a patently anti-religious ideology to develop into a mass movement. Doubtless, as we have already noted, the CPL acquired a foothold among local labour unions and the intelligentsia; but its growing importance can only be ascribed to the rôle of a regional clearing-house that circumstances have thrust upon it.

It is, therefore, not surprising that in the greatest crisis that the Republic of the Lebanon has faced since Independence, namely the civil strife of 1958, the CPL played only a very minor rôle. And this in spite of the fact that the immediate cause of the turmoil was the Lebanese Government's acceptance of the Eisenhower Doctrine specifically designed to combat Communism in the area. The opposition to the Government was almost entirely organized and led by independents, socialists, and pan-Arabists[1] and blessed by the Maronite Patriarch, Paul Ma'ushi. It is important to note that the opposition refused to include the CPL in the United National Front (UNF) formed in April 1957. In fact, Kamal Junblat, the leader of the Progressive Socialist Party, was reported to have insisted that the Front's Charter should include a call for combating Communism.[2] This suggestion, however, did not find wide support in the UNF and was not endorsed. At the same time, the Front also took care to keep the Communists at arm's length.

[1] These included: Sa'ib Salam, 'Adil Usayran, 'Abdullah Yafi, Kamal Junblat, Fu'ad 'Ammun, Henri Far'un, Charles Hilu, Nasim Majdalani, and Hamid Faranjiya.

[2] *Daily Star* (Beirut), 5 July, 1957. See text in M.S. Agwani, *The Lebanese Crisis, 1958* (Bombay, 1965), pp. 29-33.

Regardless of these rebuffs the Communists found it expedient to lend full support to the UNF. It was, however, clear that the Communists were more concerned about the Lebanese Government's involvement with the US than the domestic power struggle between President Sham'un's supporters and adversaries; and their propaganda highlighted this particular aspect. In May 1958 the Lebanese Partisans of Peace characterized the Government's complaint to the Security Council about alleged UAR interference in its domestic affairs as an invitation to foreign intervention.[3] On 14 June, the CPL indicted the United States and Britain for attempting "to turn the Lebanon into an aggressive base in the Middle East from where they could plot, pressurize and obstruct the UAR and the liberation movement in the entire Arab world."[4] After the landing of the American troops in the Lebanon the party renewed its call for "unity" and strongly urged every Lebanese to fight the "greedy invaders":

Kill them wherever you find them with bullets of your guns and machine-guns. Aim your bombs at them, attack them with everything that comes to your hands, tear them with your teeth, and make their life an inferno on our free land, so that they should depart vanquished.[5]

In its campaign against the Sham'un Government the CPL also made full use of the persistent Soviet support for the Lebanese opposition in the United Nations and outside. Sobolev, for instance, warned the Security Council on 15 July that his country could not remain "indifferent" to foreign intervention in the Lebanon, "under whatever cover such intervention is perpetrated".[6] Khrushchev's letter to Eisenhower—reminiscent of Bulganin's warning to Britain, France, and Israel at the height of the Suez War—was even more blunt:

We know that the United States has atomic and hydrogen bombs, an air force and a navy, but you are fully aware that the Soviet Union, too, has atomic and hydrogen bombs,

---

[3] *As-Siyasa* (Beirut), 28 May, 1958.
[4] Ibid., 14 June, 1958.
[5] Text of the statement in Agwani, n. 2, pp. 297-8.
[6] United Nations, *SCOR*, mtg. 827 pp. 18-22.

and an air force and a navy, and also ballistic missiles of all kinds, including intercontinental missiles.[7]

Neutralist and nationalist opinion in the Lebanon and the Arab East was doubtless impressed by these Soviet postures. But the more discerning among them were somewhat discomfited by the fact that Soviet threats were interlaced with proposals for a summit conference to thrash out Western and Soviet differences in the region on a *quid pro quo* basis. This realization eventually hastened a settlement in the Lebanon.

Taking stock of the civil war a Communist writer later underscored several gains: It prevented renewal of President Sham'un's term "despite American intervention"; strengthened the Lebanese people's faith in their own strength; heightened their political consciousness; facilitated the Iraqi revolution; and generated in the Lebanese people "a strong sense of belonging to a free, independent, and sovereign Lebanon".[8]

The Communist emphasis on the Lebanon's sovereign entity was not accidental. In the course of the civil war the opposition had continually stressed the ties of Arabism which bound the Lebanon to its neighbours and which were undermined by Sham'un's policies. The Communist lukewarmness towards pan-Arabism was evidently caused by the estrangement between the Syrian Communists and Nasser. The CPL's attitude towards Nasser further stiffened in 1959. The Communists charged that the Syrian authorities arrested the veteran Lebanese Communist, Farjallah Hilu, on 25 June 1959 and tortured him to death. On 22 July women demonstrators marched on the UAR Embassy in Beirut shouting anti-Nasser slogans.[9] The CPL was greatly outraged by this incident and compared it to the murder of Patrice Lumumba.[10]

The break-up of the UAR in September 1961 understandably pleased the CPL. Niqula Shawi, the First Secretary of the party, hailed "the victory of the Syrian people in freeing itself from the régime dominated by tyranny and dictatorship" and described it

---

[7] Khrushchev's letter to Eisenhower, 19 July, 1959. United Nations, *SCOR*, 13th year, supplement for July, August, and September, 1958, pp. 42-46.

[8] "Ibn Khaldun", "Reflections on the Lebanese Revolution", *Ath-Thaqafa al-Wataniya* (Beirut), vol. 7 (November, 1958), pp. 2-7.

[9] *As-Sahafa* (Beirut), 23 July, 1959.

[10] *L'Orient*, 7 June, 1961.

as "an event of the greatest importance for the Lebanese nation". Elaborating the last point, he observed:[11]

> The Lebanese nation, including all its various layers, was struggling against the danger of annexation and dismemberment with which Nasser's dictatorship threatened its native land.

At home the party gained some elbow-room as a result of President Sham'un's exit and the Lebanon's consequent disentanglement from the Eisenhower Doctrine. This opportunity was fully utilized to step up political and trade union work particularly in Beirut and the economically depressed southern Lebanon. A daily newspaper called *An-Nida* was launched in 1959, and the weekly *Al-Akhbar* revived. Technically speaking, the party was still illegal; but it was permitted to carry on its activities practically unhampered. However, early in 1963, the Lebanese authorities were alarmed by the influx of Communist exiles from Iraq and Syria chased out by the new Ba'thist régimes and measures were taken to curb Communist activities in the country. The party nevertheless put up candidates for the elections of *Mukhtars* and registered notable successes in some of the wards in Tripoli, Buqa' and Tyre.

Echoes of the Great Rift

In the early sixties the widening Sino-Soviet differences began to make an impact on the Arab East. As the two rivals struggled for the leadership of Arab Communist parties, the Lebanon, with its political pluralism and free Press, came into great prominence as a forum for ideological debate.

Extremists and moderates have been a familiar phenomenon in the Arab Communist parties as elsewhere in the world. In the past these differences had been resolved internally through mutual accommodation or periodic purges. But the emergence of Peking as an alternative rallying point of Communist loyalties created new tensions both in the leadership and in the rank and file. It was particularly true of the CPL because of the relatively free atmosphere of the Lebanon in which it functions. A section of the younger Communists led by Nasib Nimr was galvanized by China.

[11] Niqula Shawi's speech at the 22nd Congress of the CPSU, *Pravda*, 27 October, 1961. Excerpts in *Mizan Newsletter*, vol. 3 (November, 1961), p. 14.

This group at first challenged the old guard, which was by and large pro-Moscow, on such questions as inner democracy, periodic elections, and strict adherence to the party's principles and statutes. According to one version, the pro-Soviet faction thereupon tried to isolate the dissidents inside the party. But by 1964 the rift came out in the open.[12] In April, representatives of four Arab Communist parties denounced the "splitting and disruptive activities" of the Chinese Communist leaders.[13] The CPL made an even more stinging attack in a statement[14] issued in August accusing the diplomatic representatives of China "in the capital of a neighbouring Arab country" of having bribed and instigated certain elements against the CPL and the Soviet leadership, and added:

> The Lebanese Communists resolutely condemn the feverish disruptive activities of the Chinese leaders directed against the unity and solidarity of the Communist parties in the Arab countries. They consider it their duty at present to expose to the whole world the activities of the Peking leaders in the Lebanon, where they establish contacts with dubious elements and renegades expelled from the ranks of the progressive movement and now in the service of foreign Powers. They also contact Right-wing adventurers and some persons from among the supporters of the former pro-Fascist *Parti Populaire Syrien* (PPS) in the hope of utilizing them in their disruptive and splitting activity against the national and progressive movement.

While the Arab Communist parties were patching up their differences with Nasser following Khrushchev's visit to the UAR in May, the pro-Peking factions in the Lebanon and Syria drew closer to the anti-Nasser Ba'thists, who wielded power in Syria.

[12] *As-Siyasa*, 18 May, 1965.

[13] The signatories were representatives of the Communist Parties of Syria, the Lebanon, Iraq and Jordan. Text of the statement in *Information Bulletin* (Prague), no. 15 (1964), pp. 797-807.

[14] *An-Nida* (Beirut), 18 August, 1964. Earlier in an article written shortly before his death (16 May, 1964), the veteran Communist leader, Antun Thabit, blamed the Chinese leaders for undermining the Partisans of Peace movement ever since the Delhi session of the World Peace Council in 1961. The article was posthumously published in the *Izvestia* of 16 June, 1964. Arabic text in *An-N da*, 20 June, 1964.

Early in April, 1965, Nasib Nimr, the leader of the pro-Peking faction resigned the editorship of the Communist weekly *Al-Akhbar*. Shortly afterwards he started his own weekly organ called *Ila'l Amam*.

In the fierce battle of words raging between the rival Communist factions since the rift came to the surface, each side has tried to establish its ideological superiority over the other. It is, however, significant that whereas the pro-Moscow faction is forthright in its support to the Soviet line on co-existence and encouragement to the liberated Asian-African nations to advance towards socialism through non-capitalist economic development, the pro-Peking faction tries to present its policies in attractive disguise and with loud protestations of independence. The chief slogans of the latter group are "scientific socialism" and "democratic centralism". "We are Lebanese", proclaims Nasib Nimr, "and our plans and policies are based on Lebanese conditions and circumstances and developed in the light of Lebanon's interests." It follows from this that "what is applied in one socialist country should not be blindly adopted" by another. Every country should work out its path to social justice on the basis of scientific inquiry and analysis.[15] This is the essence of "scientific socialism" which is at once an antidote both to the "Leftist disease" caused by the belief that the Communists are the only builders of socialism, and the "Rightist disease" resulting from the belief that socialism can be established without the co-operation of Communists" and in fact by striking them down and jailing them.[16]

Secondly, the pro-Peking group points to the rival faction's utter disregard for the principles of self-criticism and democratic centralism. "Centralization alone", they maintain, "would lead to personality cult which is alien to Marxist-Leninist teachings." On the other hand, "democracy alone would lead to anarchist liberty. Democracy and centralization, in our opinion, should be dialectically inter-linked."[17]

Finally, it denies having any links with Peking, its sole criterion for supporting other socialist countries and parties being the interest of the national liberation struggles and the world progressive movement.

[15] Nasib Nimr's interview to *Al-Bayraq* (Beirut), 6 October, 1965.
[16] Nasib Nimr's interview to *Al-Ahrar* (Beirut), 18 July, 1965.
[17] n. 15.

Of the two factions the pro-Peking group maintained an assertive posture throughout 1965 and early 1966 while its rival appeared to be on the defensive. It should, however, be noted that the schism in the Lebanese Communist movement is largely a reflection of international developments and only superficially related to the facts of life in that country itself.

CHAPTER ELEVEN

IRAQ: TRIUMPH AND REBUFF

THE *coup d'état* of 14 July, 1958, which catapulted the Iraqi Communists into prominence, was in many ways a revolutionary development. Over the past years the political system of Iraq originally designed by British colonial administrators and sustained by a succession of indigenous Anglophile politicians had become politically oppressive, socially unjust, and emotionally repugnant to the Iraqi people. Haunted by the frightful memories of the Rashid 'Ali *coup d'état* (1941) and the anti-Portsmouth Treaty riots (1948), the Regent (later Crown Prince), 'Abd al-Ilah, and the perennial Prime Minister, Nuri as-Sa'id, sought security in the creation of a system which relied on suspicion, mistrust, and coercion and saw in every dissenter a potential, if not actual, agent of subversion. In external affairs they regarded the interests of Iraq as being identical with those of Great Britain—a position which did not carry much conviction to the new generation of the Iraqi *élite*. Economically, the institutions and policies adopted since Independence had proved a drag on Iraq's further progress. The Land Settlement Law of the early thirties had transformed "loyal" tribal *shaykhs* into feudal lords by assigning to them lands previously owned collectively by the tribes. This new class of feudalists became the mainstay of Iraq's oppressive polity. Against this backdrop came the massive inflow of oil revenues following the signing of a new oil agreement in 1952[1] which generated new pressures and tensions in the Iraqi body politic. The quantum of oil revenues which had steeply risen from ID 2 million in 1948 to ID 58 million in 1954 and further increased to ID 83 million in 1958[2] created a new class of entrepreneurs and merchants who resented the dominance of feudal elements in administration and politics. Nuri

[1] The agreement signed on 3 February, 1952 provided for profit-sharing between the company and the Iraqi Government on the basis of a 50:50 formula and assured production of oil "at the existing high level".

[2] An Iraqi dinar is equal to one pound sterling. Statistics are quoted from Benjamin Shwadran, *The Middle East: Oil and the Great Powers* (New York, 1959), pp. 277-78, 280.

8

as-Sa'id tried to shore up the emergent opposition through impro-vised economic policies and stricter security measures. In 1950 a Development Board was set up to undertake major irrigation and industrial projects. It was assigned 70 per cent of the oil revenues for this purpose. The Board did commendable work by way of building dams and irrigation projects; but in the absence of agrarian reform its benefits did not reach the mass of the peasantry. Besides, the Board paid little heed to industry which could have relieved urban unemployment and provided opportunities of advancement to the *bourgeoisie*. Finally, the conclusion of the Baghdad Pact outraged the susceptibilities of the younger generation of Iraqis who, unlike 'Abd Al-Ilah and Nuri as-Sa'id, felt no sentimental attachment to Britain. To them the Baghdad Pact was indeed a symbol of conti-nued British stranglehold on Iraq's freedom and sovereignty and an obnoxious impediment to Iraq's national and regional aspirations.

Communists and the July Revolution

The opposition to Iraq's unimaginative, repressive and dictatorial régime came from four political groups: the pan-Arab and re-formist Istiqlal Party; the moderate Leftist National Democratic Party (NDP), the pan-Arab Ba'th Socialist Party; and the Com-munist Party. All these groups had one thing in common; they were opposed to British influence and control on Iraq. Of the four parties the Istiqlal alone had survived the rigorous measures adopted after the 1948 disturbances. In 1954, Nuri as-Sa'id suppressed all political parties whereupon the more desperate elements went underground. The anti-imperialist euphoria created by the Suez War drew the aforementioned political groups into a tactical alliance called the United National Front. According to the Com-munist version, the Front adopted a common platform comprising:[3]

(a) Complete political and economic independence;
(b) Abolition of the Baghdad Pact;
(c) Withdrawal from the Sterling Area;
(d) Eradication of feudalism;
(e) Guarantee of democratic rights and civil liberties;
(f) Arab solidarity against imperialism and Zionism; and
(g) Friendship and co-operation with the socialist countries.

[3] From the statement of the Communist Party of Iraq dated 8 July, 1962. Text in *New Age* (New Delhi), vol. 11 (24 February 1963), pp. 14-15.

The Front established contacts with disgruntled elements in the army. Some of its constituent members even boasted of having had a direct hand in the *coup d'état*. However, considering the secretive disposition of Brigadier 'Abd al-Karim Kassem, the leader of the army revolt, it is unlikely that he would have taken the politicians into confidence about the precise nature and timing of his action. Be that as it may, the Front hailed the *coup d'état* and became its political arm from the very first day of the army take-over.

The Communist gains in the early weeks of the régime were substantial though not decisive. Hundreds of party members and sympathizers languishing in prisons were released; those in exile returned home. Restrictions on Communist activities—a perennial feature ever since the founding of the party in 1934—disappeared. Two party organs entitled *Sawt al-Ahrar* and *Ittihad ash-Sha'b* made their appearance. The party machine itself emerged intact from underground and addressed itself to the task of mobilizing public support. But the Communist Party of Iraq (CPI) was not the only beneficiary of the new order. There were the Ba'thists and the Istiqlalists, whose vociferous clamour for Arab unity was despised by the Communists. Besides, these two parties, though not as well organized, commanded greater popularity than the CPI. The NDP, which subscribed to democratic socialism, was another rival. Above all, Kassem was politically unpredictable and the loyalties of the armed forces still unresolved.

It was against this background that the CPI set out to chart its course of action. It began by making the most of the political freedom afforded by the new régime on the one hand and by demanding moderate reforms on the other. Kassem's response was guarded. He needed the Communists as a counterweight to other political groups, but was reluctant to give them conspicuous status for fear of provoking opposition at home and abroad. Accordingly, the CPI was only indirectly represented in his cabinet by the Communist-leaning Ibrahim Kubba. In contrast to this the Istiqlal found a place in the cabinet as well as the Sovereignty Council and the Ba'th and the NDP had one member each in the cabinet.[4] Though formally without any representation in the cabinet, the

---

[4] Mahdi Kubba and Siddiq Shanshal of the Istiqlal were appointed respectively to the Sovereignty Council and the cabinet. The Ba'th was represented in the cabinet by Fu'ad Rikabi and the NDP by Muhammad Hadid.

Communists were believed to have infiltrated into the army and the administration. Two conspicuous cases of this kind were Kassem's *aide-de-camp*, Wasfi Tahir, and Colonel Amin of the People's Court.

In the early weeks Kassem strongly resented suggestions made in the foreign Press that he was being soft towards the Communists.[5] Besides, he was solicitous about reassuring the West that his Government would abide by all its international obligations, political as well as commercial.[6]

Though Kassem did not deliberately favour the CPI, the latter was indirectly helped by developments which it did not engineer itself. One of these was Kassem's mistrust of Cairo and its supposed designs on Iraq. There are at least two theories about how it originated. According to one version, after Nasser's hurried visit to Moscow following the July *coup d'état,* presumbaly to sound Khrushchev on the new situation in the Arab East, the Soviet Ambassador to Baghdad gave Kassem material calculated to set him against Nasser.[7] Hasanayn Haykal, on the other hand, advances the theory that it was Sir Michael Wright, the British Ambassador to Iraq, who impressed upon Kassem that his Deputy Prime Minister, 'Abd as-Salam 'Arif, was, together with Nasser, plotting to overthrow him.[8] Whatever the truth of the case, Kassem's relations with his colleague 'Arif and President Nasser were embittered; and the pan-Arabists in Iraq turned against him.

Kassem's ill-conceived measures to bolster up his own popularity and following in the country also indirectly helped the Communists. A week after the *coup d'état* he set up a Special Supreme Military Court, commonly known as the People's Court, with the flatulent Colonel Fadhil 'Abbas al-Mahdawi as President and the Communist-leaning Colonel Amin as Prosecutor-General. Whereas Mahdawi used the Court to denigrate Nasser and his supporters in Iraq, Amin gave its proceedings a slant calculated to benefit the Communists. As the Court progressively degenerated into a judicial circus,

[5] In a speech on 14 September, 1958 Kassem sharply hit back: "Our people have their own religion and faith in God, and we will not be frightened by Communist, American, British or Fascist ideas."

[6] Foreign Minister 'Abd al-Jabbar Jumard's statement on 23 July, 1958. *Mid-East Mirror*, vol 10 (21 September 1958), p. 7.

[7] W.A.C. Adie, "The Middle East: Sino-Soviet Discords" *Survey* (London), no. 42 (June 1962), p. 140.

[8] *Al-Ahram*, 8 November, 1963.

the CPI waxed eloquent in applauding it variously as "the revolution's sword drawn against the traitors", "a school for educating the public in the spirit of democracy", "a fresh breeze which refreshed the people", and "a pride of the July 14 revolution".[9]

Another significant measure was the creation of the People's Resistance Force (PRF) under a Republican Law promulgated on 4 August, 1958.[10] Originally intended to serve as a para-military watchdog to check the activities of the opponents of the régime, the Communists increasingly infiltrated into it until they came to dominate it.

In the early months, however, the Communists played it cool. They regarded the July revolution as essentially a *bourgeois* revolution which should serve as a starting point for a socialist revolution. At the same time the CPI realized that the task was stupendous and called for laborious preparation and planning. Accordingly, it set out to cover the entire country with a network of trade unions and front organizations. At an opportune moment these could be mobilized to exert political and economic pressures on the Government. The CPI also fraternized with the Kurdish Democratic Party, which represented the younger generation of Kurds. Their leader, Mulla Mustafa Barazani, had returned to Iraq, at Kassem's invitation, after thirteen years of exile in the Soviet Union. The Kurdish community was full of excitement and hope mixed with fears of Arab nationalism destroying their identity. It naturally looked upon the CPI as a counter-weight to pan-Arabism.

Concomitantly, the CPI was waiting for a suitable occasion to push forward its political claims. Kassem's open rift with his close associate Colonel 'Abd as-Salam Muhammad 'Arif provided that opportunity. On 11 September 1958, 'Arif was relieved of his post as Deputy Commander-in-Chief of the armed forces for reasons "of public interest". On 30 September he was further relieved of his post of Deputy Premier and Minister of the Interior.[11] 'Arif was eventually arrested on 4 November on the charge of "having plotted against the safety of the homeland". It is significant to

[9] *Ittihad ash-Sha'b* (Baghdad), 13 September, 1959.

[10] According to Amin Salimov, a Soviet expert on Arab affairs, the PRF was started at the initiative of the CPI. See *International Affairs* (Moscow), vol. 9 (September 1963), p. 41.

[11] On the same day the Development Minister, Fu'ad Rikabi (Ba'th) and the Education Minister, Jabir al-'Umar, were sacked.

note that the main differences between Kassem and 'Arif, which brought about the latter's downfall, centred on relations with the UAR and future of the oil industry. 'Arif's spirited advocacy of closer ties with the UAR was disliked by both Kassem and the Communists. But curiously enough the Communists also supported Kassem against 'Arif's plea to nationalize the oil industry.[12] Indeed, the pro-Communist Minister of Economy, Ibrahim Kubba, assured the oil companies that his Government "had no intention whatever of nationalizing the Iraqi oil industry".[13]

With 'Arif having broken away and the pan-Arab Ba'th and Istiqlal consequently fallen into disgrace, Kassem had no alternative but to lean on the CPI, which fully shared his hostility towards Nasser and his Iraqi supporters. The Communists came out in full strength into the streets of Baghdad and other major towns pleading for full support to Kassem and vengeance on his enemies. The Communists projected the Cairo-Baghdad tussle as a struggle between two sets of ideologies. They juxtaposed Nasser's concept of centralized union of Arab states with their own proposal for autonomous Arab states joined together in a federation, and Nasser's neutralism with close friendship with the Communist states. They questioned the genuineness of the Arab nationalism preached by Cairo and proclaimed Kassem "as the pioneer of Arab nationalism."

Although the nationalists charged that the Communists wanted neither union nor federation but were using the latter slogan as a mask to destroy Arab nationalism,[14] it suited Kassem's strategy to endorse the Communist line on this point *in toto*. Kassem was, however, reluctant to swallow the demand for drawing closer to the Communist camp. He favoured economic and cultural agreements with the Soviet Union[15] and other Communist countries; but he wanted at the same time to steer clear of the Power blocs. Elaborating his own concept of neutralism he observed: "The important thing is: we have deleted the word 'ally' from our dictionary and replaced it by the word 'friend'. We are friends to all but ally to none".[16] In an earlier statement Kassem had maintained

[12] Benjamin Shwadran, *The Power Struggle in Iraq* (New York, 1960), p. 34.

[13] Ibrahim Kubba's statement on 9 August, 1958. *Mid-East Mirror*, vol. 10 (17 August 1958), p. 8.

[14] 'Abd ar-Rahman al-Bazzaz, *Safhat min al Ams al-Qarib* (Beirut, 1960). p. 8.

[15] The first economic agreement with the Soviet Union was signed on 11 October, 1958.

[16] *Iraq Times* (Baghdad), 12 February, 1959.

that neutralism was "inspired by the national interests of the Iraqi people".[17] Whereas the NDP hailed the latter statement as a reaffirmation of "patriotic objectives"[18] the Communist 'Aziz al-Haj issued a rejoinder warning that "it would be a mistake to think that the contents of (Kassem's) speech signified something new".[19]

Although the Communists could not prevail upon Kassem to endorse wholly their line on foreign affairs, they fared somewhat better on the home front. The CPI made great political capital out of Kassem's land reforms. It is significant that the Land Reform Law was promulgated on 30 September, 1958, the day on which Arif was demoted and Ibrahim Kubba appointed Minister of Agrarian Reform in the reorganized cabinet. The law restricted individual ownership to 1,000 *dunums* (about 250 acres) of irrigated land and 2,000 *dunums* of rainfall land; and provided for compensation to expropriated landowners through State bonds carrying 3 per cent interest and redeemable after 20 years. It was framed on the pattern of Egyptian law passed years before and which the Egyptian and Syrian Communists had disparaged as being devoid of revolutionary content. But the Iraqi Communists presented it as a great victory of the revolution. Regardless of these exaggerated claims the land reform was in fact a notable departure from the outmoded agrarian system of Iraq. It greatly enthused the peasantry. The CPI used this opportunity to step up political work in the countryside and to mobilize the poorer peasants for a speedy implementation of the reform.

It was, however, in the towns that the CPI appeared to be the strongest. With all the rival political elements except the NDP out of the way, the CPI started a vigorous drive to expand its base through recruitment of new cadres and infiltration of the army, administration, and educational institutions. Most of the new recruits came from the student community which also supplied the bulk of the manpower for massive street demonstrations. Next came teachers of schools and colleges, workers, and slum-dwellers. Much of this newly acquired support, however, sprang from emotion rather than conviction. The overthrow of the monarchy and the international crisis which accompanied it had served to create a revolutionary climate surcharged with high expectations of politico-

[17] Ibid., 11 January, 1959.
[18] *Al-Ahali* (Baghdad), 12 January, 1959.
[19] *Sawt al-Ahrar* (Baghdad), 12 January, 1959.

economic change; and many of those who lived through it were somehow persuaded to look upon the Soviet Union and the CPI as the possible midwife of that change. Greatly emboldened by these trends the Communists came to believe that there was need for "another shake-up to get complete liberties".[20]

The Mosul Revolt

Early in March 1959, the CPI was scheduled to hold a mammoth conference of the Partisans of Peace in the northern town of Mosul. The occasion was seized by elements hostile to the Communists and Kassem to unfurl the banner of rebellion against both. The revolt was led by Colonel 'Abul Wahab Shawwaf of the Fifth Brigade with Staff Brigadier Nazim at-Tabaqchali of the 2nd Division stationed at Kirkuk in the supporting rôle. Both were identified by Cairo Radio as staunch supporters of Arab unity. However, the rebel broadcasts by the Mosul Radio merely stressed the need to end Kassem's "mob dictatorship" and restore the objectives of the 14 July revolution from which the Baghdad Government had allegedly deviated.

The revolt was speedily crushed by Kassem's army supported by the Communist-dominated People's Resistance Force. Shawwaf was killed on 9 March and Tabaqchali and several other officers arrested.

The revolt was the result of the national, regional, and international conflicts touched off by the 14 July revolution. The frictions between the nationalists and the Communists in Iraq have already been noted. These were superimposed by the war of nerves between Cairo and Baghdad. Nasser's Port Sa'id speech (23 December 1958), in which he roundly accused that the UAR and Iraqi Communists were working for the interests of a foreign Power, lent a new dimension to an otherwise regional contest for leadership. Thereupon, Moscow came out openly on the side of Kassem and its relations with Cairo were seriously strained. Undaunted by this new handicap, Cairo's "Voice of the Arabs" mounted a powerful broadside against Kassem inciting all his internal enemies to overthrow "the tyrant".

The savage war of words between Baghdad and Cairo now reinforced by heated exchanges between Khrushchev and Nasser greatly strenghened the hands of the Iraqi Communists, who took

[20] *Labour Monthly* (London), vol. 40 (December 1958), pp. 560-1.

up the cudgels on behalf of Kassem. While the Communists dubbed Nasserites as "Rountree friends", Mahdawi declared in the People's Court that "the Arab caravan is unaffected by barking dogs, some of which claim to be Arabs".[21] Simultaneously, the CPI evinced growing impatience with what they described as Kassem's "hesitation and tardiness" in liquidating the "enemies of the revolution". On 2 March 1959, the *Sawt-al-Ahrar* darkly hinted at what the Communists had in mind:

> The people have considered the Communists as the vanguard of the new era...There is nothing more dangerous than coming in the way of the Revolution. This is open treason, and treason can lead only to one fate, known to all.

The outbreak of the Mosul revolt seemed to have vindicated the Communist standpoint. No longer contented with verbal persuasion, the CPI now took matters into its own hands in order to achieve what Kassem had been hesitant to undertake on his own. The entire party machine was geared to action in a drive to terrorize anti-Communist elements. "Soldiers' Committees" were set up to run the Communist-dominated army units; Committees for the Protection of the Republic were installed in Government offices and enterprises; urban workers were organized in "People's Defence Committees"; volunteers were sent to the countryside to organize "Leagues of Peasants"; and "Vigilance Squads" went round the capital terrorizing those found wanting in revolutionary zeal.[22] Concomitantly, the *Ittihad ash-Sha'b* (9 March) called for "maximum firmness to protect the Republic", "merciless blows to be delivered to the enemies of the people", withdrawal from the Baghdad Pact, and execution of the verdicts passed by the People's Court.[23] 'Aziz al-Haj added to this long catalogue the demand for expanding and arming the People's Resistance Force.[24] Implicit in all these demands was the Communist desire to have a voice in the governance

[21] Quoted in M. Perlmann, "Nasser by the Rivers of Babylon", *Middle Eastern Affairs* (New York), vol. 10 (April, 1959), p. 154.

[22] *New Statesman* (London), vol. 57 (11 April, 1959), p. 494; Amin Salimov, "Iraqi *coup:* cause and effect", *International Affairs* (Moscow), vol. 9 (September, 1963), p. 39.

[23] This referred to the death sentences earlier allotted to 'Arif and Rashid 'Ali al-Gaylani by the People's Court and which remained to be carried out.

[24] *Sawt al-Ahrar*, 11 March, 1959.

of the country, though it remained unuttered for the time being. In the meantime the Communists backed their demands with mammoth demonstrations which completely paralysed public life in Baghdad for three consecutive days (9 to 11 March).

These militant tactics of the CPI appreciably undermined Kassem's authority in the country. It also gave rise to speculation abroad about the imminence of a Communist take-over. *Al-Ahram* reported that a committee of five consisting of Khalid Bakdash, 'Afif al-Bizri, Colonel Mahdawi, Wasfi Tahir, and Ahmad Salah al-'Abdi had been formed in Baghdad to prepare the ground for Communist rule in Iraq.[25] Soon after, President Nasser spoke of a "Communist masterplot" to set up a "Red Fertile Crescent" comprising Iraq, Syria, Jordan, the Lebanon, and Kuwait and with Baghdad as the seat of the "Arab International".[26]

In Iraq itself, while the Ba'th and the Istiqlal went completely underground, the NDP now suddenly awoke to the hazards of Communist ascendancy. Its official organ *Al-Ahali* sharply criticized the "excessive" measures taken by the PRF, particularly the searches carried out by night in the name of safeguarding the Republic, and demanded that the organization be immediately disbanded.[27] This brought the Communists into collision with the only rival political organ still in circulation. In a cutting retort the *Ittihad ash-Sha'b* upheld the PRF as "the sharp weapon and the vigilant eye" of the Republic and dubbed its critics "enemies of the nation".[28]

In the meantime the CPI pressed for the realization of its demands. Kassem conceded some of them but deftly evaded the rest. Large-scale arrests of pro-Nasser elements were carried out and those accused in the Mosul revolt were referred to the People's Court. On 24 March, Kassem announced Iraq's formal withdrawal from the Baghdad Pact which had in any case ceased to be operative since 14 July, 1958. The Eisenhower Doctrine was renounced on 14 May. While Kassem had occasionally spoken of having "frozen

[25] *Al-Ahram*, 16 April, 1959. The suggestion that Major General Ahmad Salah al-'Abdi, Kassem's Chief of Staff and Military Governor-General of Baghdad, was in league with the Communists was indicative of the panicky state of the Cairo Press. 'Abdi was in fact the staunchest anti-Communist in Kassem's Government and his most trusted man.

[26] Nasser's interview to R. K. Karanjia in *President Gamal Abdel-Nasser's Speeches and Press-Interviews, 1959* (Cairo, n.d.), pp. 536-7.

[27] *Al-Ahali*, 19 March, 1959.

[28] *Ittihad ash-Sha'b*, 22 March, 1959.

the Pact", he was, for some inexplicable reason, reluctant to annul it until the Communists forced the issue soon after the Mosul revolt. Even so the announcement was couched in conciliatory terms expressing the hope that it "would help the maintenance of friendly and cordial relations with the Pact members on a sound basis". By the end of May the withdrawal of the British personnel from the Habbaniya air base was accomplished. Shortly after that Kassem announced his Government's intention to withdraw from the Sterling Area.

At this juncture the CPI decided to make a display of its newly acquired strength and influence. The occasion was provided by the second congress[29] of the Iraqi Partisans of Peace held in mid-April. Among the participants of the mammoth congregation were representatives of district peace committees, the General Students' Union, the Women's League, and several trade unions. Delegations were also invited from many countries including Syria, the Lebanon, Jordan, Saudi Arabia, and the Sudan.[30] The Government provided special travel facilities to delegates coming to Baghdad from all parts of the country. The congress was inaugurated by no less a person than Kassem himself.

Presenting his report, the secretary of the congress, 'Aziz Sharif, stressed the point that the Partisans were not "a closely defined group working solely for peace" but that they were engaged in the wider patriotic struggle. The objectives of the congress were summed up in the new slogan adopted by it: "Peace and the safeguarding of the Republic."[31] At the end of a two-day meeting the sponsors of the congress organized, on 17 April, a massive procession of about a million people from all over Iraq comprising students, soldiers, workers, peasants, writers, civil servants, and shopkeepers. All nationalities including Arabs, Kurds, Assyrians, and Armenians were distinctly represented. Among the highlights of this unprecedented procession were the delegations from provinces, the largest being from Mosul, and a contingent of the People's Court headed by Colonel Mahdawi. Slogans of the congress were splashed on

[29] The first congress was held secretly in July, 1954.

[30] Foreign Arab delegations were composed as follows: Syria: Najah as-Sa'ati, Ahmad Sulayman al-Ahmad; Lebanon: George Hanna, Husayn Muruwwah and Nakhla Matran; Jordan: Yahya Hamudah and Dr 'Abd ar-Rahman Shuqayr; Saudi Arabia: Ali Abdul Karim; Sudan: Muhammad Khayr. See *Al-Ahali*, 26 April, 1959.

[31] *I-: Times*, 19 April, 1959. Special Supplement.

colourful banners in Arabic, Russian, Chinese, and English. As it passed by the Ministry of Defence, Premier Kassem came out four times to acknowledge the cheers of the crowd. The congress served to advertise the meteoric ascendancy of Iraqi Communism and Kassem's acquiescence in it.

Clamour for Power

The CPI was, however, not taken in by the marginal concessions granted to it as a result of its steadfast support to Kassem against the Shawwaf revolt. The fact that Kassem could now ill afford to lose Communist backing encouraged the CPI to confront him with an outright demand for share in authority. Late in April, the *Sawt al-Ahrar* bluntly stated that "the present stage dictates the participation of the CPI in the Government".[32] The *Ittihad ash-Sha'b* also bitterly complained that "our party has remained, longer than expected, the target of a discriminatory policy which served no interest".[33]

The Communists also raised the general question of legalizing the political parties. After the July revolution the United National Front had been granted quasi-legal status; but no such recognition had been accorded to its component members. Of the latter only three, namely the CPI, the NDP, and the Kurdish Democratic Party, survived the Mosul rebellion. The Communists demanded that these parties be legalized. Refuting the charges that such a course would enable one of them to swallow up the rest, they cited the example of the Chinese Revolution which "proved that parties based on the people could march ahead in unity not only during the stage of the patriotic democratic revolution but beyond that".[34]

As a corollary to legalization of the Leftist parties the Communists advanced the proposal for a coalition Government to be drawn from these elements. Implicit in this idea was the Communist claim to the leadership of the entire Iraqi Left. As Ibrahim Kubba, the pro-Communist Minister of Agrarian Reform, put it "the only way to silence imperialism and to frustrate its aggressive designs is to expedite the participation of the CPI in the government".[35]

The prospect of a Leftist coalition dominated by the Communists

---

[32] *Sawt al-Ahrar*, 28 April, 1959.
[33] *Ittihad ash-Sha'b*, 30 April, 1959.
[34] Ibid., 6 and 7 May, 1959.
[35] Interview to *Ittihad ash-Sha'b* published on 11 May, 1959.

appalled an influential section of the NDP. Soon the party was divided into two factions, one strongly supporting partnership with the Communists and the other fiercely opposing it. Whereas the former suggested the creation of an Indonesian style "guided democracy" in which "all democratic parties" would share authority on the basis of a programme dictated "by the present revolutionary stage of our Republic",[36] the latter supported Kassem's line that all party political activity be suspended in order to consolidate the revolution.[37] This provoked the CPI to issue a statement on 22 May denouncing the moderate faction of the NDP for having directly or indirectly helped the ideas opposing party life and encouraging political passivity among the masses.[38] The moderates were further accused of having "engineered" peasants' deputations to Kassem complaining against the alleged atrocities of the Communist-sponsored General Federation of Peasants' Associations in the countryside in order to discredit the Communist Party.[39]

By June, the controversy between the moderate and the extremist wings of the NDP ended in a split. The latter joined the CPI in presenting a formal memorandum to Kassem asking for the reactivization of the United National Front as the second best alternative to the legalization of political parties. According to the Communist version the memorandum was signed by "representatives of patriotic parties, trade unions, associations and democratic organizations".[40] The official organ of the NDP immediately disclaimed association with the UNF which, it observed, consisted only of the CPI and its supporters who had "borrowed this name after they discovered that the overwhelming majority of the people support suspension of party activities during the transition period".[41] The CPI was also assailed for having injected politics into trade unions and violence in public life. "It is the duty of all sincere

[36] *Al-Ahali*, 9 May, 1959.

[37] The statement was issued on 20 May, 1959.

[38] Extracts from the statement in the monthly *New Age* (New Delhi), vol. 8 (July, 1959), p. 20.

[39] *Ittihad ash-Sha'b*, 16 June, 1959.

[40] *Iraq Times*, 30 June. 1959. The term "patriotic parties" was an euphemism for the CPI, the Kurdish Democratic Party, and the extremist wing of the NDP. The NDP signatories were Naji Yusuf, Dr Ahmad al-Chalabi, Dr Salah Khalis, 'Abd al-Majid al-Windawi, Dr Jalil al-Wardi, Na'if al-Hasan, and Husayn Ahmad al-Amili.

[41] *Al-Ahali*, 1 July, 1959.

members of the public", wrote *Al-Ahali,* "to raise their voices in condemnation of the acts of violence and barbarism to which some political groups have lately made recourse and which, alas, have taken the place of scientific debates for the settlement of differences."[42]

But the NDP was not alone in resisting the Communist moves. Kassem himself was reluctant to allow any more latitude to the CPI. On the contrary, he had initiated measures calculated to counterbalance Communist influence. Amnesty was granted to a large number of political detainees, mostly belonging to Right-wing groups, on the occasion of the '*Id al-adha* festival. Announcing the decision, on 11 June, Salah al-'Abdi, the Military Governor-General of Baghdad, roundly warned the Communists "not to interfere in anything which is outside their concern, thereby inadvertently becoming a factor causing fear, anxiety and confusion".[43] The CPI quickly protested that this decision did not serve the interests of the Republic nor the security of the citizens.[44] Secondly, Kassem's Government proceeded to tighten the control of the Ministry of Defence on the People's Resistance Force. Originally the PRF was intended to serve as an ancillary organ of the armed forces; but in practice it had developed, under Communist direction, as a parallel, if not a rival, force to the regular army. In an unusually forthright statement marked for its candour, Kassem clarified, before a PRF rally on 5 July 1959, his standpoint on a variety of issues in which the CPI was deeply involved. He explained that the PRF was created after the pattern of "the medieval knights who were characterized by chivalry, nobleness, high virtues, and readiness to help the poor" (nothing could have been more repugnant to the Communists than this comparison!); and rebuked the Communist elements in it for going "beyond their duties" and indulging in "rash acts". The Partisans of Peace also came in for severe criticism. "How can we possibly term ourselves Peace Partisans," observed Kassem, "if we are unable to protect the individual's freedoms or if we commit aggression on the individual's freedoms?" He also assailed the CPI for practising violence in the name of combating feudalism and imperialist plots and added that there was "no longer any feudalism or imperialism in this

[42] Ibid., 5 and 7 July, 1959.
[43] *Iraq Times,* 12 June, 1959.
[44] *Ittihad ash-Sha'b,* 13 June, 1959.

country" and that "anyone who tells you that feudalism exists in Iraq from now on is a liar." Besides, he emphasized that it was the function of the army to deal with any plots that might exist and that no one should "take the law into his own hands". Finally, he firmly rejected the Communist demands for legalization of political parties and reactivization of the UNF. No parties were expected to carry out their activities during the transitional period and the Communists were admonished to note this "from this day on". As regards the UNF, Kassem observed:

> Let me talk to you frankly.....If the parties were existing during this period, I would have encouraged any front that would have existed. I will encourage the creation of such a front after the period of transition.[45]

Kassem's tirade against the Communists was, however, mingled with gentle entreaties to abandon the path of sectarianism and violence and work for the consolidation of the Republic. Obviously, he wanted to avert a showdown with the Communists. Although intensely outraged by this public censure, the CPI considered discretion as being the better part of valour. A meeting of the Politbureau, called on 8 July, issued a statement at the end of its two-day closed-door deliberations proclaiming that the party placed "its entire energies and forces at the disposal of the Government of the Revolution, in an unconditional manner, for the defence of the Republic against threats and against the dangers of plots and aggression". At the same time, it deplored "feverish endeavours on the part of the imperialists and their collaborators to disseminate intrigues and fabrications and to sow the seed of mischief between the patriotic forces, putting them one against the other and, in turn, undermine confidence and spread doubts between the people and the Government".[46] The Communists also refused to yield on the issue of the UNF. On the contrary, party newspapers were "flooded" with messages of support for the Front; and the *Ittihad ash-Sha'b* claimed that the organization already commanded the support of a quarter million people.[47] In order to bring further pressure on Kassem the Communists

[45] Text of Kassem's speech in *Iraq Times*, 7 July, 1959.
[46] Text of the statement in *Iraq Times*, 12 July, 1959.
[47] *Ittihad ash-Sah'b*, 12 July, 1959.

spread rumours that 'Arif and Gaylani were going to be released shortly and the Rightists re-installed in power.

Kassem, who had been suffering from exhaustion and nervous strain for the past several weeks, at last succumbed to Communist pressure. In the new cabinet announced on 13 July 1959 he included two Communist sympathizers: Dr Nasiha Dulaymi, President of the League for the Defence of Women's Rights (Minister of Municipalities) and Faysal as-Samir, President of the Teachers' Union (Minister of Guidance).[48] Some members of the old cabinet, identified as conservatives, were dropped. On the following day Kassem announced that political parties would be restored on the next Army Day (6 January 1960) and ground prepared for the adoption of a permanent national constitution. Was the CPI satisfied with these concessions? The events of the following day showed that it was not.

The Kirkuk Adventure

While Baghdad was engaged in a week-long celebration of the first anniversary of the July revolution, Communist elements in Kirkuk took the law into their own hands and started an orgy of violence against their opponents. Taking advantage of the traditional Arab-Turkoman antagonisms, the Communists instigated the Arabs against the Turkomans, who had been known for their allergy towards Communism. The CPI and the conservative *Hizb at-Tahrir at-Turkamani* (Turkoman Liberation Party) had never seen eye to eye with each other on any issue. The immediate cause of the flare-up was, however, the release of Turkoman detainees under an amnesty proclaimed by Kassem. The Turkomans, jubilant over this development, enthusiastically participated in the festivities attending the revolution's anniversary. Deeply angered by this, the Communists resorted to arson and murder. According to official figures, 41 people including women and children were buried alive and 79 killed by other means.[49]

The Egyptian and the Ba'thist Press came out with the theory

---

[48] A section of the foreign Press indicated that 'Abd al-Latif Shawwaf and 'Awni Yusuf, the other two new Ministers in Kassem's cabinet were also Communist. Shawwaf was formerly Director-General of the Dates Association. Yusuf, a Kurdish lawyer, was identified as an old-time Communist who had fifteen years in jail under the Monarchy. *Al-Ahram*, 17 July, 1959.

[49] *Iraq Times*, 5 August, 1959.

that the Kirkuk massacre was not an isolated aberration. The CPI
had prepared a blueprint to liquidate the "enemies" of the revolution in the entire country. But the plan misfired and action could
be taken only in Kirkuk.[50] Subsequent confessions of the CPI
itself lend some credence to this theory.

In the beginning the Communists were totally unapologetic
about the massacre. The *Ittihad ash-Sha'b* of 20 July observed
that the Kirkuk killings were the result of "armed reactionary
raids on the premises of the unions and democratic organizations",
that the Communists were "compelled to exercise their legitimate
right of self-defence when local authorities failed to protect their
lives, properties and democratic rights" and that "such provoca-
tions" had previously occurred in Samawa, Musayyab, Hindiyya,
and Samarra.

But Kassem's strong disapproval of the Kirkuk incidents persuaded the Communists to have second thoughts. Speaking on the
occasion of Thanksgiving Service at St Joseph's Church, Baghdad,
Kassem made a frontal attack on the CPI:[51]

> The recent incidents in some towns and villages were but the
> outcome of cruelty and blind fanaticism. The recent events
> in Kirkuk are things which I utterly condemn.... We have at
> our disposal forces capable of crushing any anarchist elements
> which might come up against the people.... I will bring to
> severe account those who trespassed on the freedom of the
> people in Kirkuk.

At a Press conference held on 29 July, Kassem showed maps
seized from the Communist-dominated General Students' Union
in which houses belonging to the victims of the Kirkuk holocaust
were marked out, and maintained that similar plans had been made
for Baghdad and other places in Iraq. He observed that "even

[50] See *Al-Ahram*, 19 August 1959 and *As-Sahafa* (Beirut), 8 August 1959. An
eminent Egyptian journalist who must remain anonymous told this writer two
years later that the Mosul and Kirkuk incidents were not entirely the work of the
Communists and that the British agents who had infiltrated the demonstrators
on both occasions did most of the dirty job. It enabled the British to undermine
the position of the Ba'thists, the Nasserites, and the Communists, their real
foes, and to safeguard the vital oil interests. Though somewhat plausible, this
thesis is difficult to prove.
[51] *Iraq Times*, 20 July 1959.

9

Hulagu did not commit such atrocities" and pledged "to chase them [the anarchists] until they revert to the path of justice".[52] Soon afterwards he demanded that the Communist Party purge its ranks.[53]

Thereupon the CPI hurriedly called an enlarged meeting of the Central Committee to review the entire party line. After an agonizing reappraisal of the events of the past year the committee decided in favour of a tactical retreat. In a new policy statement[54], the party admitted of serious "Leftist deviations" and drastically modified its stand on major issues. First, it acknowledged that the army had carried out the 14 July revolution, whereas the Communists had only helped to "consolidate" it. Secondly, it disclaimed any desire to dominate the United National Front.[55] Thirdly, the party confessed to have made the mistake of "underrating the capabilities of the national government" which happened to be "practically the centre around which the national forces gathered". Fourthly, it regretted its clamour for participation in the cabinet without "reckoning with concrete reality", namely the balance of forces in the country and the international situation. It was "an abortive and sectarian act" which damaged the unity and solidarity of the national forces". Fifthly, it underlined the party's miscalculation:

> The situation was the result of a miscalculation by us, namely, the overrating of our own strength and the underrating of the role of the government and the other national forces in defending the Republic. As a result of this miscalculation our party concentrated its efforts on mobilizing the masses with the intention of taking the defence of the Republic in hand and leading it on the path of democracy. This is in itself right and proper. But from time to time this was pursued too strictly and another problem which is just as fundamental was lost

[52] Ibid., 31 July 1959.

[53] Ibid., 5 August 1959.

[54] Substantial excerpts from the statement are reproduced in Arnold Hottinger, *The Arabs: Their History, Culture and Place in the Modern World* (London, 1963), pp. 325-27; Arabic text in *Ittihad ash-Sha'b*, 4 August 1959.

[55] In an explanation bordering on apology the statement said that after the exclusion of the Istiqlal and the Ba'th from the Front the CPI had offered full co-operation to the NDP. But while negotiations on this subject were going on, the NDP decided to suspend its political activities thus leaving the CPI no choice but to carry on the Front with the help of the Kurdish Democratic Party.

sight of, namely, lasting solidarity with the government and with other national forces.

Finally, the Kirkuk incident was ascribed to "Leftist deviations", which Lenin had once decried as "an infantile sickness of revolution".

Reprisals: First Phase

Unmellowed by the CPI's belated self-criticism Kassem proceeded to quash Communist power and influence in Iraq. This was done in two stages: in the first stage the Communist-dominated PRF and sundry committees were abolished and Communists were removed from leading positions in various front organizations; in the second stage, the party itself was split in order to isolate the militant hard core from the pliable moderates. After the split the party was left with no choice but to lie low in order to mend its machine and prepare for the next round to retrieve lost positions.

Even as Kassem mounted a verbal attack on the "anarchists" and "terrorists"—a convenient euphemism for the CPI—the Military Governor-General of Baghdad, Major-General Salah al-'Abdi, was charged with the operation to constrict Communist power and influence. 'Abdi started by dissolving the Communist-sponsored "Committees for the Defence of the Republic" in various branches of the administration. The "Committees" had been functioning as party cells exercising arbitrary control on the administrative machinery. 'Abdi also reassured Government officials about security of tenure and protection against political intimidation so long as they functioned "within the limits set by the authorities".[56] Towards the end of July the PRF also was immobilized and wearing of PRF uniform by citizens was "strictly" prohibited. Besides, all arms licences were cancelled and holders of authorized as well as unauthorized arms were ordered to surrender them.[57] And to top it all, a new set of military courts was created to deal with the "anarchists". These constituted an unobtrusive counterweight to Mahdawi's Court, which was designed to deal with the "reactionaries".

This concerted operation encouraged nationalists and Right-wing elements to settle scores with the CPI. As the former raided the

[56] *Iraq Times*, 27 July 1959.
[57] *Iraq Times*, 30 July 1959.

offices of trade unions and front organizations the authorities allowed retribution to take its course. Having been put in a tight corner, the Communists now began to preach the virtues of national unity, the futility of harping on sectarian interests, and the need to concentrate on basic issues.[58]

Kassem then turned to major front organizations. During the past year there had been a mushroom growth of such organizations under Communist inspiration and guidance. The CPI had also entrenched itself in important professional bodies such as the Lawyers' Union. The opponents of the Communists charged that the latter had secured leading positions in trade unions through intimidation and pressed for fresh elections.[59] Kassem endorsed the suggestion. Consequently, the CPI met with further reverses. The first defeat was suffered in the election to the presidency of the Lawyers' Union on 28 August when 'Abd-al-Razzaq Shabib defeated his Communist rival 'Aziz Sharif with 456 votes against 267.[60] The Communists did better in the election of the Journalists' Union. Muhammad Mahdi al-Jawahiri[61] was elected President of the Union, but only after agreement had been reached on a unified list for the new Executive Committee representing all shades of opinion.[62] Finally, the headquarters of the General Federation of Trade Unions was closed and its chief, Sadiq al-Falahi, arrested.

Despite these serious set-backs the outlook for the CPI was not altogether bleak. For Kassem's intention, at this stage, was not to blot out the CPI but to curb its soaring ambitions and to tame it into a pliable instrument for counteracting the Nasserites. The anti-Communist drive was, therefore, intended to clip the wings of the CPI and not to destroy it. At the same time, to reassure

[58] Editorial comment in *Ittihad ash-Sha'b*, 10 August 1959.

[59] See *Al-Ahali*, 9 August 1959.

[60] The Communists ascribed their defeat to the two rulings given by the Iraqi Court of Cassation on the eve of the election. One of these rulings enfranchized some 150-200 lawyers who had been disenfranchized by the Government on political grounds following the July revolution; and the other one disenfranchized all government-employed lawyers. The result, according to the Communists, "revealed the revival of reactionary elements".

[61] Jawahiri, a poet and writer, was also a leading figure in the Partisans of Peace movement.

[62] Shortly before the elections, the Government imposed a ban on publication of incendiary material in the Press. This blunted the edge of another vital Communist weapon.

the Communists that he was not veering to the Nasserites he allowed death sentences against seventeen army officers and civilians, charged with the Mosul revolt, to be carried out.[63] And as if to keep the balance even, three Communists, found guilty of the Kirkuk killings by a military court, were executed shortly afterwards.

This negative equilibrium was, however, shattered by the Ba'th's attempt on Kassem's life on 8 October 1959. Kassem escaped with a fractured shoulder; but the experience gave him a severe jolt. Disturbed by this renewed offensive of the "Rightists" in spite of his sustained drive against the CPI, Kassem pounced upon the Ba'th with concentrated wrath and vengeance. In a statement issued from his bed in the hospital Kassem made the belated revelation that the Communists alone were not responsible for the Kirkuk massacre. He charged that the Ba'thist agents had set up cells in Kirkuk and that these had "added fuel to fire".[64]

This marked shift in Kassem's attitude to his political foes gave the CPI some respite. The Communists joined Kassem in denouncing the Ba'th, and the slogan of struggle against the "enemies of the Republic" was revived. The Government, too, reciprocated by halting the campaign against the Communists. In the elections of the General Students' Union held in November the Communist-sponsored "unified democratic list" swept the polls by securing 75 per cent of the votes cast.[65] This thumping victory heartened the *Sawt al-Ahrar*, and it asserted that "the slogan of non-interference in politics [by students] behind which the enemy forces conceal themselves is but a part of conspiratorial endeavours to isolate the students from the national tasks".[66]

Reprisals: Second Phase

By the end of 1959 Kassem had accomplished the abridgement of Communist power and influence to manageable proportions. The time had now come to deal the *coup de grâce*. Earlier in July

[63] The executions were carried out on 20 September 1959. Among the persons executed were Brigadier Nazim at-Tabaqchali and Colonel Mustafa Rifa't Sirri.

[64] *Iraq Times*, 7 December 1959.

[65] About 63,000 students voted in the election. Of these 13,000 were from the Baghdad University and affiliated colleges; 18,000 from Baghdad secondary schools; and 32,000 from secondary schools all over the country.

[66] *Sawt al-Ahrar*, 28 November 1959.

Kassem had promised, under Communist prodding, to restore political parties by January 1960. He now availed himself of this opportunity to split the CPI.

The ground had indeed been prepared for the elimination of the CPI in the months following the Kirkuk incidents. The stratagem now employed for this purpose was to detach a handful of moderate elements from the bulk of the militant Communists, who could then be denied legal status. Kassem found in Da'ud as-Sayigh[67], a founder-member of the CPI reputed for his political flexibility, a ready ally to carry out his design. Sayigh's splinter faction made its public appearance with the publication of its daily organ *Al-Mabda'* in November 1959. Sayigh took the line that the "immortal 14 July Revolution" had brought Iraq to the stage of "national liberation". The "socialist revolution" was yet to come. But in the meantime it was the duty of the progressives to observe the laws of the Republic and to carry out "the directives of the leader". Turning to the CPI, he observed: "It is not a progressive attitude to show ostensible consent but harbour the opposite feeling".[68] In an interview to Sayigh, on 23 November, Kassem expressed his satisfaction with the former's "balanced approach". As the time for legalizing the political parties drew near, *Al-Mabda'* came forward with the suggestion that all classes except the working class could have more than one political party representing different trends thereby implying that the Sayigh group alone be recognized as the Iraqi Communist Party.[69]

On 1 January 1960 the new Law of Association and Parties was proclaimed. The law was apparently liberal; but some of its provisions appeared to be loaded against the Communists. Article 7 required the parties to adopt "peaceful democratic means".

[67] A lawyer by profession, Sayigh hailed from a Christian family. Unlike many Communist leaders he had never been to a Communist country. The CPI sources accused him of having founded a dissident faction of "opportunist and politically backward elements" called the Iraqi Communist Brotherhood in 1942. He was consequently expelled from the party. In 1956 he reportedly atoned for "opportunistic factional activity" and was readmitted to the fold. But during the second half of 1959 when the party was "undergoing a crisis", Sayigh "resumed his subversive activities" and was again expelled. See *World Marxist Review* (Prague), vol. 3 (April 1960), pp. 63-65.

[68] *Iraq Times*, 22 November 1959; and *Al-Mabda'* (Baghdad), 22 November 1959.

[69] *Al-Mabda'*, 29 December 1959.

Party elections were to be conducted in "a free atmosphere" and in the presence of a magistrate (Article 10).

Parties were further required to maintain a register of membership and minutes of all the constituent bodies (Article 14). Members of the armed forces, judges, foreign service officials, heads of administrative units, and students of primary and secondary schools were forbidden to join political parties (Article 31). Article 40 prohibited non-governmental military or semi-military associations. The law also disallowed affiliation of parties to alien groups with headquarters outside Iraq without special permission and receiving of funds from abroad. The Ministry of Interior could refuse licence to an applicant subject to appeal to the Court of Cassation within fifteen days of such refusal.[70]

The split in the CPI came out in the open in the second week of January when both factions applied to the Ministry of Interior for licence in the name of the CPI. While Da'ud as-Sayigh applied on behalf of the splinter group, Zaki Khayri put forward the case for the militant majority group.[71] Since the Sayigh group had applied two days in advance for recognition as the CPI and no two parties could be licensed under the same title, the Khayri group styled itself the *Hizb al-Ittihad ash-Sha'b* (Party of People's Unity). The manifestos of the two groups bore some striking similarities. Both stood for land reform, speedy industrialization, ending of exploitation by foreign capital, and encouragement to indigenous capital and industry. But the two groups did not see eye to eye on crucial issues. While the Khayri group stood for restricting the freedom of feudal and reactionary classes, its rival advocated peaceful resolution of class conflicts among the national classes through a moderate programme of reforms. The former pleaded for "freedom of expression and ideology", the latter for absolute loyalty to "the revolutionary and democratic leader, 'Abd al-Karim Kassem". Above all, the Sayigh group proclaimed that it did not

[70] Text of the Law in *Iraq Times*, 6 January 1960.

[71] The Khayri group's application for licence was signed by 15 founding members: Tawfiq Ahmad Muhammad, Zaki Khayri, Husayn Ahmad ar-Radhi, 'Aziz Ahmad ash-Shaykh, 'Abd ar-Rahim Sharif, Kazim al-Jassim, Dr Khalil Jamil al Jawad, 'Amir 'Abdullah, 'Abdul Qadir Isma'il, Karim Ahmad ad-Daud, Ilyas Hanna Kohri, Muhammad Husayn 'Abd al-'Ays, Dr Husayn 'Ali Al-Wardi, Ahmad Mulla Qadir and 'Abdul 'Amir 'Abbas. The Sayigh group's application was backed by 12. The law required a minimum of 10 founding members to support each application.

consider Marxism-Leninism "a rigid theory" and that it believed in its creative application and struggled against Rightist and Leftist deviations.[72]

Soon after, an acrimonious wordy duel started between the two rivals in the columns of *Al-Mabda'* and *Ittihad ash-Sha'b* speaking respectively for the Sayigh and Khayri factions. The Khayri group denounced its rival as an "artificially contrived party"; the latter returned the compliment by branding its opponent as "a band of gangsters and opportunists". Again, the Khayri group charged that Sayigh was out to disrupt the party and that he had applied ahead of other parties in order to confront the CPI with a *fait accompli* and to compel it to fall in line with the splinter faction. Sayigh, in turn, retorted that it was the Khayri group that had been persistently playing the rôle of a splitter—its disruption of the NDP in 1959 being an illustration of this—and maintained that the "least" condition for settlement was that the Khayri group "unmask and condemn the persons responsible for the past mistakes, crimes and acts of sabotage lest these are repeated in the future".[73]

Aside from Kassem's unconcealed patronage[74], the Sayigh group also attracted the support of the NDP. And the NDP organ, *Ath-Thawra*, which had supported the CPI in the pre-Kirkuk period, now championed the cause of the splinter faction pleading that it had "no blood-stained hands" and was opposed to the "criminal methods which the other group practised".[75]

As was widely expected, the Government eventually recognized the Sayigh group as the Communist Party of Iraq.[76] The decision was announced on 9 February. At this the organ of the Khayri group cuttingly wrote that "the existence of martial law and the mentality of the majority of people in the government contradicted the concept of party activity".[77] Its opponents, on the other hand, declared that "the Communist Party headed by Zaki Khayri was now illegal and must liquidate its secret work which, if continued,

[72] See *Al-Mabda'*, 12 January 1960; and *Ittihad ash-Sha'b*, 20 January and 6 February 1960.

[73] See *Ittihad ash-Sha'b* and *Al-Mabda'* of 24 January 1960.

[74] The Sayigh group was reported to have received £5,000 from Kassem for its election campaign. See *Guardian* (Manchester), 6 January 1960.

[75] *Ath-Thawra*, 11 January 1960.

[76] The other two parties recognized by the Government were: the National Democratic Party and the Kurdish Democratic Party.

[77] *Sawt al-Ahrar*, 11 February 1960.

would constitute high treason".[78] Stating the reason for rejecting
the Khayri group's application, the Ministry of Interior said that
the party's draft regulations contravened Article 4 of the Law of
Association and Parties which required that no party should aim at
spreading disunity among the different Iraqi nationalities and religious groups or be prejudicial to the country's independence.[79]
According to the *Ittihad ash-Sha'b*, the Ministry had specifically
asked the party to delete the term "revolution" and "Marxist-
Leninist doctrine" from its programme.[80]

Having been rebuffed by the Ministry of Interior, the Khayri
group made a direct appeal to Kassem to intervene in the matter.
It also tried to secure recognition under the contrived label of the
Republican Party.[81] But Kassem refused to oblige. Thereupon the
Communists took to verbal defiance. Zaki Khayri angrily
declared that his party was "the victim of unjustifiable discrimina-
tion" and added with a touch of scorn:[82]

> For twenty-five years our party required no licence to carry
> out its duties towards the people.... It is of course common
> knowledge that licences by themselves cannot make parties—
> much less a Communist Party. The Communist Party is ours
> and not that of the opportunist and renounced faction which
> has assumed the name of our party.

In another statement Khayri warned the Government that "mere
words about democracy will not convince anyone unless they
are backed by the right of working class and the working people
in general to legal political organization".[83] These angry protestations further strengthened Kassem's resolve to suppress completely
the militant Communists.

What was Kassem's motive in splitting the Communist Party?
He was possibly trying to exterminate the Communists by playing
off one faction against another. Having used the Communists

[78] *Ath-Thawra*, 11 February 1960.

[79] Quoted in *Mideast Mirror*, vol. 12 (28 February 1960), p. 12.

[80] *Ittihad ash-Sha'b*, 9 February 1960.

[81] The application for the Republican Party was backed by frontmen like
'Abd al-Fattah Ibrahim and Muhammad Mahdi al-Jawahiri. It was turned
down on 28 March 1960.

[82] *Ittihad ash-Sha'b*, 2 March 1960.

[83] Quoted in *World Marxist Review*, vol. 3 (April 1960), pp. 63-65.

against the Nasserites and the Ba'th, he perhaps discovered that the CPI had become too strong in the process to subserve him. Or did he aim to rally the Communist rank and file under his own protégé Da'ud as-Sayigh? Whatever his motives might have been, the phantom Communist Party patronized by him proved to be still-born. For Sayigh was able neither to attract the support of the Communist rank and file, which remained loyal to the Khayri group, nor to gain recognition in the Communist world. On 28 April, Sayigh confessed his inability to call a party congress within the legally prescribed period of three months and asked for a six months' extension.[84] Besides, both Moscow and Peking denounced the Sayigh group. While the Chinese broadcasts charged that it was "void of any sincerity", Radio Prague branded it "a gang of traitors".[85]

Retreat to Underground

Although Kassem's attempt to divide the CPI had proved infructuous his refusal to lend the main party a legal aura dealt a serious blow to Communist prestige in Iraq. The CPI still remained intact, but the tide of public opinion had definitely turned against it. Kassem used this opportunity to dislodge the Communists from the positions still occupied by them in public life.

In a staggered process of elimination, Communist-sympathizers were dropped from the cabinet one after another. Ibrahim Kubba, the Marxist Minister of Agrarian Reform, was "excused from his duties"—an aphorism for dismissal—in February 1960. In a cabinet reshuffle effected in November, Nasiha Dulaymi, who had been earlier demoted to Minister of State, lost her job. Two other Left-leaning Ministers, 'Abd al-Latif Shawwaf and Yusuf 'Awni, were also excluded from the cabinet. Faysal as-Samir, Minister of National Guidance, followed in May 1961.

Simultaneously, the Government turned the screw on various front organizations. The Partisans of Peace were disbanded in February 1960. They reappeared in April after Kassem proclaimed that they did not come under the law governing political parties, but were finally outlawed in May 1961. The Communist-dominated Peasants' Association had been disrupted following the appearance

[84] See *Mideast Mirror*, vol. 12 (1 May 1960), p. 27.
[85] *New York Times*, 29 February 1960 and *Al-Hayat* (Beirut), 26 February 1960.

of a rival organization backed by the Government. The Communists were also squeezed out of leading positions in the trade unions of oil and dock workers, railwaymen, and teachers through Government-manipulated union elections, though they put up stiff resistance. The severest of all tests came in November 1960, when, following Communist reverses in the elections of the Tobacco Workers' Union, thousands of workers staged anti-Government demonstrations leading to violent clashes. They protested that the elections had been rigged in order to defeat Muhammad Ghabban, the militant President of the Tobacco Workers' Union. Several workers were killed or injured and more than a hundred arrested in the course of the conflict. The General Students' Union and the Women's League were banned in January 1961.

In the meantime circulation of the *Ittihad ash-Sha'b* was banned in the southern provinces in May 1960 following an attack by the Communist weekly *Al-Hadhara* on the Shi'i divine Muhsin al-Hakim.[86] The newspaper was eventually banned in October and its Editors-in-Chief, 'Abd al-Qadir Ismail al-Bustani and Majid Mahmud, put under house arrest.[87] Towards the end of December strict censorship was imposed on all newspapers and periodicals.

In the army, too, the CPI's position was greatly eroded. Brigadier Taha Shaykh Ahmad, who as Director of the Army Planning had served as a communication line between the CPI and the Army, was now posted to an unimportant position in the Ministry of Defence. Mahdawi of the People's Court had for some time toyed with the idea of a new political party with the collaboration of Majid Muhammad Amin and Wasfi Tahir, but the plan did not materialize.[88] The Court itself lost its political significance after 1960.

In the lower echelons of the armed forces and administration, however, pockets of Communist influence persisted. This was particularly true of the Air Force[89] and the Ministries of Education

[86] Shaykh Muhsin al-Hakim had invited Communist wrath when in answer to a written question from a citizen he observed: "Communism is blasphemy or atheism ... and no Muslim is ever allowed to embrace it." Facsimiles of the Shaykh's answer reportedly fetched as much as £10 a piece in Baghdad. *Al-Hadhara* (Baghdad) retaliated through a cartoon depicting the Shaykh as a donkey. See *Jerusalem Post* (Jerusalem, Israel), 1 April 1960.

[87] *Iraq Times*, 3 October 1960 and *Al-Hayat*, 18 October 1960.

[88] *Al-Ahali*, 15 January 1960.

[89] Air Commodore Jalal Al-Awqati, Chief of the Iraqi Air Force, was des-

and National Guidance, and, to a lesser extent, of the Ministries of Planning and Agrarian Reform. But these were effectively neutralized by anti-Communist forces which came to the fore in the wake of Kassem's rebuffs to the CPI. With Kassem's connivance they set up a network of their own, terrorizing and chasing the Communists across the whole country. An Iraqi Communist wrote in the fall of 1960 that in the year following the Kirkuk incidents, over a hundred Communists were assassinated in Baghdad, Mosul, and other places and that the number of Communist detainees in Kassem's prisons totalled twice that under Nuri's régime.[90]

The rift between Kassem and the Communists having proved irreparable, the CPI effected a planned retreat to underground.

The CPI and Kassem: An Appraisal

During Kassem's rule the fortunes of the CPI went up and down as in a game of snakes and ladders. But after the Kirkuk incidents there were more snakes than ladders and some of them quite deadly at that.[91]

Analysing the causes of Communist failure, Amin Salimov, a Soviet specialist in Arab affairs, observed:

In the first year of the revolution the ruling circles of the national bourgeoisie fought the enemies of the Republic and the reactionaries with the help of the peoples' revolutionary forces; from mid-1959 onwards, they used the reactionary and Right-wing forces to fight the people's democratic forces. When the ruling circles realized they were equally threatened from Right and Left, they tried to 'balance' between the two. Prime Minister Kassem conducted this policy of 'balancing' until the very end.

The CPI, too, blamed its débâcle on Kassem's deviation, after initial "democratic reforms", into "fatal dependence on reactionary forces".[92] Whereas Salimov's analysis merely highlights Kassem's

cribed by the correspondent of the Christian Science Monitor (28 April 1960) as a Communist sympathizer.

[90] See New Age (New Delhi), 12 February 1961, pp. 8-10.

[91] Salimov, n. 22, p. 41.

[92] CPI statement dated 8 July 1962. Text in New Age, 24 February 1963, pp. 14-15.

peculiar rôle, the CPI statement is plain oversimplification. The reasons for Communist failure in Iraq were indeed varied and complex.

Paradoxically, the chief source of Communist weakness was the vast number of followers it had acquired after Kassem's quarrel with Cairo and the pan-Arabists came out into the open. It was the incompetence of the leadership to come to grips with this mass of new recruits, coupled with the youthful over-enthusiasm of the new converts, which drove the party towards adventurism. Secondly, even in the exceptionally favourable conditions of post-revolution Iraq, the CPI was never really able to outlive its sectarian past. It was mistrustful and intolerant towards all other parties including the Left-leaning NDP, which came in for ridicule as "a party of the Iraqi *bourgeoisie*" ridden with contradictions.[93] The Kurdish Democratic Party was likewise dubbed *bourgeois*.[94] The CPI's misguided endeavours to eliminate or undermine its political rivals roused deep antagonism against it. Thirdly, the CPI permitted the tendency among the minority groups like the Kurds and Shi'is to act on communal impulses to go unchecked. This explains Communist excesses in Mosul, Kirkuk, and several Shi'i pockets in southern Iraq. The pan-Arabists even attributed the hostility of the CPI to Arab nationalism to the fact that a number of top Iraqi Communists belonged to minorities of foreign origin: 'Abd al-Qadir Isma'il al-Bustani was of Indian origin; 'Aziz al-Haj and Muhammad Mahdi al-Jawahiri belonged to Iranian stock; and Wasfi Tahir was a Turkoman.[95] Fourthly, the Iraqi Communist triumvirate comprising Zaki Khayri, 'Adil Salam, and 'Abd al-Qadir Isma'il al-Bustani seldom functioned as a single-minded team. Whereas Khayri was a disciple of "Fahad", who was reputed to be the only Communist in the Arab East who did not take orders from Khalid Bakdash, Bustani had long been a protégé of the Syrian Communist chief.[96]

Finally, the Communists fell a prey to Kassem's waywardness. At one time observers in Iraq and abroad had suspected that Kassem

[93] Mohammad Salim, "Three Years after the Iraqi Revolution", *World Marxist Review*, vol. 4 (October 1961), pp. 35-41.

[94] Sami Mahmud, "Combating the Terror in Iraq", *World Marxist Review*, vol. 4 (June 1961), pp. 90-91.

[95] Radio Cairo's "Voice of the Arabs" quoted in *Iraq Times*, 19 April 1959.

[96] See *As-Sahafa*, 24 April 1959.

was a Communist. Some had even ventured to give his card number.[97] Kassem always denied his being a Communist, and perhaps did so truthfully. He had seized power in the midst of widespread discontent against the *ancien régime*. But he proved no better visionary than Nuri. He adopted the milder if naïve path of allowing the new forces to have free interplay under his personal umpireship. In fact, he regarded himself as more than an umpire. He imbibed megalomaniac notions of being a saviour carrying out a divine mission and eventually degenerated into a tyrant of the classical Greek type who would solicit support from whichever quarter it came in order to keep his opponents down. He pitted them one against another in an endless series of civil strife which left the country exhausted and confused. The CPI, having initially become a wilful partner in this diabolical sport, could not escape its disastrous consequences.

The 1963 Massacre

Ever since the bloody incidents of Mosul and Kirkuk, the Ba'th Socialists, Nasserites, and other anti-Kassem elements had been secretly planning to topple the régime. After successive set-backs during 1960-61, the CPI, too, was driven to desperation. The party's new strategy envisaged a line of least resistance to Kassem in public life coupled with an orderly retreat of its militant core to the underground whence to prepare for a fresh initiative. In the circumstances, the Ba'th as well as the CPI was striving for the common objective of overthrowing Kassem's dictatorship though from different motives.[98] But the Ba'thists outpaced the Communists, with disastrous consequences for the latter.

The bitter rivalry between these two parties went back to the early months of the 1958 revolution when the CPI had savagely attacked the Ba'th for its pan-Arab proclivities. The Communist role in suppressing the Mosul revolt further widened the cleavage between the CPI and the Ba'th.

Hence the Ba'thist leadership which seized power on 8 February 1963 was determined to wipe out the Communists. The CPI antici-

---

[97] Fa'iq as-Samarrai, former Iraqi Ambassador to Cairo, reportedly told Nasser that Kassem's card number was 37. See R. K. Karanjia, *Dawn or Darkness* (Bombay 1959), p. 12.

[98] Amin Salimov later wrote that by late 1962 the Iraqi national *bourgeoisie* began to apprehend the possibility of "a shift to the Left". Hence its decision to act. *International Affairs* (Moscow), vol. 9 (September 1963), p. 43.

pated this, and instantaneously took up arms. But this time the Communists were on the defensive and fighting with their backs to the wall. Their supporters in the army were outnumbered by their enemies. The Soviet-trained pilots of the Iraqi Air Force were opposed to the *coup d'état*, but they too were neutralized by the ground personnel which had switched to the opposite camp. In an all-out offensive, the National Council of the Iraqi Revolution called upon the army, police, and the paramilitary National Guards to treat the Communists as Kassem's allies and to annihilate them. Armed with meticulous lists of the Communists the Ba'thists combed their hideouts "street by street, quarter by quarter, and city by city".[99] The Communist resistance was toughest in Basra, Najaf, and the Kazamayn area of Baghdad. *Pravda's* correspondent, P. Demchenko, who was in Baghdad at that time, witnessed the ironical spectacle of the CPI being crushed with Soviet-made tanks and machine-guns. Scores of Communists, among them members of the CPI's Central Committee, were shot dead. These included Salam 'Adil, the First Secretary of the party; 'Abd al-Qadir 'Isma'il al-Bustani, formerly editor of the *Ittihad ash-Sha'b*; Muhammad Husayn 'Abd al-'Ays, editor of the Communist weekly, *Sawt ash-Sha'b*;[100] and Hasan 'Uwayni.[101] Kassem himself was executed after a summary trial carried out before a television camera. Wasfi Tahir, Taha Shaykh Ahmad, and Fadil 'Abbas al-Mahdawi met with similar fate.

Notwithstanding the telling blows it sustained in February, the CPI made some desperate attempts, first in March and again in July, to retrieve lost ground. In the latter case, it tried to capture the important Rashid Military Camp near Baghdad, where a thousand Communist detenus had been languishing in prisons. The venture was, however, foiled by the army's prompt intervention. The Ba'thists alleged that the insurgents had a plan to announce withdrawal from the Tripartite Unity Charter, to disband the

[99] G. H. Jansen in *The Statesman* (New Delhi), 26 February 1963. Haykal states on King Husayn's authority that an American espionage service which was in touch with the Iraqi Ba'th conveyed to the latter, on a secret broadcasting service, the names and addresses of the Iraqi Communists. *Al-Ahram*, 8 November 1963.

[100] The *Sawt ash-Sha'b* had been started in August 1959.

[101] Another ten Communist leaders were executed on 2 July 1963 for their rôle in the Mosul clashes in March 1959.

National Guards, and to revive the People's Resistance Force following seizure of power.[102] More arrests and executions followed.[103] Later, the Communists bitterly recalled that "in one year alone punitive expeditions executed more patriots than did the Monarchy in its last twenty-five years".[104]

The ordeal left the CPI in utter disarray. The Ba'thist régime revived Nuri's penal code outlawing all Communist activities. Some of the Communist detenus "volunteered" confessions mingled with denunciation of the party.[105] Among them was Ibrahim Kubba, an eminent Marxist who had served as Minister of Agrarian Reform under Kassem, who indicted the CPI for its ideological muddle and opportunistic alliance with Kassem's dictatorial rule.[106] A number of Iraqi Communists fled to Syria and, following a Ba'thist *coup d'état* there in March, to the Lebanon. From there they dispersed into Eastern Europe. Those who stayed behind in Iraq went into hiding.

Search for a Viable Policy

Around October 1964 an enlarged meeting of the Central Committee of the CPI—the first since the fateful events of 1963—was secretly convened. In the meantime, Iraq had witnessed another political shake-up. In a swift *coup d'état* on 18 November 1963 President 'Arif smashed the Ba'thist régime. The Communists were heartened by the development; but their hopes were soon dampened as the new régime carried out the executions of two Communist trade unionists whose original death sentences had been commuted by Kassem to seven years' imprisonment.[107] This provoked the CPI to denounce quickly the duumvirate of President 'Arif and Premier Tahir Yahya as "Fascist" and call for continued battle

[102] *Al-Jamahir* (Baghdad), 5 July 1963.

[103] Three members of the Central Committee were hanged on 21 July 1963 following a court martial. They were identified as Jamal al-Haydari, 'Abd al-Jabbar Wahbi and Muhammad Saleh al-'Abbasi.

[104] Nadji, "The Situation in Iraq and the Position of the Communist Party", *Peace, Freedom and Socialism* (Prague), vol. 8 (June 1965), p. 58.

[105] See letters to this effect by 'Isam al-Qadi and 'Abd as-Sattar Mahdi Muhammad Rida in *Iraq Times*, 6 March 1963.

[106] *Iraq Times*, 22 March 1963.

[107] The trade unionists, Karim Husayn and 'Abdullah Rashid, were executed on 24 December 1963. See *Peace, Freedom and Socialism*, vol. 7 (February 1964), pp. 87-88.

against these forces.[108] A fuller assessment of the new situation emerged from the deliberations of the Central Committee in the fall of 1964.

The Central Committee's statement[109] indicated a clear shift in Communist policy and tactics supported by an elaborate diagnosis which traced the party's recent blunders to "dogmatism and Left-sectarianism". The new policy formulations covered a wide spectrum of national, regional, and international issues. Surveying the international scene the statement forcefully deprecated the "factionalist activities of the Communist Party of China" and called for "an active ideological struggle against them". This set at rest widespread suspicion of the CPI's inclination towards the Chinese Communists in the Sino-Soviet ideological conflict. As a corollary to this, the Iraqi Communists endorsed the Soviet thesis that the world balance being favourable to the forces of peace, liberation, and socialism, the way had opened for the developing countries to "non-capitalist development leading to socialism". Its validity was borne out by the advance of the UAR and Algeria from political independence to "important social changes". The rulers of Iraq were called upon to emulate this "vanguard" of the Arab revolutionary movement. In this changed context, the party saw in the movement of Arab unity "a new and more progressive content" and fully supported the Co-ordination Agreement between Cairo and Baghdad. Finally, the party adopted a conciliatory posture on domestic issues. For the first time, it made a clear distinction between the short-lived Ba'thist terror and 'Arif's régime which supplanted it. 'Arif was given due credit not only for ending "the nightmare of Fascist rule" but also for stopping the war against the Kurds and restoring the National Oil Company Law.[110] At the same time, the party warned the Government to pay attention to the "serious defects" in its policy such as continued detention of "patriots", emergency conditions, and military courts before "it is too late". It also extended the hand of co-operation

[108] The CPI secretly distributed, in Baghdad, a circular to this effect in January 1964. Text in *Information Bulletin* (Prague), No. 7 (1964), pp. 268-9.

[109] Text in *An-Nida* (Beirut), 16 October 1964. For an English version see *Peace, Freedom and Socialism*, vol. 7 (November 1964), pp. 82-85.

[110] Originally adopted in Kassem's time and put in abeyance by the Ba'thist régime, the National Oil Company Law sought to put an end to the monopolies of the foreign oil companies by wresting from the latter the vast unexploited areas covered by the concessions.

to all organizations and groups determined to uphold national independence.

The Central Committee's accent on moderate reforms and conciliation with pan-Arabism, however, did not find favour with the hardliners in the party and eventually forced it thoroughly to re-examine the situation. This came about in April 1965 when a fresh policy statement was issued. It demanded that "the dictatorial military régime of "Arif-Yahya" be replaced by "a provisional government of national coalition" which would terminate the legacy of past dictatorship. 'Arif's espousal of a single-party system on the UAR pattern was singled out for sharp criticism; and a call was issued to all "democratic" and "anti-imperialist" forces— including those who had joined the officially sponsored Arab Socialist Union—to coalesce in a united national front. The UAR was also warned that while the party commended its contribution to world peace and national liberation movement, it reserved the right to offer "constructive criticism" of its failures such as the "incorrect attitude" to the Iraqi national liberation movement "and the support still being rendered to 'Arif's dictatorial régime".[111]

Beneath this hurriedly contrived tough posture lay the inner party struggle between those who believe that any headlong clash with 'Arif's régime will only help the Rightist elements and jeopardize peaceful co-existence between the USA and the USSR, and those who see better prospects for the party in a Communist-Ba'th alliance directed against the 'Arif régime. The name of Abd as-Sattar Kawsi, *alias* Abi 'Ubayda is associated with the former group; those of 'Aziz al-Haj and Zaki Khayri with the latter.[112] In the strictly local context, the conflict centres on the party's status *vis-à-vis* the Government-sponsored Arab Socialist Union (ASU). Should the CPI go the Egyptian way and dissolve itself in the wider interest of national cohesion? Or should it forge a united front with other Leftist elements to defy the amorphous ASU? The choice is rendered immensely difficult by the simple fact that the CPI even in its present emasculated state is far more organized and far stronger than the Communist factions in Egypt. The temptations of moral and material support from the two rival centres of world Communism scarcely make it less difficult.

111 See Nadji, n. 104, pp. 58-59.
112 *Al-Jarida* (Beirut), 18 May 1965.

The CPI and the Kurds

The coming to power of Kassem in 1958 had brought the Kurdish Democratic Party (KDP) and the CPI closer to each other. Both had been eager to gain the favour of the new ruler though not for identical reasons. The Kurds had hailed the destruction of the old régime, for it ended the Baghdad Pact,[113] which they had regarded as an "anti-Kurdish alliance". But the upsurge of Arab nationalist sentiment that accompanied the revolution posed a far more potent threat to Kurdish national interests. For Iraq's merger into a larger Arab entity, as advocated by the pan-Arabists, was bound to submerge the Kurdish national identity. The Communists, too, were apprehensive of being swallowed up by the rising tide of Arab nationalism. It was this common fear of Arab nationalism which formed the basis of partnership between the Communists and the Kurds. They, in turn, became Kassem's natural allies after he openly clashed with Nasser.

With Kassem's approval Mulla Mustafa Barazani returned to Baghdad, in October 1958, from his long exile in the Soviet Union. Barazani reassembled the KDP, which had fallen into disarray as a result of political repression and absence of vigorous leadership, and adopted a radical programme promising drastic land reform and close co-operation with the socialist countries in external and economic policies.[114] The KDP's Leftward swing was further accelerated by the rise of Hamza 'Abdullah in the party hierarchy. 'Abdullah had been close to the CPI since the forties. He now strove to co-ordinate the activities of the two parties and their various front organizations. In March 1959, the Kurds fought by the side of the Communists to put down the Mosul revolt engineered by pro-Nasser army officers.

The triangular alliance, however, proved to be short-lived. The KDP soon discovered that despite his verbal sympathy Kassem had no intention to grant autonomy to the Kurdish provinces. The Communists, too, were not prepared to underwrite all Kurdish claims for fear of antagonizing Kassem. The Kurds also sensed imminent peril to their security in the large-scale shipment of Soviet arms to Iraq.

The parting of the ways came soon after Mosul. Barazani first

[113] Dana Adams Schmidt, *Journey among Brave Men* (Boston, 1964), p. 125.
[114] Hassan Arfa, *The Kurds: A Historical and Political Study* (London 1966), p. 130.

proceeded to curb the influence of Hamza 'Abdullah in the party. Following this the KDP's relations with the CPI began to cool down. Early in 1960 the CPI organ *Ittihad ash-Sha'b* came forward with a strong condemnation of "the narrow nationalistic tendencies and separatist inclinations that have gripped the minds of some chauvinistic Kurds".[115] The resultant estrangement between the two parties led to the expulsion of Hamza 'Abdullah and his associates from the KDP by the fourth party Congress held in October.

Soon after, the KDP's differences with Kassem came out into the open. Kassem had tried to mollify the Kurds by giving official recognition to the KDP in February 1960. At the same time, he continued to evade the substantive Kurdish demand for autonomy. In desperation the Kurds took up arms in March 1961. By September the conflict developed into a large-scale war between the Iraqi army and Barazani's guerrilla fighters. On 10 October Kassem indicted the KDP for "undermining security, creating schism among various nationalities and jeopardizing national unity" and formally disbanded the party.[116]

During the eighteen months of Kurdish armed struggle against Kassem, Barazani purged the KDP of Communist elements. This period also witnessed the rise of Ibrahim Ahmad, the urbane intellectual who deftly employed his knowledge of Marxian ideology to wean the Kurdish youth from the CPI. The Communists tried to counteract this by the slogan of "self-government for the Iraqi Kurdistan within the Republic of Iraq".[117] After Kassem's fall, political adversity impelled the Iraqi Communists to seek refuge in the Kurdish region where they were disarmed by Barazani's forces. Relations between the KDP and the CPI improved for a while when, early in 1963, the Ba'thist régime's combined offensive against the Kurds and the Communists prompted the Soviet Union to champion the Kurdish cause strongly. But prospects of an equitable settlement with the Baghdad Government following the cease-fire of June 1966 revived Barazani's antipathy towards the CPI.[118]

[115] *Ittihad ash-Sha'b*, 21 January 1960.

[116] *The Jerusalem Times* (Jerusalem, Jordan), 11 October 1962.

[117] Resolution of the Central Committee of the CPI adopted in March 1962 and quoted in Jabbar Ali, "The Iraqi Communist Party and the Kurdish Question", *World Marxist Review*, vol. 5 (August 1962), pp. 18-24.

[118] Barazani told the correspondent of the Cairo weekly, *Akhbar al-Yawm* (29 October 1966) that he fought for Kurdish autonomy in order to safeguard his people against "lunatic attacks by Communists and Ba'thists".

The CPI has no doubt suffered a serious set-back in the Iraqi Kurdistan. But it is by no means permanently incapacitated. In the major Kurdish towns of Arbil, Kirkuk, and Sulaymaniya, pockets of Communist influence still persist. Besides, in the KDP itself the domineering and conservative Mulla Mustafa has been at loggerheads with radical leaders like Ibrahim Ahmad and Jalal Talbani. The return of peace and normalcy in this war-ravaged region is likely to bring these latent differences to the fore and thus create new opportunities for the Communists to utilize to their advantage.

CHAPTER TWELVE

JORDAN: THE CHRONIC STALEMATE

THE united front tactics which the Communist Party of Jordan (CPJ) had been pursuing since 1952 at last began to yield handsome dividends in 1956. By that time nationalist sentiment in Jordan had been greatly stirred by the termination of the Anglo-Egyptian Treaty of 1936, Nasser's emphatic call to the Arabs to resist the Baghdad Pact, and the Egyptian arms deal with Czechoslovakia. The fight against the Pact was led by the Communists, the Ba'th, and the National Socialists. As soon as the Government yielded to public pressure on the question of the British-sponsored military alliance[1] the opposition came forward with the demand that the Anglo-Jordanian Treaty of 1948, under which Britain paid an annual subsidy of £12 million to Jordan in return for bases at Amman, Mafraq, and 'Aqaba, be abrogated and the sovereignty of Jordan restored. The campaign against the treaty was spurred by the offer of Saudi Arabia, Syria, and Egypt, in January 1956, to replace jointly the British subsidy. By the middle of 1956 street demonstrations in Jordan, reinforced by the anti-British propaganda carried out by the Cairo Press and radio, made it practically impossible for the Government to function. Under the circumstances the King had no alternative but to dissolve the parliament and hold fresh elections.

The 1956 Elections

Having played an important rôle in stirring public sentiment against the Baghdad Pact and the Anglo-Jordanian Treaty, the Communists were determined to translate their recently acquired popularity into concrete political gains. As in the case of previous elections they fought under the guise of the National Front (*al-Jabha al-Wataniya*). The broad alliance with the Ba'th and the National Socialist Party (NSP) was preserved intact. On the chief election issue, namely abrogation of the treaty, there was complete agreement among the three parties. They were also united on the question of liberalizing the political set-up in the country. At the

[1] See above, ch. 7.

same time differences did exist on several issues. Whereas the Ba'th and the Front were anti-royalist, the NSP favoured constitutional monarchy. As to possible alternatives to the British subsidy, the Ba'th was in favour of forging economic ties with non-aligned Egypt and Syria, whereas the Front emphasized the virtues of Soviet aid and the NSP stood for aid from friendly Arab countries without having to sacrifice Jordan's political identity. Disagreements also cropped up on the question of distribution of seats. These differences were, however, not carried to the breaking-point. Instead, electoral adjustments were effected, ideological differences side tracked, and the need for general accord on ridding the country of British influence emphasized.

The October 1956 elections were the freest ever held in the Kingdom of Jordan. For the first time the Government did not put up its own candidates and the contest was not between the parties and the authorities but among the parties alone. In the circumstances the victory of the opposition at the polls did not come as a surprise. What was indeed extraordinary, the Front, which had fielded only eight candidates, won three seats. Of these, one was returned unopposed from Bethlehem area. On the contrary, the Ba'th having contested many more seats secured only two. The NSP with its eleven seats emerged as the largest group in the 40-member parliament. Even more impressive was the Front's share of the votes cast in the elections. Of the 405,000 votes actually cast, the Front secured 51,389, the Ba'th 34,200, and the National Socialist Party 72,467.[2]

The Nabulsi Cabinet

Shortly after the announcement of the election results Sulayman Nabulsi, the leader of the NSP, was called upon to form a cabinet. The united front having survived the electoral test, Nabulsi formed a coalition Government in which the Front deputy, 'Abdul Qadir Salih, was assigned the portfolio of Agriculture. Salih thus became the first Communist to hold a cabinet post in the Arab East.

With the assumption of office by the Nabulsi cabinet the struggle between the King and his opponents entered the last phase. The King had manifestly lost much ground. His worst critics now controlled the Government. The case for Anglo-Jordanian alliance had

[2] A. H. H. Abidi, *Jordan: A Political Study, 1948-1957* (Bombay, 1965), p. 209.

been irretrievably lost in view of Britain's armed assault on Egypt. Yet the King had not lost the whole game. For after all, instead of resisting the recent changes, he had, at least outwardly, taken credit for ushering them in. He had dismissed Glubb; and it was under his orders that the elections were conducted in a free atmosphere wholly immune from customary malpractices. Again, at the time of the Suez War, the King readily offered armed assistance to Nasser although Premier Nabulsi had advised caution on practical grounds.[3] By deftly manipulating these strong points, Husayn was able to project himself as a nationalist King. But now that he was required to make the ultimate choice between royal prerogatives and constitutional rule he decided to fight back rather than surrender.

Conflict with the King

In the ensuing tussle between King Husayn and the cabinet the former chose his weapons skilfully and with deadly effect. At home the King fell back on the Bedouin army to retrieve his position. Here, too, he had to contend with the anti-royalist "Free Officers" and an unpredictable Chief of Staff. But by and large the officers and men of the army remained loyal to the King. Outside Jordan the increase of Soviet influence in the Arab East following the Suez war had weakened the Cairo-Damascus-Riyadh Axis. Scared by the prospect of Soviet ascendancy in the area, King Sa'ud now appeared favourably disposed to "combat Communism" with American aid, if necessary. Husayn found in him an invaluable ally who had the triple distinction of being technically non-aligned, traditionally anti-British, and a friend of the United States.

Against this backdrop, Husayn initiated a series of calculated moves designed to oust the Nabulsi cabinet. He tactically endorsed the Parliament's decision (28 November 1956) to terminate the Anglo-Jordanian Treaty and to sign an Arab Solidarity Agreement with Egypt, Syria, and Saudi Arabia which substituted Arab for British subsidy. Having thus established his credentials as an ardent nationalist, he launched a tirade against domestic Communists and Communism in general. Early in February, the King wrote a letter to Nabulsi pointing to the danger of Communist infiltration which opened the way for "a new type of colonialism" and urged

---

[5] Nabulsi calculated that while Jordan's active support could scarcely improve the position of Egypt it would have provided a plausible excuse to Israel and Britain's ally Iraq to march their troops into Jordan.

the Government to adopt a policy aimed at creating a "strong national structure free from Communist propaganda and Bolshevik teachings".[4] Much as the Nabulsi Government resented Husayn's refusal to function as a constitutional monarch, it offered to meet the King's demands half-way rather than precipitate a headlong clash with the latter. Accordingly, the Government moved to ban the Communist weekly *Al-Jamahir*[5] as well as publication and sale of other Communist literature. Likewise, the recently started news bulletin of the *Tass* Agency was disallowed and exhibition of Soviet films prohibited. This tactical retreat was clearly intended to blunt the edge of the King's offensive against the cabinet in the name of combating Communism.

At the same time Nabulsi refused to yield ground on the crucial issues of democratization of the régime and implementation of the Arab Solidarity Agreement. Again, while the King adopted an equivocal attitude on the question of the Eisenhower Doctrine, the cabinet took the stand that Arab defence should be the "sole concern" of the Arabs. Nor was the King satisfied with the Government's perfunctory measures against the Communists. To press forward his argument, the King wrote to the signatories of the Arab Solidarity Agreement to join him in resisting "all propaganda that belied our beliefs, faiths and religion". But Nabulsi refused to be coerced. On the contrary, he proceeded to improve Jordan's relations with the Communist bloc. On 24 March, he told a visiting delegation of Chinese Trade Unions that his Government intended to recognize the People's Republic of China. A few days later the Government decided to establish diplomatic ties with the Soviet Union. With this rapid succession of moves and counter-moves an open showdown between the King and the cabinet appeared imminent. On 8 April 1957 an armoured-car regiment surrounded the capital reportedly at the instance of the Chief of Staff, Major-General 'Ali Abu Nuwar and other "Free Officers" of the army. Two days later the King demanded, and obtained, the resignation of the Nabulsi cabinet. On 13 April, the anti-royalist officers staged

[4] Quoted in Benjamin Shwadran, *Jordan: A State of Tension* (New York, 1959). Shwadran adds that this letter "may have had two alternative objectives. The King's strong anti-Communist and anti-Nabulsi position might persuade the British to continue the subsidy; or, if the British were irrevocably determined to withdraw it, the Americans might appreciate his stand and offer assistance, which would enable him to preserve his throne." pp. 346-7.

[5] *Al-Jamahir* was started in December 1956.

a revolt at Zarqa, a military camp adjacent to Amman. The bulk of the Bedouin army, however, remained loyal to the King and the revolt was crushed expeditiously.

Husayn claimed that the abortive *coup d'état* was the work of some political parties which were getting "support from outside sources 'including' a foreign power outside the Arab world" and were trying to infiltrate into the army in order to subvert the régime and "to swing Jordan into the Red Axis".[6] On the other hand, 'Ali Abu Nuwar, who had in the meantime fled to Syria, told *Al-'Alam* (Damascus) on 22 April that Husayn's action was intended "to liquidate certain liberal military and civilian elements and to impose the Eisenhower Doctrine on Jordan".

Following Nabulsi's fall the National Front, the Ba'th, and the NSP formed a Committee of National Guidance which demanded restoration of the Nabulsi Government, categorical rejection of the Eisenhower Doctrine, and expulsion of the US Ambassador, Lester D. Mallory, and the Military Attaché, Colonel James Sweeney. These demands were duly backed by massive demonstrations in Nablus, Ramallah, Jericho, Jerusalem, and Amman on 24 April. But the King, who had already purged the army of "Free Officers", was now in a far stronger position than on 13 April to engage his opponents. In a swift move, he called upon Ibrahim Hashim, a trusted friend of the Hashimite throne, to form a new cabinet, dissolved the Parliament and all political parties, and proclaimed martial law in the Kingdom. The army was given extensive powers to deal with the opposition. Over 200 people were arrested. Early in May the Arab Students' Congress and all trade unions were disbanded. The Leftist deputies Yaqub Zia' ad-Din (Jerusalem), Fayiq Warrad (Ramallah), and 'Abdul Khaliq Yaghmour (Hebron) were tried by a military court and sentenced to various terms.

The King's all-out offensive against the opposition was backed up by the US Government, which promptly offered him military and financial assistance. On 24 April, President Eisenhower proclaimed that the "independence and integrity" of Jordan was "vital" to US interests. On the following day the Sixth Fleet was ordered to sail towards the eastern Mediterranean. Soon after, the US Ambassador to Amman announced aid worth $10 million to assist Jordan "in economic development and maintenance of political stability".

[6] See John Law's interview with King Husayn in *U.S. News & World Report* (Washington, D. C.), 5 July 1957, pp. 41-42.

The Balance-Sheet

The events of the mid-fifties were a landmark in the history of the Communist movement in Jordan. It would, however, be incorrect to ascribe Communist successes in 1955-56 to ideological factors. For even at the peak of its influence the CPJ did not muster more than a thousand card-carrying members. But they were able to raise many more sympathizers and general supporters. This they could achieve partly through their solid organization and zealous drive but mostly because of the party's resolve to embrace the nationalist cause and to be in the forefront of the patriotic struggle. This tactical shift was part of the general trend in the Arab East resulting from a reassessment of revolutionary potentialities of Arab nationalism. The initiative in this regard was taken by the Soviet Union as reflected in its policy towards Egypt and Syria. The CPJ, like other Communist parties in the region, made necessary adjustments to clear the way for collaboration with the nationalist forces. A broad front with the Ba'th and the NSP was the logical outcome.

It must, however, be noted that the Communist-dominated National Front was merely a minor partner in the Nabulsi cabinet. Besides, Nabulsi himself was no revolutionary. At best he was a cautious politician wedded to emancipation from the British, moderate reforms, and constitutional monarchy. His party's alliance with the pan-Arab Ba'th and the Communists primarily rested on their common antipathy towards the British and distrust of the King rather than on any all-embracing national programme. None the less, it gave the Communists enormous political prestige. But before the CPJ could cash in on this, the King's decisive intervention wrecked the party's immediate prospects.

Sectarian Interlude

The Communist line during the next five years was determined by the chastening experience of 1957, the Iraqi revolution of the following year, and what the party described as the "reign of black terror" imposed by the Jordanian régime. Following a succession of stunning blows the party had sustained in 1957, it ceased all public activities and went underground. It remained practically inert until the middle of 1958, when the Iraqi revolution propelled it into action.

By early 1959 the rift between Baghdad and Cairo polarized the nationalists and the Communists in the Arab East into mutually hostile camps. Jordan was no exception. Taking advantage of the split between the Communists and the nationalists the Jordanian régime resumed its anti-Communist drive with renewed zest. In April, the police claimed to have unearthed the secret party head-quarters in the Nablus area. Two Communist leaders—'Abdullah Sulayman al-Bayya and Muhammad Mahmud Sa'da—and 16 other party members were rounded up. More arrests followed in the months of July and August. Over 80 Communists were taken into police custody in July. These included Muhammad Sa'id Sa'd, a Central Committee member, Ibrahim Yusuf Mahmud, and Mahmud Jabir.[7] Wadi' Michael 'Ammarin and Yunus Husayn were arrested early in August, as they arrived in Jordan after confabulations with the Iraqi comrades in Baghdad.[8] By December it was officially con-firmed that the recent anti-Communist drive had resulted in the detention of 200 Communists.[9] Jordan, according to a Communist statement, had been turned into "a large prison dominated by terror, torture, vagrancy and total economic destruction".[10]

Isolated from the nationalists and paralysed by continued re-pression, the CPJ adopted a distinctly sectarian posture. In a belated appraisement, the party secretary, Fu'ad Nassar, blamed the vacil-lations of the NSP and the Ba'th no less than "the dollar, the US Sixth Fleet, and the Eisenhower-Dulles Doctrine" for the 1957 débâcle. Nassar indicted the NSP and the Ba'th—labelled respective-ly "the party of the national *bourgeoisie*" and "the party of the petty *bourgeoisie*"—for ignoring repeated warnings by the party against "reactionary conspiracies" in the beginning of 1957. On the con-trary the former "entered into a compromise with the reactionaries" and the latter declined to co-operate with the Communists "believing that mass action would 'strengthen' the Communists". In the same breath, however, Nassar called for a national front wedded to "extirpation of the British and US imperialist rule, abolition of the reactionary monarchist régime and establishment of a national democratic system". Needless to say, the Communist call fell on unresponsive ears.[11]

[7] *As-Sahafa* (Beirut), 25 July 1959.

[8] *Al-Hayat* (Beirut), 9 August 1959 and *Ad-Difa'* (Jerusalem), 10 August 1959.

[9] *Al-Hayat*, 6 December 1959.

[10] Text of the statement in *New Age* (New Delhi), 27 March 1960, p. 11.

[11] "F. N.", "What the Jordanian Communist Party Is Fighting for", *World Marxist Review* (Prague), vol. 4 (July 1961), pp. 57-60.

Towards Re-alignment and Revival

By 1962 the wheel of shifting political alliances in the Arab East having come full circle, the Arab Communists once again took to fraternizing with the nationalists. The Communist reverses in Iraq, the promulgation of far-reaching socialist laws in the UAR (July 1961), and the new Soviet line commending a gradualist path to socialism—all these served to bring about a marked change in Communist outlook.

In Jordan, the new Communist line was reflected in improved relations with the Ba'th and the Nasserites. The UAR, Algeria, and Syria came to be identified as "progressive" states. Fullthroated support was extended to the Arab summit conferences held in 1964, and the creation of the Palestine Liberation Organization (PLO) was fervently welcomed. All "national and progressive forces" of the country were invited to co-operate in formulating a progressive charter with the aim of establishing a "national democracy in Jordan". Towards that end the CPJ submitted the outline of a broadbased programme comprising (*a*) support for Arab solidarity against "the intrigues of imperialism and its flunkey, Israel",[12] (*b*) promotion of unity among liberated socialist and friendly countries, and (*c*) radical and progressive measures and reforms in the field of industry, agriculture, and education.[13]

In the meantime a marked relaxation in the attitude of the Government towards the opposition stimulated Communist activity. In August 1963 the Government of Jordan, on its own initiative, established diplomatic relations with the Soviet Union at ambassadorial level. This was in sharp contrast to King Husayn's contention, in 1957, that diplomatic ties with the Soviet Union would lead to "growth of Communism in the country".[14] In April 1965 the King even approached the Soviet Union for economic and technical assistance. Simultaneously amnesty was granted to 1,566 political detenus and 150 political exiles. The latter included Fu'ad

---

[12] It is important to note that while advocating close co-operation with the "liberated" Arab states and Arab solidarity against imperialism the CPJ does not subscribe to the view held by Nasserites that Jordan should merge into a larger Arab entity. On the contrary, it believes that Jordan possesses sufficient mineral and other resources which, if properly tapped with the help of friendly nations, could release the country from dependence on foreign subsidies. *At-Taqaddum* of December 1964 quoted in *Al-Ittihad* (Haifa), 5 February 1965.

[13] Text in *Information Bulletin* (Prague), no. 39 (1965), pp. 23-25.

[14] Law, n. 6, pp. 42-43.

Nassar, 'Abd ar-Rahman Shuqayr, Yaqub Ziyadni, Amal Nafih, 'Isa Madnat, and Fayid Warrad—all leading Communist figures.[15] The Communists, however, viewed these gestures sceptically and continued to function secretly. In 1964 a clandestine journal called *At-Taqaddum* was started.

With the setting up of the PLO and a host of terrorist organizations pledged to liberate Palestine through guerrilla warfare and the resultant friction with Israel, it would seem as if Jordan were heading towards another crisis. If it does, the Communists are not likely to remain disinterested spectators. Perhaps the drama of 1957 will be repeated. But in view of the unchanged power equation in Jordan and the Arab Eastern region, it would be safe to assume that its outcome is unlikely to vary substantially.

[15] *An-Nahar* (Beirut), 7 April 1965.

PART THREE
THE IDEOLOGICAL ISSUES

CHAPTER THIRTEEN

COMMUNISM AND NATIONALISM

THE interplay of Communism and local nationalisms has been frequently touched upon in the foregoing chapters. It may nevertheless be useful to sum up the broad features of the Communist-nationalist relationship before we pass on to examine the related phenomenon of the interaction between Communism and pan-Arabism.

Communism made its début on the Arab scene at a time when nationalism, whether local or pan-Arab, had already come into its own. On the face of it the two creeds were strikingly incongruous in motivation, background, and ideological content. Whereas the driving force behind the nationalist upsurge was the impulse to redeem national identity, Communism was primarily moved by the urge to foment a proletarian revolution transcending national boundaries. Secondly, whereas nationalism was the product of a sustained process of political, economic, and intellectual evolution, Communism was a wholly exotic plant sought to be abruptly transplanted in the unfamiliar Arab soil. Another source of conflict between Communism and nationalism lay in their intrinsic differences as to the goals of national struggle. Whereas the nationalists put the highest premium on wresting political freedom from the colonial Powers, the Communists conceived of national struggle as an intrinsic part of a global conflict between Communism and world capitalism. This divergence of objectives was inevitably reflected in the respective methods of struggle of the two creeds: the nationalists commended unity of national ranks; the Communists resorted to class struggle.

Paradoxically, however, there was also considerable common ground between Communism and Arab Eastern nationalisms. To begin with, the Bolshevik Revolution evoked keen, sympathetic interest in the nationalist circles. So did Lenin's stirring call that the way to destroy imperialism was by the union of the proletarian revolution in Russia with the nationalist revolutions of the East. Rashid Rida, an orthodox Muslim scholar and a conservative nationalist, expressed this sentiment as follows:

11

Bolshevism is only another name for socialism, and socialism means the liberation of the workers from the capitalists and oppressive governments. Muslims must hope for its success, since they too are workers and suffer from the same oppression, and if socialism succeeds, the subjugation of peoples will end. True, Communism is not in conformity with Islamic law, but neither are the activities of the European governments.[1]

Rida's reaction signified not so much a considered endorsement of the Communist doctrine as an emphatic protest of nationalist sentiment deeply outraged by British and French imperialist policies. But the important point is that Arab nationalism tended to look on Bolshevism as a potential ally in the anti-imperialist struggle.

Secondly, Communism, like nationalism, found its most ardent supporters neither in the teeming peasantry nor in the far less numerous industrial proletariat but in the politically articulate middle class, comprising lawyers, doctors, teachers, technocrats, and army officers, and in the sprawling student community. And since the middle class was the common fountainhead of the Communist and nationalist movements, the differences between Communists and nationalists tended to be "less clear-cut in real life than in the text books".[2] Furthermore, with the passage of time the gap between the nationalist and Communist programmes and attitudes has progressively narrowed. The advent of political independence coupled with mounting internal pressures impelled the nationalist leaders and parties to adopt positive policies to promote socio-economic welfare. The nationalists also tended to share the Communist distrust of private enterprise which came to be regarded "as the evil demon behind Western imperialism and expansion".[3]

Communism and Pan-Arabism: The Early Phase
Some of the aforementioned considerations also determined the

[1] Quoted in A. H. Hourani, *Arabic Thought in the Liberal Age 1798-1939* (London, 1962), p. 304.

[2] W. Z. Laqueur, "The National Bourgeoisie: A Soviet Dilemma in the Middle East", *International Affairs* (London), vol. 35 (July 1959), p. 330.

[3] Morroe Berger, "The Middle Class in the Arab World", in W. Z. Laqueur, ed., *The Middle East in Transition* (London, 1958), p. 69.

attitudes of Communism and pan-Arabism towards one another. In a sense both regarded local nationalism (*wataniya*) as an unavoidable evil which needed to be constantly guarded against and eventually subordinated to higher goals. But there the parallelism ended. Whereas the Communists desired to subject *wataniya* to proletarian internationalism, the pan-Arabists aspired to merge it into comprehensive Arab nationalism (*qawmiya*).

The rise and growth of Communist movements coincided with a politically frustrating yet intellectually productive phase in the evolution of pan-Arabism. Born and reared in the Fertile Crescent in the late nineteenth and early twentieth centuries, the Arab nationalist movement initially sought to create a sovereign Arab entity out of the disaffected Arab provinces of the Ottoman Empire. A significant turning-point in its career came in 1916, when, following a secret understanding with the British, a band of Arab nationalists rose in rebellion against the Turkish authorities. The nationalists' hope of securing an independent Arab state comprising the Fertile Crescent and the Arabian Peninsula, kindled by British assurances, was, however, belied by the arbitrary fragmentation of the Ottoman provinces by Britain and France under the cover of the Mandates System. As a consequence of this, the Arab unity movement was paralysed for the time being. But the idea underlying it not only survived the ordeal but acquired, in the course of the next two decades, a measure of theoretical sophistication and intellectual appeal at the hands of a host of nationalist thinkers.[4]

The enormous intellectual output of the inter-war period was, however, more concerned with the exploration and elaboration of the determinants and rationale of Arab nationhood than with questions of methods and timing, forms and structures, and other aspects of the mechanics of national action.[5] In any case, even the most ardent champions of Arab nationalism did not believe that unity was round the corner; and the Communist-nationalist dialogue was in fact conducted, in this period, on a purely theoretical level. The sole exception to this was a joint resolution adopted by the Communist parties of Syria and Palestine in 1931 which treated the question of pan-Arabism in an unusually positive and forthright manner. "The gist of the Arab national question", it con-

---

[4] For an able treatment of this subject, see Hourani, n. 1, ch. 11.

[5] Fayez A. Sayegh, *Arab Unity: Hope and Fulfilment* (New York, 1958), p. 81.

tended, "consists in the fact that the English, French, Italian, and Spanish imperialists have dismembered the living body of the Arab peoples, hold the Arab countries in a state of feudal fragmentation, deprive each and every one of these countries of the prerequisites of an independent political and economic development, and block the national political unification of the Arab countries." The Arab peoples were bound together by a "common language, historical conditions, and a common enemy"; and their fusion in the revolutionary struggle had created "all the prerequisites to cast off the imperialist yoke, to achieve national political independence, and to create a number of states, which, thereafter of their own free will, could unite on the basis of federal principles".[6] There is no evidence, however, to show that the thesis set forth in this resolution was backed with concrete action or sustained even on a theoretical plane.

In actual fact, the Communists, like the nationalists, were opposed to the Mandates System and to the British presence in Egypt, but unlike them they did not question the boundaries drawn by the Mandatory Powers in the Fertile Crescent. As for the claims advanced on behalf of Arab nationalism, they regarded them as wholly unrealistic and lacking in material basis. The Communist case was authoritatively stated by Khalid Bakdash in 1939 as follows:[7]

> Most of our politicians and writers have scarcely discussed our national problems scientifically. They believe that by ignoring the factor of geography they, in fact, eliminate its effect on the rise and development of nations. They do not realize that in doing so they behave like an ostrich which buries its head until it ceases to see the enemy. It then thinks that the enemy is not seeing it whereas it is the ostrich which is not seeing the enemy. It is geography that separates Syria from Algeria and Iraq from Egypt. It has shaped and continues to shape the culture, economic and intellectual life and psychological fabric of each country.

The Communist concern for factors of diversity and particular-

[6] Text of the resolution in Ivar Spector, *The Soviet Union and the Muslim World: 1917-1956* (Mimeographed, Washington, D. C., 1956), pp. 75-82.

[7] Quoted in Muhammad 'Ali az-Zarqa' and Ilyas Marqas, *Khiyana Khalid Bakdash l'il Qawmiya al-'Arabiya* (Cairo, 1959), p. 31.

ism in the Arab world was perhaps only one of the reasons for its antipathy towards pan-Arabism. The preponderance of non-Arab elements in the Arab Communist movement was another reason. For example, Jewish, Greek, and Italian elements remained dominant in the Egyptian Communist movement for about a quarter century. The Kurds and the Armenians were proportionately far more numerous than the Arabs in the Communist Party of Syria and the Lebanon. A similar situation obtained in Iraq, where, in addition to Kurds and Armenians, the Jews also took a leading part in organizing and leading Communist activities. Yet another reason was the secretive and clandestine character of the Arab Communist parties in the early formative years. Above all, the Soviet Union made no secret of its contempt for Arab nationalism. The small Soviet Encyclopaedia published in 1930, for instance, described pan-Arabism as an ideology of the national *bourgeois* intelligentsia which was used by Britain against Turkey in the First World War.[8]

The Slogan of Solidarity

The first discernible change in the Communist outlook on pan-Arabism occurred during the Second World War, when the Communist parties in the Fertile Crescent abandoned the posture of total rejection of Arab unity in favour of its partial acceptance. The national charters adopted by the Communist parties of Syria and the Lebanon, in January 1944, spoke of the need and value of Arab solidarity and commended promotion of economic and cultural co-operation between the Arab lands. Later in the year, the Communist Party of Iraq also incorporated this approach into its national programme. The new Communist line, however, embodied two distinctive features: it conceived of unity as a means of strengthening the struggle for liberation from imperialist domination; and it stressed the unity of the Arab peoples, workers, intellectuals, and students, not of governments.[9]

The reasons for this shift in policy, though unstated, were not difficult to perceive. The exigencies of the war had persuaded Britain to underwrite formally the Arab desire for "a greater degree of unity than they now enjoy". The British pledge to that effect was

[8] Quoted in *Mizan Newsletter* (London), vol. 2 (March 1960), p. 7.
[9] See Al-Hakm Darwaza, *Ash-Shuyu'iya al-Mahalliya wa Ma'arkat al-Qawmiya* (Beirut, 1963), pp. 128-32, 146.

contained in a major policy statement by the British Secretary of
State, Anthony Eden, which said:

> It seems to me both natural and right that the cultural and
> economic ties between the Arab countries, and the political
> ties too, should be strengthened. His Majesty's Government
> for their part will give their full support to any scheme that
> commands general approval.[10]

Eden's statement evoked warm response in Baghdad, Amman, and
Cairo. The Amir of Transjordan came forward with his "Greater
Syria" plan which proposed to unify Syria, the Lebanon, Palestine,
and Transjordan under the Hashimite sway. This was supplemented
by Nuri as-Sa'id's Fertile Crescent project which envisaged a federation of "Greater Syria" and Iraq. The Government of Egypt, on
the other hand, pressed for widening the scope of unity so as to
include all the independent Arab states.

The Communists saw in these developments an attempt by the
British, the Arab monarchs, and the old-guard politicians to strengthen their respective positions in the area. It was also clear that the
popular sentiment in the Arab East viewed these moves with hope
and excitement. This confronted the Communists with a serious
dilemma: while continued repudiation of pan-Arabism would have
isolated them from the mainstream of Arab politics, an unqualified
acceptance of it would be tantamount to wilful collusion with their
proclaimed adversaries. Hence the new Communist line which endorsed the slogan of Arab unity only to forestall the moves of its
British and indigenous exponents.

Accordingly, in the closing years of the war, the Communists
campaigned strongly against the various projects of Arab unity.
They were critical of the frequent consultations between Arab
statesmen on this subject and decried those who conceived of Arab
unity "under the sponsorship of this or that foreign Power".[11]
The Egyptian Communist Party, which did not even nominally
subscribe to pan-Arabism, demanded Egypt's "withdrawal from
the Arab League, the instrument of the imperialists".[12]

[10] Quoted in Sayegh, n. 5, pp. 117-18.
[11] Khalid Bakdash, *Ba'd Masa'ilina al-Wataniya* (n. p., 1943), pp.
8-16.
[12] Darwaza, n. 9, pp. 114-16.

A Stride Forward

In the decade following the war the Communist mistrust of the ideas of Arab unity continued unabated, although with this difference that criticism was now directed not at the pan-Arab ideology but at its manifest symbol, the Arab League. However, as the years passed, Communist criticism became increasingly sterile and irrelevant to changing political realities. It was indeed a period which marked a steep decline in the authority and prestige not only of Britain and France but of the entire generation of politicians who had owed their sudden rise to prominence originally to social status and subsequently to the patronage of the Mandatory Powers. France was ousted from Syria and the Lebanon; Britain's treaty privileges were subjected to relentless popular pressure in Egypt and Iraq. But the creation of Israel proved to be a political catastrophe for the entire West. On the other hand, the failure of the Arab Governments to save Palestine sealed the fate of the ruling *élite*, which had been habitually amenable to Western influence.

In these circumstances it would have been a logical course for the Communists to make common cause with Arab nationalism. They had indeed done so in the case of local nationalist movements. A comparable adjustment of policy in respect of pan-Arabism had to wait until the autumn of 1955. An explanation for this change must be sought partly in the fact that the new generation of nationalists which was gradually coming into prominence in the Arab East was, because of its relatively humble social origins and upbringing, more amenable to radical ideas and influences than its predecessor. Secondly, in its immediate context Arab nationalism was, after all, an anti-imperialist force with immense revolutionary potentialities. But perhaps the most decisive factor was the initiative of the radical nationalists to draft Soviet support against ceaseless Western pressures. In this realignment of forces the interests of pan-Arabism, local Communists, and the Soviet Union converged.[13]

Needless to say that these were not the reasons given by the Communists themselves for the sudden shift of policy. In fact, they offered no explanation at all. It was perhaps to overcome the embarrassment implicit in the *volte face* that Khalid Bakdash mingled the announcement of a new policy with an unseasonable tirade against

[13] See above, chs. 8 and 9.

the Zionists and the PPS.[14] Speaking before the Syrian Parliament on 6 October 1955, Bakdash said:

> The effrontery of the Zionists has reached a stage where they pose to be a nation but deny the existence of the Arab nation even though the Arabs possess the ingredients of nationhood which also satisfy the requirements of scientific socialism and are as distinct as the mid-day sun. It must be added that this Zionist habit of disclaiming the existence of Arab nationalism conforms to the attitude of the PPS gang.[15]

Notwithstanding these prevarications the Communist parties of the region formally confirmed the change of policy by adopting resolutions to that effect. The Communist Parties of Syria and the Lebanon said in a joint resolution adopted on 22 April 1956:

> The Arab aspiration for unity is not the product of expediency or sentimentalism. Nor is it the result of political propaganda carried out by some party or section of people. Rather it is the expression of real necessity and the result of objective histori- cal development independent of sentiments or wishes. The existence of common territory, language and history, of com- mon consciousness as reflected in the Arab culture, and of economic factors which link one country to another—all these factors have historically evolved, despite serious obstacles, into bases of friendship and unity between various parts of the Arab land. They are the actual foundations on which the issue of Arab unity rests.[16]

In September the Central Committee of the Communist Party of Iraq emphasized the same points in its report to the National Con- gress adding that Iraq's isolation from the rest of the Arab world was "the creation of the imperialists. It is both unnatural and temporary because it is against the logic of historical national development and economic liberation."

In Egypt, however, the faction-ridden Communist movement was slow to respond. In the beginning, the Communists perfunctorily

[14] See above, ch. 5, n. 4.
[15] Darwaza, n. 9, p. 164.
[16] Ibid., pp. 165-66.

talked of Arab nationalism as "a stage in the anti-imperialist struggle" and "a battle-cry against the common enemy". It was only after the short-lived merger of the principal factions into the Communist Party of Egypt that an unequivocal switch-over to pan-Arabism was effected. A study entitled *The Meaning of Nationalism* written by "Khalid" and "'Abbas", and widely circulated among party members, observed, among other things, that economic diversity should not obstruct Arab unity, since it was the artificial creation of imperialist domination and since "prior to imperialist domination there did exist a common Arab market in one form or other". On the crucial question of Egypt's national identity, it pleaded that "whatever superficial distinction we in Egypt make between ourselves and the rest of the Arabs is nothing but a relic of our insular attitude towards Arab nationalism".[17] In the traditionally separatist Lebanon, too, the Communists swore allegiance to pan-Arabism. A leading publicist[18] decried those who wanted to "snatch away the Lebanon from the Arab world", adding:

> They will not succeed since it is impossible to separate the Lebanese history from the Arab history or to isolate its soil from the Arab soil, its language from the Arabic language, its heritage and glories from the Arab heritage and glories, its tradition from the Arab traditions, and all aspects of its social, political and economic life from the Arab life.

While espousing the Arab nationalist cult, the Communists endeavoured to give it a revolutionary twist. As the Syrian Communist Party put it, the motto of Arab unity was the motto of struggle for "liberation from imperialist tyranny". Secondly, the Communists conceived of comprehensive Arab unity not as an end in itself but as a means to "basic democratic reforms" and "peaceful evolution towards socialism". Similarly, the Egyptian Communists expressed the belief that Arab nationalism would destroy "all traces of imperialist exploitation, raise the standard of living of the Arab people and join the socialist camp in the task

[17] Darwaza, n. 9, pp. 164-66, 170-74; and Ibn Khaldun, Pseud., "An Attempt to Understand Arab Nationalism", *Ath-Thaqafah al-Wataniya* (Beirut), vol. 6 (June and July 1957), pp. 9-11, 62-64.

[18] Ibn Khaldun, Pseud., "Lebanon. . . and Arab Politics", *Ath-Thaqafah al-Wataniya*, vol. 6 (March 1957).

of securing world peace".[19] Ihsan Sarkis, a Syrian ideologist, drew a distinction between nationalism of the oppressing nations and nationalism of the oppressed nations. The former breeds imperialism, the latter resists it. Arab nationalism belongs to this latter category. As for the latent contradictions between "the national *bourgeoisie*" and the "toiling masses", Sarkis maintained that these could be resolved by conscious endeavours as was being done in Egypt and Syria. Thus he saw in the Egyptian experiment the example of a *bourgeoisie* that was trying to resolve its contradictions *vis-à-vis* the working class by means of administrative control over trade and industry, labour regulations, and general direction of the national economy. The *bourgeois* class in Syria was likewise trying to curb the excesses of indigenous capital.[20]

The Merger and Its Aftermath

The Communists had good reasons to be satisfied with the radical domestic and foreign politics of Egypt and Syria. They had equally good reasons to believe that the merger of Syria and Egypt, hotly canvassed by the Syrian Ba'th, was likely to weaken rather than strengthen their bargaining position *vis-à-vis* Damascus and Cairo. The diverse motivations of the principal partisans of merger have been discussed in a previous chapter.[21] Suffice it to say here that the Communists made little or no positive effort towards the creation of the United Arab Republic. At the same time political expediency demanded that they should not openly obstruct it. Both the Soviet Union and the Arab Communists had gained in prestige and popularity by lending vocal support to Arab nationalism, and any precipitate retraction from that position was bound to do them incalculable harm.

However, within months of the merger, the Communists made it clear that they were not exactly pleased with what the union had brought in its train. Khalid Bakdash refused to dissolve the Communist Party of Syria, as required by the laws of the UAR, and left for Eastern Europe in disgust. Moscow, too, became lukewarm towards Cairo. K. Ivanov, a Soviet specialist in Arab affairs, even ventured to refute Nasser's thesis (though Ivanov tactfully ascribed it to the

[19] Darwaza, n. 9, pp. 166-67, 173-74.

[20] Ihsan Sarkis, "The Substance of Arab Nationalism", *Ath-Thaqafah al-Wataniya*, vol. 7 (January 1958), pp. 29-31.

[21] See above, ch. 9.

"foreign *bourgeois* Press") that the Iraqi-Jordanian Federation was in effect "a pro-Western centre of Arab unity competing with Cairo and Damascus". As for Arab nationalism itself, Ivanov theorized:

> Being Marxists, we are by no means inclined to make a fetish of Arab unity as such and to ignore the fact that the idea may, in certain circumstances, be used for some time also by the reactionaries, who seek to arrest the progressive development of the Arab peoples.[22]

The Rift with Nasser

The Communist disapprobation of the UAR at first voiced in soft notes became distinctly loud and jarring in the months immediately following the Communist-backed Iraqi *coup d'état* of 14 July 1958. Ever since the Iraqi development, the Communists had begun to think that the time had come to redress the adverse effects of the merger on their movement in the region. The initiative came from the side which had been hurt most by the creation of the UAR: the Communist Party of Syria. The Bulgarian Radio reported, on 20 July, Khalid Bakdash's trenchant criticism of the bases of Syro-Egyptian union. Early in September the Politbureau of the Communist Party of Iraq came to Bakdash's rescue by formally proposing that the cause of Arab unity could be best served by adopting the federal model of the United Arab States (comprising the UAR and the Yemen) which allowed for maximum regional autonomy. It was thus implied that the unitary principle on which the UAR was founded was unacceptable to the Communists. The Egyptian Communists, too, rushed to indicate their preference for the federal idea. By the end of September it was clear that the Communists were opposed not only to Iraq joining the UAR but to the continuation of the original union itself. After this it was not long before the Communists began to question the desirability of any kind of union. In October, an Iraqi Communist, 'Aziz al-Haj, bluntly stated in an article published in *Al-Adab* (Beirut) that it was "not absolutely necessary for a people belonging to one nationality to form a single state" and added that unity "at this historical stage should not mean a united state. It should rather mean unity of struggle for liberation from imperialism."

[22] K. Ivanov, "A New Arab State", *International Affairs* (Moscow), vol. 3 (March 1958), pp. 53-58.

It was now Nasser's turn to hit back. In a hard-hitting speech delivered at Port Sa'id on 23 December 1958, he bracketed the Communists with the Zionists and imperialists. The point was duly taken up for further elucidation by the UAR radio and Press. Cairo's appreciation of the Communist motives was pointedly conveyed by *Al-Akhbar* in these words:

> What is the aim of imperialism? It is to keep the Arab nation disunited and disintegrated so that it can swallow each part of it easily. This is also the aim of Zionism and the Communists in the Arab countries. ... The Communists in the Arab countries consider that their ideology can triumph not in a united nation but in a disintegrated one. Hence the Arab nation must be broken up; separatism must be fostered; and agents of division and disunity must be fostered so that the (Arab) body can be dismembered.[23]

At this the Soviet Premier Khrushchev took up the cudgels on behalf of the Arab Communists. In a direct reference to Nasser's criticism, Khrushchev told the 21st Soviet Communist Party Congress (January-February 1959) that it was "foolish to see in everything the 'machination of the Communists' ":

> The struggle against Communist and other progressive parties is a reactionary affair. An anti-Communist policy does not unite national forces, but disunites them, and consequently weakens the efforts of the whole nation in defending itself against imperialism. It is incorrect to accuse the Communists of opposing the national interest of the Arab peoples. It is also naïve to place Communism on the same footing as Zionism. Everyone knows that the Communists, including those in Israel, are conducting a struggle against Zionism.[24]

The task of elucidating the Arab Communist standpoint on the question of Arab unity was, however, left to Khalid Bakdash who told the Congress that Arab unity was, "first and foremost, a movement for liberation from imperialism". Secondly, it should take into account "objective conditions in each Arab country". And,

[23] *Al-Akhbar* (Cairo), 30 December 1958.
[24] *Mizan Newsletter* (London), vol. 1 (February 1959), Appendix A, pp. 2-3.

finally, Arab unity "should be built on a genuinely democratic basis".[25]

The reasons for this marked shift in Communist policy lay in the new balance of power which obtained as a result of the Iraqi *coup d'état.* Now that the Communists were securely entrenched in Iraq, they no longer felt the need to play second fiddle to Nasser. In fact, they could use this opportunity to secure concessions in Syria. These, in fact, were the ideas underlying the demand that Arab unity should take the form of a loose federation.

After the Mosul uprising of March 1959—by which the pro-Nasser elements in Iraq had unsuccessfully attempted to bring down Kassem's pro-Communist régime—the antagonism between Nasser and the Arab Communists reached a point of no return. At this juncture Khrushchev used the occasion of an Iraqi economic delegation's visit to Moscow to state bluntly that the interests of all the Arabs could not coincide and that "attempts under the flag of nationalism to ignore the interests of separate classes of the population and the interests of the working people" were "futile".[26] In the meantime the Communist Party of Iraq abruptly dropped the slogan of federalism and declared that the achievement of unity of the Arab nation "will take several paths and proceed according to different steps, all of which will consolidate the Arab liberation movement and lead it towards a true democratic unity".[27] Accordingly, the Syrian Communists urged a reconsideration of the union of Syria and Egypt. "It has become necessary", declared Khalid Bakdash, "to establish in Syria a united front to restore democracy and review the bases of unity between Syria and Egypt. The Syrians must also strive to establish fraternal relations with Iraq."[28] When Syria indeed seceded from the UAR in the autumn of 1961, Bakdash hailed the event as "a great victory" of the Syrian people and complimented the Soviet Union on being "the first of the Great Powers to recognize the Syrian Arab Republic".[29]

[25] Ibid., p. 10.

[26] Quoted in *Mizan Newsletter,* vol. 2 (March 1960), p. 8.

[27] Statement by Salam 'Adil, Secretary of the Iraqi Communist Party, in *New Age* (New Delhi), vol. 7 (7 June 1959), pp. 7, 11.

[28] From Bakdash's address to the Hungarian Party Congress quoted in *Al-Hayat* (Beirut), 5 December 1959.

[29] Quoted in *Mizan Newsletter,* vol. 3 (November 1961), p. 12.

The Emerging Equilibrium

Three years later, leading Communist theoreticians met in Prague to re-examine the whole question of Pan-Arabism. In the intervening period, the fortunes of Arab Communism had dwindled considerably. In Iraq, they fell out with Kassem and were eventually crippled by the Ba'thists in February 1963. In Syria, the Right-wing secessionist régime was succeeded by an anti-Communist Ba'thist junta in March 1963. With the Nasserites and the Ba'thists working at cross-purposes and the Communists rapidly losing ground, conservative elements in the Arab East at last got the opportunity to reassert their own claims to leadership. It was this adverse turn of events that forced the Communists and radical Arab nationalists to seek reconciliation.

Reviewing the events of the recent past the Prague symposium[30] ascribed the break-up of the UAR to diverse factors. It was argued that the experiment had failed partly as a result of the attempt of the Egyptian *bourgeoisie* to dominate Syria and partly because of the Syrian *bourgeoisie's* opposition to the socialist decrees of July 1961. Refusal to make allowance for the objective conditions prevailing in Syria and Egypt was another cause of disaffection.

Turning to the present, the symposium noted the emergence of two distinct trends on the issue of Arab unity: "the *bourgeois*-nationalist trend and the revolutionary-democratic trend". The *bourgeois*-nationalist trend was in the main represented by Nasser's UAR and the Ba'th Socialist party. The former linked the problem of unity with social progress but also insisted that Arab unity "must be achieved under Egyptian leadership"; the Ba'th's concept on the other hand was "vague, Utopian [and] inimical to the people, to the working class, and to the anti-imperialist national liberation movement". All in all, this trend reflected the psychology of "the small and middle class *bourgeoisie*". In contrast to this "the revolutionary-democratic trend" combined the struggle for Arab unity with that of social progress and anti-imperialism as evidenced by Ben Bella's National Liberation Front and the Arab Communist parties. In other words it linked the issue of unity with the national-

[30] The following Communist leaders participated in the symposium: Khalid Bakdash, Zahir 'Abd as-Samad, 'Umar Siba'i, and Murad Quwatli (Syria); Anwar Mustafa and 'Aziz al-Haj (Iraq); Swaya Sawaya, Jamil Haddad, and Sa'id Trablusi (Lebanon); Fu'ad Nassar and Farid Sa'id (Jordan). Text of the statements in *Peace, Freedom and Socialism* (Prague), vol. 7 (July 1964), pp. 74-81.

liberation struggle and the victory of socialism throughout the Arab world.

All this, however, did not mean that co-operation with non-socialist elements was ruled out or that unity must wait until the triumph of socialism in the Arab world. On the contrary, "a revolutionary progressive union of two or more countries can be achieved as they advance along the non-capitalist way even before socialism has triumphed throughout the Arab World". Thus the whole question of Communist-nationalist partnership turned on the issue of "non-capitalist development". The Communists maintained that by removing "economic differentiations and unevenness between various Arab countries", the method of non-capitalist development would pave the way for genuine Arab unity.[31] According to this thesis the UAR qualified as a "progressive" régime. After the overthrow of the Aflaq-Bitar-Razzaz faction of the Ba'thist régime in Damascus, Syria was also elevated to that status. Cairo and Damascus reciprocated by showing cautious solicitude for local Communism. In the meantime, the prospect of immediate unity being uncertain the three parties concerned settled on the unambitious but mutually acceptable motto of "unity of objectives". This idea has been further elaborated by Lutfi al-Khuli, an Egyptian Marxist. In a conference of representatives of Arab revolutionary movements held in Cairo in 1966, Khuli pleaded for unity in terms not of immediate political unification but of a revolutionary front based on specific goals such as complete liberation of Arab lands from imperialism, feudalism, and capitalism, social reforms, and co-ordinated economic planning. The conference was of the view that the front should take the form of a coalition of various national organizations in the Arab world. In the UAR the cohesion of national revolutionary forces was reflected in the Arab Socialist Union, but this pattern was not considered obligatory for other countries. Finally, the conference agreed that this blueprint by no means exhausted all forms and methods of co-operation. The search for these would continue in the light of changing conditions.[32]

[31] Fu'ad Nassar, "On Arab Unity", *Peace, Freedom and Socialism*, vol. 7 (February 1964), pp. 19-20.

[32] Lotfi El-Kholi, "Perspectives of Co-operation and Unity of the Progressive Forces in the Arab Countries", *Peace, Freedom and Socialism*, vol. 9 (October 1966), p. 29.

All in all, the current Communist approach to Arab nationalism is essentially the product of an overall slump in the fortunes of the Arab Left; and it may well turn out to be yet another transient phenomenon in the erratic history of Communist-nationalist relationship.

CHAPTER FOURTEEN

IDEOLOGY, STRATEGY, AND TACTICS

THE Arab Communist movement was originally a child of the intellectual curiosity of a handful of middle-class intellectuals who were mesmerized by the Bolshevik Revolution and its slogan of proletarian revolution though few of them could relate it to the realities of life in the Arab East. Thus the pioneering Communists in Egypt styled themselves the standard-bearers of the proletariat. In Syria and the Lebanon, Communism made its début as a movement of romantic visionaries who viewed the Bolshevik Revolution not as a forerunner of the world proletarian revolution but as a summation of the humanistic and egalitarian ideals of the French Revolution.

The revolutionary ecstasy which gripped the minds of the early Arab converts to Communism proved extremely short-lived. In Russia, too, hopes of an imminent upsurge in the East most fervently voiced at the Baku Congress in September 1920 yielded to a realistic appraisal of the world around. Even before the Baku Congress, Lenin took a practical view of the national liberation movement in the colonial East. He admitted that the peoples of the colonies were faced with problems "the solutions of which you will not find in any Communist book". "You will have to tackle these problems", he added, "and solve them by your own independent experience."[1] Soon after, the Soviet leadership also realized that in the colonial East the much-expected revolutions were not round the corner. The Sixth Comintern Congress in fact envisaged a prolonged struggle involving three stages: (i) liberation from colonial rule; (ii) struggle of the workers and peasants to carry out social revolution; and (iii) seizure of power by the Communists.

It was in the context of these broad objectives that the strategy and tactics of the Communist movements were evolved. Stalin took special interest in developing the Communist concepts of strategy and tactics. He designated this subject "the science of leadership in the class struggle of the proletariat". In his definition, strategy is "the determination of the direction of the main blow of

[1] *Lenin on the National Liberation Movement* (Peking, 1960), pp. 10-11.

12

the proletariat at a given stage of the revolution, the elaboration of a corresponding plan for the disposition of the revolutionary forces (the main and secondary reserves), [and] the fight to carry out this plan throughout the given stage of the revolution". Tactics, on the other hand, are "the determination of the line of conduct of the proletariat in the comparatively short period of the ebb or flow of the movement, of the rise or decline of the revolution, the fight to carry out this line by means of replacing old forms of struggle and organization by new ones, old slogans by new ones [and] by combining these forms. . . . " While tactics vary from time to time, strategy remains "essentially unchanged throughout a given stage".[2]

The programmes and activities of the Arab Communist parties represented local adaptation of these principles. After a brief spell of soaring revolutionary effervescence the Communists switched to the practical tasks defined partly by local compulsions and partly by the exigencies of the world Communist movement. The evolution of Arab Communism to date can be broadly divided into six distinctive phases. The period from the rise of the Communist parties in the early twenties to 1936 was the period of doctrinaire bigotry when the proletarian character of the movement was stressed. Then began the era of national fronts which after the Nazi attack on the Soviet Union resulted in Communist collaboration with the imperialist Powers. After the war the Communists once again struck a sectarian posture carrying a surcharge of Cold-War politics. Stalin's death and subsequent changes in the Soviet world view brought the Communists into close relationship with radical nationalist elements in the Arab East. But the Communist successes in Iraq in 1958 induced them once again to unfurl the flag of sectarian revolt resulting in a series of disastrous set-backs. These reverses together with Soviet exhortations for moderation on the question of national-liberation movements and the passing of the revolutionary initiative into the hands of the radical nationalists persuaded the Communists to abandon the goal of proletarian revolution in favour of peaceful transition to socialism and to reconcile themselves to an admittedly junior rôle in the revolutionary struggle.

The Doctrinaire Phase: 1920-1935

In the initial period the Communist parties of the Arab East were mostly preoccupied with questions of ideological purity and

[2] J. V. Stalin, *Problems of Leninism* (Moscow, 1947), pp. 67-70.

organizational viability. On the ideological side, the Communist programmes represented local adaptations of the Comintern policies. The sharp fluctuations in the manifestos of the Egyptian Communist Party between 1921 and 1923 were indicative of the rapid reappraisal of the colonial question by the international Communist movement. While the earlier programme called for a unified struggle against the alien imperialist and the native capitalist, the latter broadly conformed to the modest reformist programme of the Wafd Party.[3] After the Sixth Comintern Congress (1928) the pendulum once again swung in the direction of revolutionary militancy. The new mood was reflected in the programmes adopted by the Communist parties of Syria, Palestine, and Egypt in the early thirties.[4] The manifesto of the Egyptian Communist Party designated the Wafd "the party of *bourgeois*, landowning, counter-revolutionary national reformism... a party that deceives the entire population, the party of national treasons". It further proclaimed that "between the camp of the Wafd and the camp of the people's anti-imperialist and agrarian-peasant revolution lies an impassable gulf". In a similar vein the Palestinian and Syrian Communists proclaimed that "the *bourgeoisie* and the *bourgeois* landowning elements are incapable of a revolutionary struggle against imperialism. They veer more and more in the direction of a counter-revolutionary deal with it within the framework of limited pseudo-constitutional concessions which only disguise the imperialist domination". Accordingly, the Syrian National Bloc was accused of having betrayed the Druze uprising of 1925 and the Palestinian Arab High Committee of having entered upon the road of traitorous competition with Zionism in bargaining for concessions from British imperialism.

Another distinctive feature of the Communist programmes was the central place they assigned to the industrial workers in the overall strategy of revolution. It is a curious paradox that in an area where the landless peasantry was far more numerous than the proletariat, the Arab Communists tirelessly harped on the necessity of the proletariat leading the revolutionary struggle. The Communist stance was rooted in the doctrinaire belief that the proletariat was in all circumstances endowed with greater firmness and consistency

[3] See above, ch. 1.
[4] Text of the programmes in Ivar Spector, *The Soviet Union and the Muslim World: 1917-1956* (Mimeographed, Washington, D. C., 1956), pp. 75-82, 82-91.

than all other social classes. Besides, there also existed a marked discrepancy between Communist theory and practice in regard to the peasantry in general. Lenin had observed in 1920 that, in the colonial East, the task for the Communists was to wage a struggle, not against capitalism, but against mediæval survivals. "It would be utopian", he had said, "to think that proletarian parties, if indeed they can arise in such countries, could pursue Communist tactics and Communist policy in these backward countries without having definite relations with the peasant movement and without effectively supporting it."[5] In the Arab East, however, the Communists made no serious attempt to enlist peasant support. Their interest in peasantry was confined to verbal platitudes. The Egyptian programme of 1923 admitted the need for a peasant front which would campaign for radical land reforms involving confiscation of holdings exceeding 100 feddans and distribution of the surplus land among the landless peasantry. But in practice no advance was made in that direction. The Sixth Comintern Congress in fact upbraided the Communists for having failed to draw "the masses of agricultural workers" into the revolutionary struggle.[6]

Prodded by the Comintern, the Communists partially revised their formulations on the peasants' rôle. The Syrian and Palestinian Communists came forward with the thesis that there could be "no lasting victory for national and political independence without an agrarian peasant revolution and the establishment of workers' and peasants' government". But even so the working class was to retain its hegemonic status. The Egyptian Communist Party, too, adopted the slogan of agrarian revolution but admitted that organizing the peasants was immensely more difficult than organizing the workers. This difficulty, it was suggested, could be overcome by evolving a new strategy of the revolution under which "a united and organized struggle of the workers will swing the fellahin masses and will help to find the correct and skilful transition from economic struggle and economic strikes to demonstrations, political strikes, and to other forms of struggle which might develop".

The Communist theory and practice during this period, though unfructuous in terms of immediate gains, did yield some positive results. As a consequence of Communist activities and propaganda the urban intelligentsia and the working class got acquainted

[5] Lenin, n. 1, p. 23.
[6] See above, ch. 1.

with the Marxian doctrine. The Communists also gained a foothold in the trade unions of Syria, the Lebanon, and Palestine. Above all, the Communist movement threw up a set of professional revolutionaries who carried on the struggle in the coming decades.

The First Breakthrough: 1936-1945

After years of self-imposed sectarian isolation the Communists began to move into the mainstream of Arab politics in the course of the late thirties. The ground for this headway was prepared by the Soviet reassessment of the European situation in the wake of Hitler's rise to power. This was reflected in the thesis of the Seventh Comintern Congress exhorting Communists everywhere to forge a worldwide anti-Fascist front. The victory of the proletarian revolution could wait until after the "towering menace of Fascism" was fully annihilated. In the circumstances, the Arab Communists were required to make peace with their two principal foes: the French and British imperialists and the national *bourgeoisie*. The Communist feat lay as much in effecting these seemingly incompatible compromises as in translating them into concrete political gains. Except for a brief reversal caused by the Nazi-Soviet Pact this policy was consistently pursued until the conclusion of the Second World War.

The policy of fraternization with the imperial Powers secured for the Communists a measure of political freedom hitherto non-existent in Egypt and the Fertile Crescent countries. And they seized this opportunity to gain the leadership of the trade union movement and to canvass support among the intelligentsia and the student community, formerly a breeding ground of pro-Fascist tendencies. But the collaborationist line also created some political handicaps. The lukewarm attitude of the Communists towards national independence on grounds of political expediency greatly outraged nationalist sentiment. This was particularly true of Syria and the Lebanon, where the Communists openly pleaded that independence should await the conclusion of the war.

What the Communists lost by incurring the displeasure of the nationalists was more than offset by the success of the national front tactics. The concept of national front, implicit in the Comintern thesis, found its most eloquent exponent in the Syrian Communist leader, Khalid Bakdash. In an unprecedented departure from the orthodox Communist theory and practice it envisaged national unity between all sections of the people regardless of class or party affiliation, on the basis of a common programme of moderate reforms. The programmes of the Communist parties of Syria and the Lebanon, adopted in 1944, went so far as to avoid even the use of the term socialism.

The tactics of compromise and moderation greatly augmented the strength of the Communist parties. By the end of the war, party membership in Syria and the Lebanon rose to 10,000 and 15,000 respectively. In Egypt the largest Communist faction, MELN, and the Arab wing of the Palestinian Communist Party, the League for National Liberation, commanded a thousand card-carrying members each. Besides, the Communists dominated large trade unions in Egypt and the Fertile Crescent.

The Tug of War: 1946-1954

The Communist tactics during the early post-war years were determined by the changed local and international conditions. With the destruction of the Nazi power in Germany it was no longer necessary to condone the British and French colonial presence. On the contrary, the advent of the Cold War between the Communist and capitalist.blocs necessitated an all-out war against the remnants of colonialism in the Arab East. Internally, the seething discontent generated by economic hardship and post-war retrenchments brought about a new balance of forces pregnant with revolutionary possibilities.

The Communists now completely reversed the wartime line on national liberation. At the same time, the national front tactics was retained although in a vastly modified form. As in the earliest phase the national *bourgeoisie* was singled out as the chief villain; and the choice of partners in the national front was to be strictly governed by that assumption. Secondly, the isolation and disestablishment of the *bourgeoisie* being the immediate goal, the Communists did not insist on identity of views on other issues between the various components of the national front. Thus the Egyptian Communists forged an alliance with such Right-wing extremists as the Muslim Brothers and Ahmad Husayn's Socialist Party. Thirdly, unlike in the previous years, the Communists insisted upon complete freedom of action for themselves as a necessary condition of co-operation with other forces.

Owing to the serious set-back caused to the Communist position by the precipitate Soviet backing to the partition of Palestine, the efficacy of the new tactics could not be tested until the beginning of the fifties. In Syria the Communists allied themselves to the Ba'th and Hourani's Arab Socialist Party in an attempt to resist the military dictator, Adib Shishakli. The Iraqi Communist Party drew closer to the National Democratic Party and the Istiqlal. In Jordan the Communist front organization called the National Front (*Al-Jabha al-Wataniya*) even secured two parliamentary seats in the 1954 elections.

Although the National Front tactics continued to yield political dividends, the Communist line on foreign affairs found few supporters outside the party circles. The Communists accepted the Cominform's thesis that as between the forces of "good" and "evil" represented respectively by the Soviet Union and the United States, neutrality was not only undesirable but utterly unacceptable. In a local adaptation of the argument it was maintained that the idea of alignment with Russia was "nearer to Arab hearts" than the idea of siding with the British. "Russia never subjugated our country and does not snatch our bread or deprive us of our freedom and independence".[7] Needless to add, few non-Communists were prepared to endorse this view wholly; but there were many who readily co-operated with the Communists in resisting Western manoeuvres to draw the Arabs into Cold-War alliances. And to that extent there existed a common meeting ground between Communism and radical Arab nationalism.

A notable feature of this period is the mushroom growth of front organizations, the Partisans of Peace being the most effective of them all. Though actuated by Soviet foreign-policy interests the Partisans' movement came handy as a non-sectarian projection of the National Front theme. It served as a potent means of popularizing Soviet international policies on the one hand and broadening the sphere of Communist influence on the other. The "Peace Appeal" was articulated in broad humanitarian, not ideological, terms and a wide cross-section of people, not excluding the clergy, came under its spell.

The Second Breakthrough: 1955-1958

By the mid-fifties, the unmistakable radicalization of Arab politics as evidenced by the outright rejection of the Western-sponsored

[7] *At-Tariq* (Beirut), vol. 8 (October-November 1949), p. 28.

military alliance by all Arab states except Iraq, the Czech arms deal, and the nationalization of the Suez Canal, rendered some of the basic Communist assumptions wholly unworkable. The unyielding attitude of the younger generation of Arab nationalists in regard to the question of national sovereignty and independence utterly disproved the Communist thesis about the innate compromising propensities of the national *bourgeoisie*. A re-evaluation of Arab nationalism was also necessitated by the interest of Soviet security. With the consummation of the Baghdad Pact the Soviet Union had no option but to make common cause with the Arab neutralists.

Communist thinking on the immediate objectives and corresponding tactics of the revolutionary movement crystallized during the year 1955 and was duly sanctified by the Twentieth Party Congress of the Soviet Communist Party the following year. At the outset a clear distinction was made between *national* liberation and *social* liberation, the former representing attainment of complete national sovereignty, the latter signifying the accomplishment of socialist transformation. It was then argued that the ground for social revolution could not be prepared until national sovereignty was firmly established. Hence the necessity to give top priority to the question of national liberation.

The next postulate of the new Communist thesis was that the national *bourgeoisie* in Egypt and Syria, by virtue of its having moved out of the imperialist orbit, was qualified to lead "the Arab liberation movement striving for effective realization of national sovereignty". In other words, the Communists should reconcile themselves to junior partnership in a "strong, broad, and solid national front with a common patriotic programme acceptable to it".[8] The concept of national front also was modified to meet new requirements. The working class was dethroned from its exalted position in the front. Secondly, the national front was to be treated as an *enduring*, not opportunistic device. Thirdly, the national front alliance, resting on a real community of interest, namely national liberation, must be *sincere*.[9]

As for the next stage of development, it was stipulated that the

---

[8] Khaled Bagdache, "The October Revolution and the Arab East", *For a Lasting Peace, For a People's Democracy* (Bucharest), 18 November 1955.

[9] A Bennigsen, "The 'National Front' in Communist Strategy in the Middle East", in Walter Z. Laqueur, ed., *The Middle East in Transition* (London, 1958), pp. 362-7.

transition of different countries from capitalism to socialism could be achieved by *peaceful means*. Towards that end the Moscow conference of Communist parties (November 1957) declared that in a number of capitalist countries it was possible to "win State power without a civil war". However, in conditions in which the exploiting classes resorted to violence, the possibility of "non-peaceful transition to socialism" could not be excluded. In such cases, the "severity and forms of class struggle" would depend on the degree of resistance of the "reactionary circles".[10]

Finally, it was conceded that in the era of national liberation it was not obligatory for revolutionary nationalism to align itself with the Socialist camp. This concept was elucidated by George Hanna in an article published shortly after the Czech arms deal. He pleaded that the threat to Arab independence stemmed from Western, not Soviet, source. Secondly, ideologies could not be treated as articles of import or export. A free nation evolves its own ideology according to its needs and circumstances. Thirdly, co-existence between different social and political systems was both a desirable and a practical goal. In these circumstances it was in the interest of the Arab states to be friendly with "any country which reciprocates this friendship without a price tag on it".[11] While accepting the validity of non-alignment the Communists also insisted that this should not add up to equating the East with the West. Such an attitude would be both unrealistic and contrary to Arab national interest since "you cannot equate the forces you are fighting against with those who support you in the struggle".[12]

During this period, the Communists achieved respectability and influence in Egypt, Syria, and Jordan and a large measure of clandestine co-operation with the non-Communist elements constituting the Iraqi National Front. The Egyptian Communists gained an un-

[10] Text of the declaration in Robert V. Daniels, *A Documentary History of Communism* (New York, 1960), vol. 2, pp. 270-3. Emphasis added.

[11] George Hanna in *At-Tariq*, vol. 4 (October 1955), pp. 2-4; and "East is East", in *Middle East Forum* (Beirut), vol. 31 (1956), pp. 10, 37.

[12] "Ibn Khaldun" "Misconceptions about Nationalism and Internationalism", *Ath-Thaqafah al-Wataniya*, vol. 7 (May 1958), pp. 2-5. To Clovis Maqsud's argument that complete opposition to the West would lead to the Communists taking over the leadership of the nationalist movement, the author replies: "What does this mean except that imperialism should not be resisted lest the leadership of the liberation movement passes into Communist hands? Surely, such views are spread by imperialism and its agents."

precedented measure of freedom short of legal recognition. In Syria, the Communists joined hands with the Ba'th and the radical army officers in an attempt to wipe out Right-wing politicians. During 1957, the Syrian Communists and the Russians appeared to be working at cross-purposes, the former pressing for a share in political authority and the latter seeking to promote Soviet influence through the "red millionaire", Khalid al-'Azm. But Syria's merger with the UAR had a chastening effect on both. In Jordan, the peak of the national front era was reached in 1956-57, when the Communists scored some electoral victories and a seat in the Nabulsi cabinet. The greatest beneficiary of the new line was the Communist Party of Iraq which suddenly rose to prominence following the July 1958 *coup d'état*.

The Extremist Interlude: 1958-1963

Paradoxically, the effectiveness of the national front tactics in resisting external pressures proved to be the main cause of its destruction. It emboldened the Syrian Communists to ask for a share in political authority. In Egypt, the Communists resented the emergence of the national *bourgeoisie* as the conspicuous beneficiary of the post-Suez Egyptianization of the vast majority of foreign business and industrial concerns. Nasser and the Ba'th, on the other hand, grew apprehensive of their own staggering dependence on the Soviet Union and of the influence and prestige it indirectly bestowed on local Communism. Their concerted move to rush through the union of Syria and Egypt was deeply resented by the Syrian Communists, whose freedom of action it abridged. However, it was only after the Iraqi *coup d'état* of July 1958 that the Communists made bold to declare a full-scale war on "*bourgeois* nationalism".

An early indication of the new Communist line was given by Khalid Bakdash at a symposium held in Prague in June 1958 where he derisively referred to the *bourgeois* nationalists and Right-wing socialists who "assert that socialism in the Arab countries cannot be built by the Communist Party". He found fault with the land reforms in Syria and Egypt which, in his opinion, merely strengthened "the class of kulaks". The national *bourgeoisie*, he maintained, possessed neither the economic nor political resources to adopt more vigorous measures.[13] This thesis was slightly amended

[13] Haled Bagdash, "The Crisis and the Problems of the Middle East", *World Marxist Review* (Prague), vol. 1 (September 1958), p. 69.

in the wake of the Iraqi revolution in order to accommodate the national *bourgeoisie* of Iraq. A distinction was thus made between the reformist and compromising *bourgeoisie* represented respectively by the Egyptian ruling class and the Ba'th and the anti-imperialist *bourgeoisie* of Iraq. This explained, in Bakdash's view, the polarization of the Arab national movement into the *bourgeois*-democratic and the national-liberation camps with Cairo and Baghdad as their respective rallying centres.[14]

The Communists, then, re-examined their tactics in the light of this analysis. This resulted in two significant departures. Firstly, it was stipulated that instead of playing a junior rôle in the national-liberation struggle the Communists should seize its leadership. Secondly, the entire concept of national front was thoroughly radicalized disqualifying the reformist national *bourgeoisie* for its membership.

This approach was soon reflected in the practice of the Iraqi Communist Party. It began by eliminating the Ba'th and the Istiqlal from the United National Front and proceeded to pressurize the Left-wing National Democratic Party into acknowledging the Communist hegemony. Simultaneously, the Communists mobilized their total strength in order to seize State power.

The swing towards the extreme Left evoked sharp reactions in Cairo and Damascus, where the Communists were firmly suppressed. In Jordan, the authorities took advantage of the Communist-nationalist cleavage to intensify police operation against the underground Communist network. In Iraq itself, the Kirkuk massacre, which was but the logical outcome of the adventurist strategy, thoroughly discredited the Communist Party.

By 1961, the wild expectations roused by the Iraqi revolution having been dampened by Kassem's sustained anti-Communist drive, the 1958 thesis on political polarization was partially amended. While re-evaluating the character of the Iraqi national *bourgeoisie*, the revised thesis retained its essential premises. It was stated that the Communists had erred in over-emphasizing the positive aspects of the Iraqi *bourgeoisie* which were typical only for the pre-revolutionary period. This enabled the *bourgeoisie* to consolidate its position after the July revolution and brought to the surface its reactionary potentialities. The dual nature of the *bourgeoisie*, it was maintained, called for more cautious tactics than hitherto employed. To that end the following guidelines were recommended:

[14] See above, ch. 9.

An alliance unrelated to the attitude of the *bourgeoisie* with regard to imperialism and feudalism leads to the Right, to defeatism and to infringement on the people's rights and weakening of national independence. Struggle without taking into account the attitude of the different groups of the national *bourgeoisie* leads to sectarianism and Left tendencies which weaken the anti-imperialist front and can force the *bourgeoisie* to look for allies in the enemy's camp.[15]

The confrontation between the nationalists and the Communists brought to the fore their latent differences on the question of non-alignment. Here, too, the Iraqi revolution played a crucial rôle in determining the attitudes of the two sides. Whereas the nationalists saw in it a vindication of the policy of non-alignment, the Communists offered it as a justification for drawing closer to the Soviet camp. Khalid Bakdash went a step further and expressed doubts about the eligibility of the non-aligned national *bourgeoisie* for Soviet aid. "We must not forget", he argued, "that the national *bourgeois* often uses the assistance rendered by the socialist camp in bargaining with the imperialists for favourable terms."[16] For a while, Moscow, too, appeared willing to use economic aid as a lever to secure concessions from the nationalist régimes but was careful not to press it to the breaking-point.

The tragic consequences of the extremist posture became unmistakably clear by 1963, when not only the Communist dream of seizing power in Iraq stood completely shattered but the very survival of Communism as an organized political force in the Arab East became uncertain. The point was driven home by the large-scale massacre of the Iraqi Communists at the hands of the Ba'thist National Guards following the downfall of Kassem. With that the Communist movement in Iraq was completely paralysed. The outlook for Communism in the rest of the Arab East seemed scarcely less unpromising.

The "New Road" to Socialism: 1964

Arab Communism traversed the path of adventurism born of an exaggerated concern for ideological purity and a wild overestima-

---

[15] Mohammad Salim, "Three Years after the Iraqi Revolution", *World Marxist Review*, vol. 4 (October 1961), pp. 34-39.

[16] Bagdash, n. 13, p. 69.

tion of its own strength, and it was manifestly overtaken by developments at home and abroad. In the first place, there occurred a marked shift in the Soviet approach to the problems of the Asian-African countries. Its early indications were contained in the statement of Moscow conference of 81 Communist parties convened in November 1960.[17] The new approach rested on the twofold assumption that although on the global scale the forces of socialism had acquired an edge over those of imperialism, the development of monstrous means of mass annihilation nevertheless posed a serious threat to the entire human race. The superior position of the Socialist camp coupled with the frightening risks of a nuclear holocaust called for a new strategy of world revolution based on the principles of peaceful competition between the Socialist and capitalist countries. In this context, the statement fervently underscored the need to shun dogmatism and sectarianism in theory and practice, to "develop Marxism-Leninism through scientific analysis", and to apply it "creatively according to the specific conditions". Applied to the Asian-African world the Soviet line implied that it was no longer necessary or desirable to promote revolution by the use of force and that the balance of forces in the present-day world being favourable to the Socialist camp, the revolutionary transformation of the newly independent states could be accomplished by peaceful means.

Another development which greatly baffled the Communists was the sharp shift in the course of the Egyptian revolution signified by the nationalization decrees of July 1961. By transferring all enterprises above the level of small shopkeepers, artisans, and farmers to State ownership or control, it effected the transition from mixed economy to socialistic economy. Besides, the ceiling on private ownership of land was slashed down from 200 to 100 feddans and a 42-hour week declared for the workers. Ironically, the scope of these changes far exceeded the blueprints ever commended by any Arab Communist party. To drive the point home Nasser asserted that "there is no closed road beginning with capitalism and ending in Communism. . . . We are forming a new society which is not capitalist or Communist."[18] To this Hasanayn Haykal sarcastically added that there were two kinds of "Left" in Egypt: One is the

---

[17] Text of the statement in David Floyd, *Mao against Khrushchev* (London, 1964), pp. 296-307.

[18] *The Times* (London), 25 August 1961.

theoretical Left which represents the desire for change resulting from theory alone; the other is the *practical* Left which represents the desire for change resulting from the problems of real life.[19]

The publication of the Egyptian Charter in May 1962 marked the crystallization of the theoretical basis of Nasser's Socialist practice. The Charter further took the wind out of the Communist sails by firmly rejecting the capitalist path to economic development on the ground that local capitalism was no longer capable of competition without the customs protection paid for by the masses and that the only hope left for local capitalism to develop was to relate itself to world monopolies. Hence a Socialist solution envisaging people's control over the means of production was the only way to economic and social progress. In a passage carrying Marxian overtones the Charter proclaimed:

> The socialist solution to the problem of economic and social underdevelopment in Egypt—with a view to achieving progress in a revolutionary way—*was never a question of free choice*. The socialist solution was a *historical inevitability* imposed by reality, the broad aspirations of the masses and the changing nature of the world in the second part of the 20th century.[20]

At the same time, the Charter clearly indicated its fundamental difference with the Marxian doctrine by advocating peaceful resolution of class antagonism, private ownership of land "within limits that would not allow for feudalism", individual freedom, and respect for spiritual values. The Charter was indeed projected as a blueprint of the "Third Road" between capitalism and Communism and a contribution to world's revolutionary ideology derived from "Arab revolutionary experience".[21]

The shift of emphasis in the Soviet approach to national-liberation movement from revolutionary struggle to peaceful methods of persuasion and compromise together with Egypt's spontaneous swing towards the Left induced the Arab Communists to reconsider the whole gamut of their strategy and tactics. The result has been a series of daring and unorthodox formulations that are more

---

[19] *Al-Ahram* (Cairo), 29 June 1962. Emphasis added.

[20] *The Charter* (Cairo, Information Department, 1962), pp. 51-61. Emphasis added.

[21] Muhammad Hasanayn Haykal in *Al-Ahram*, 15 June 1962.

in the nature of working hypotheses than immutable dogmas. The new line of thought emanates from the assumption that the idea of proletarian revolution is not a practical proposition for the Arab East in the existing conditions. Secondly, the immense increase in the power and influence of the Socialist camp has practically obviated the need for a violent revolution and opened up the prospects of peaceful transition to Socialism. This can be achieved in successive stages through constant interaction of the Socialist camp and the progressive forces in individual countries. In the current stage of development in the Arab East the Communists should strive for the creation of national-democratic Governments wedded to a programme of peaceful transition to Socialism to be achieved by a broadbased national front.

In this context, it has been argued that the transition to Socialism can be achieved only by adopting the path of non-capitalist development. In Egypt the ground had been prepared for such a course by the nationalization decrees of July 1961. According to Anwar 'Abd al-Malik, these measures marked the victory of the national-liberation movement and the beginning of the "nationalitarian" as distinct from the nationalist phase. "It is no longer so much a matter of driving the other out as it is of reaffirming one's own national existence." The task for the Communists in this phase was "to find a foothold in every measure the military takes, so as to help steer it in the direction of democracy and more freedom of action".[22] Khalid Mohi ad-Din, on the other hand, sees in the theory and practice of the Egyptian Revolution a conscious commitment to "the scientific socialist programme".[23]

A parallel development took place in Syria. The Central Committee of the CPS adopted a resolution in June 1964 commending "the concrete successes" achieved in economic and social fields since Independence, such as nationalization of foreign enterprises, the Central Bank of Issue and major spinning and weaving mills, land reform, and formation of the public sector. The Communists had serious doubts about the capacity of the Ba'thist régime to

---

[22] Anwar 'Abd al-Malik, "Problems of Socialism in the Arab World", *Nuovi Argomenti* (Rome), March 1963-February 1964, English translation in US Department of Commerce, *Translations on International Communist Developments*, no. 572, 17 March 1964, pp. 57, 66-67.

[23] Khaled Mohei El-Din, "The Course of the Egyptian Revolution and Its Future", *Peace, Freedom and Socialism* (Prague), vol. 9 (August 1966), p. 22.

effect further "progressive measures";[24] but these were removed by
the extensive nationalization measures, adopted in January 1965,
which placed all large-scale industrial enterprises and most of the
medium-sized factories and the remnants of foreign enterprises
under public ownership. The Syrian Communists promptly endorsed these measures as the "prerequisites" for Syria's progress
"along the non-capitalist way of development". The source whence
they emanated, said Khalid Bakdash, was immaterial, and added:
"We want to eat the grapes, not to kill the watchman.[25]" The CPS
called upon all members and sympathizers to exert every effort in
order to uphold this development and to contribute to its success.

The next important departure in the Communist theory concerns
the concept of national front. Although there are varying shades
of emphasis in the formulations adduced by a host of Arab Communist leaders, most of them seem to agree that the Arab working
class, because of its small size and limited influence, cannot assume
the leadership of the national front in the present phase. The example of Egypt, as Lutfi al-Khuli put it, shows that "the revolution
in the direction of socialism has depended not so much on the working class becoming the leading force as on social necessity connected
with the consolidating and upholding the national gains against
imperialism and neo-colonialism". Moreover, owing to the favourable international position of the Socialist camp, it is now possible
to effect radical socio-economic changes in the direction of Socialism
by the combined efforts of all classes aspiring to national regenera-
tion and social progress and not merely by the working class.[26]

In like manner, Khalid Bakdash admits that "from the standpoint of its weight in the country, its political consciousness and
organization, and its ability to marshall its allies, especially the

[24] Text in Al-Akhbar (Beriut), 9 August 1964.

[25] Khaled Baghdash, "Syria's New Road", Peace, Freedom and Socialism, vol.
8 (March 1965) pp. 6-10. Even the Iraqi Communists, still smarting under the
impact of recent reverses, have come round to the view that since the State
sector in the country already accounts for three-fourths of all industrial production (excluding oil industry) there exists a basis for non-capitalist development. See Mounir Ahmid, "The Situation in Iraq and the Position of the Communist Party", in Peace, Freedom and Socialism, vol. 7 (December 1964),
pp. 34-38.

[26] Lotfi El-Kholi, "Perspectives of Co-operation and Unity of the Progressive
Forces in the Arab Countries", Peace, Freedom and Socialism, vol. 9 (October
1966), pp. 27-28.

peasants, Syria's working class has not yet grown to the task of heading national-liberation movement and leading it forward to the next higher stage". The task must therefore be carried forward by the combined endeavours of all progressive democratic forces.[27] Elaborating the same theme the Jordanian Communist leader, Fu'ad Nassar, contends that the national-liberation movement has now reached the stage where it can take action—even before the proletariat has come to the fore—not only against colonialism but also against imperialism and capitalism resulting in "one or more country taking the non-capitalist road". He further adds that "the fact that in the UAR, Syria, and Algeria the socio-economic changes are not being carried out under the leadership of the proletariat should not blind us to the nature of those changes".[28]

What, then, of the future of the Communist parties and the proletariat? On the face of it, the Egyptian Communists have carried their line of reasoning to its logical conclusion and voluntarily dissolved their party organizations. The Arab Socialist Union (ASU) has since become synonymous with the national front. This apparent loss has been to some extent compensated by the formation of a hard core of "revolutionary vanguard" within the ASU "consisting entirely of Socialists who support the National Charter and who are imbued with the ideas of scientific Socialism".

Moreover, the fact that this "cadre party" is being organized and trained mostly by "ex-Communists" and with official blessing has placed the Communists in an influential position. At the same time, the Egyptian Communists concede that the national front might take different forms, depending on the concrete conditions and on the balance of class forces obtaining in other Arab countries.[29]

That the national front need not necessarily follow the Egyptian pattern is manifested by the example of the Syrian Communist Party, which, while conceding that it is "no longer the only national force advocating Socialism and struggling for it", asserts that it is "destined to play an important, though not necessarily the leading, role in the advance towards Socialism".[30] The Syrian Communists,

[27] Khaled Baghdash, "Some Problems of the National-Liberation Movement", *Peace, Freedom and Socialism*, vol. 7 (August 1964), pp. 51-52.
[28] Fu'ad Nassar, "Anti-Imperialist Struggle of the Arab People", *Peace, Freedom and Socialism*, vol. 9 (September 1966), pp. 18-19.
[29] Lotfi El-Kholi, n. 26, p. 28.
[30] See Khalid Bakdash's interview to *L'Humanité* (Paris), 6 September 1964.

13

therefore, clearly reject the course of political self-effacement. This view is shared by the Communist Parties of Iraq and Jordan. Fu'ad Nassar, Secretary of the Communist Party of Jordan, indeed goes so far as to maintain that considering the larger variety of objective conditions in the Arab world "it is not excluded that development in one or another country will proceed under proletarian leadership".[31]

The future of the working class is, of course, closely tied to the future of the Communist parties. Like the Communist parties, the working class must be reconciled to playing a junior rôle during the national-democratic phase. Does this not detract from the basic tenets of Marxism which regards the proletariat as the sole instrument of Socialist revolution? The Communists say it does not since national democracy is merely a transitional phase during which the continuous expansion of public ownership of means of production, the impact of the Socialist world system, and the growing influence exerted by the ideas of scientific Socialism will gradually tilt the balance of forces within the national front alliance in favour of the proletariat and pave the way for "the establishment of the hegemony of the proletariat in that alliance".[32]

Finally, the attitude of the national-democratic state towards the rival Power blocs. Two distinct viewpoints have so far crystallized on this subject. The one represented by the Egyptian Communists advocates friendly relations with the Socialist countries "based on mutual benefit, non-interference in internal affairs, and respect for national sovereignty", but would be satisfied with absence of anti-Communism on the part of the national-democratic state since "the danger to Arab countries lies not in Communism but in imperialism".[33] The other viewpoint shared by the rest of the Arab Communists holds that close co-operation between the national-democratic state and the Socialist camp is indispensable, for "were it not for the existence of the world Socialist system and its vanguard, the Soviet Union, countries like Syria, Algeria, the UAR, Ghana, Burma and others could not have launched such a bold offensive against capitalism, nor could there have been any question of the

---

[31] See Mounir Ahmid, n. 25, p. 36 and Fu'ad Nassar, n. 28, pp. 18-19.

[32] Fu'ad Nassar, n. 28; and Khaled Baghdash, "Problems of the National-Liberation Movement of the Arab Peoples", *Peace, Freedom and Socialism*, vol. 7 (September 1964), p. 60.

[33] Lotfi El-Kholi, n. 26, p. 28.

non-capitalist development for the newly-free states of Asia and Africa".[34]

These doctrinal innovations have been proudly portrayed as the Communists' "contribution to the treasure-store of Marxism-Leninism". On closer scrutiny these may, however, turn out to be no more than an attempt to make political virtue of an inescapable necessity. It nevertheless brings out the Arab Communists' hitherto unsuspected talents to improvise, innovate, and come to terms with ideologically unpleasant realities. It must, however, be added that current theoretical formulations are still in a fluid state and by no means universally accepted. They are indeed being challenged by small but growing pro-Peking factions, the self-styled upholders of the orthodox Marxian tradition. But that belongs to the next chapter.

[34] Baghdash, n. 25, ;

CHAPTER FIFTEEN

THE IMPACT OF THE SINO-SOVIET RIFT[1]

THE implications of the current cleavage in the world Communist movement for the Arab East can be viewed from two angles: its bearing on the international power equation in the region and its impact on Arab Communism. Although seemingly incongruous the two approaches are, in fact, complementary, one to another, for the simple reason that the two Communist giants now contending for the international Communist leadership also happen to be world Powers in the conventional sense of the term.

The emergence of the Soviet Union and China on the Arab Eastern scene must be seen in the context of the region's international significance. Situated at the junction of three continents, the Arab East has always been the hotbed of Big-Power rivalries throughout its recorded history. In modern times, the void created by the progressive decline of Ottoman power during the eighteenth and nineteenth centuries tempted Britain, France, Russia, Germany, and Italy to enter into a frantic race for spheres of influence in the area. In the process, the Ottoman Empire itself totally disappeared from the scene at the end of the First World War. From its ruins emerged the modern nation states of the Arab East.

The Second World War eliminated Germany, Italy, and France from the race. Britain still held out, though it scarcely possessed the means to carry on the show. Of the old Powers, only the Soviet Union now seemed to have the means to influence the course of developments in the area; and the prospect of the Soviet Union employing those means to promote its own interest inevitably brought the United States on the scene. In the post-bipolar period of international politics, the situation in the Arab East, as elsewhere in the world, is again in a state of flux. Blocs are defreezing and their constituents trying to find their own level. In this context, the respective aims and strategies of the Soviet Union and China in the Arab East acquire considerable significance.

[1] This chapter is based on the present writer's article entitled "The Soviet Union, China and West Asia", in *International Studies* (Bombay), vol. 6 (April 1965).

The Soviet Union and the Arab East

The Soviet Union's relations with the Arab East have been largely determined by the ceaseless interplay of ideology and national interest. From Tsarist Russia, it inherited the urge to gain access to the warm-water ports of the Mediterranean and the Persian Gulf. Turkey and Iran, bordering on Russia's southern flank, bore the brunt of this inexorable southward drive. With the advent of the Bolshevik Revolution, Russia's geo-political interests got inextricably mixed up with the dominant impulse to lead the oppressed people of the colonial world against their imperialist masters. The latter found expression in the stirring appeal issued by the Baku Congress of September 1920 calling upon the peasants and workers of the entire Near East to take up arms against their new colonial rulers and to join the Russian workers and peasants' army in order to "defeat the English, French and American capitalists" and to secure freedom.[2]

But having found no encouraging response to these fiery summons, the Russians addressed themselves to the more practical task of sorting out their relations with their southern neighbours. As for the Arab countries of the farther south, the Soviet Union relegated them to a relatively junior position in the overall strategy of the international Communist movement. For one thing, most of the countries in the area were under the direct or indirect control of Britain and France. Besides, the Arab proletariat was weak and disorganized. The theoreticians in Moscow also did not think much of the weak and indecisive *bourgeoisie* of Egypt, Iraq, Syria, and Palestine. But when Ibn Sa'ud established an independent kingdom in Arabia in 1926, the Soviet Union lost no time in extending diplomatic recognition to it. Shortly afterwards, the Soviet Union concluded a treaty of friendship with the ancient Imamate of Yemen. Evidently, these overtures were inspired by practical, rather than ideological, considerations. The thirties saw an enormous upsurge against British and French domination in the Fertile Crescent and Egypt. But it drew inspiration mostly from Berlin and Rome. Only in Syria were the circumstances propitious for the local Communists to make some headway through a broad-based national front. It was not until 1941 when the Soviet Union joined the Allies against

[2] Of the 1,891 delegates who attended the Congress only three were Arabs. See Ivar Spector, *The Soviet Union and the Muslim World: 1917-1956* (Mimeographed, Washington, D. C., 1956), pp. 26-27.

Hitler that the former got an opportunity to establish Soviet legations in Cairo, Damascus, Beirut, and Baghdad. Soviet victories following Stalingrad served to create an image of Soviet prowess. In the decade after the war, Soviet policy was marked by rapid changes dictated by shifting exigencies. It backed Syria and the Lebanon against the French, and Egypt against the British. In the fall of 1947, it took a sharp turn and threw its weight on the side of the Zionist demand for the creation of Israel. Between 1948 and 1952 it assumed a strictly neutral attitude towards the Arab-Israeli conflict, followed by qualified support to the Arabs during 1953-54. As for Arab neutralism, Moscow scarcely cared to conceal its profound distaste. On 13 November 1949, Egypt's Nahas Pasha, while referring to the two Power blocs, observed: "Which camp should Egypt join? Certainly Egypt cannot join the imperialist camp since the British imperialists are in occupation of Egypt and constitute a menace to its independence." He added that if a war broke out, "Egypt retains the freedom to determine its policy". This pronouncement was apparently an unembellished plea for neutralism. But Soviet writers interpreted it as "the Egyptian leader's inclination to keep the door open to join the imperialists".[3]

The watershed in the Soviet Union's relations with the Arabs lies in the post-Stalin era. Towards the end of his life, Stalin had perceived the value of neutralism in a world infested with anti-Soviet alliances. The consummation of the Baghdad Pact in 1955 confirmed the validity of this approach. In the Arabs of Egypt and the Fertile Crescent who were putting up stiff resistance to the Baghdad Pact, the Soviet Union saw its natural allies. It is important to note that it did not extend unqualified support to Arab neutralism until after the Pact was finalized. In an all-out attack on the Pact, the Soviet Foreign Ministry declared on 16 April 1955 that it had no choice left but to win to its side the uncommitted Arab states. The Soviet Union then proceeded to open its heart and purse to them.

The Soviet support to Arab nationalism as a counter to the "iron belt" of the Baghdad Pact has a parallel in early Soviet history. In the twenties, the Soviet Union had signed treaties of friendship with Turkey, Iran, and Afghanistan primarily to forestall British designs to draw them into an anti-Bolshevik alliance. Molotov sought to achieve similar results by different means in 1939, when

[3] *At-Tariq* (Beirut), vol. 8 (October-November 1949), p. 24.

he tried to impress on Berlin that "the area south of Batum and Baku in the general direction of the Persian Gulf should be recognized as the main area of Soviet aspirations".[4]

As for the Arab attitude towards the Soviet Union, it was aptly summed up in Mustafa Nahas Pasha's observation in 1944 that the Soviet Union was, after all, four thousand miles away.[5] The Soviet Union had no common frontier with the Arab states. Nor was there any political, economic, or cultural intercourse between the Arabs and the Soviets. Arab Communist movements were also not in a position except during the later years of the Second World War, to project the Soviet image in an appreciable measure. But the Baghdad Pact pulled down all these barriers at one stroke. It suddenly dawned on the Arabs that the Soviet Union was not quite as far off as Mustafa Nahas had once thought. The interests of resurgent Arab nationalism coalesced with those of the Soviet Union. The first casualty of this new alliance was the Western embargo on supply of arms to the Arab states. Then followed a succession of reverses for the West leading to Iraq's defection from the Baghdad Pact.

Emergence of China

Unlike the Soviet Union, China is a new-comer in Arab East. Kuomintang China had maintained diplomatic missions in quite a few Arab capitals, presumably to keep the semblance of a Big Power. A chaotic China had no time or resources to cultivate interests in a far-off region. And the Arabs reciprocated this lack of interest. Egypt, for instance, did not care to establish a diplomatic or consular mission in Taiwan, although the latter had an Ambassador in Cairo until 1955. The situation did not substantially improve even after the Communist take-over in China. During the Korean crisis, the Arab countries either took an attitude hostile to China or observed strict neutrality. When the vote was taken in the UN General Assembly on the crucial US draft resolution which branded the People's Republic of China an aggressor, Iraq and the Lebanon voted in favour; Egypt, Syria, and the Yemen abstained. Saudi Arabia was not content with "abstaining"

[4] *Nazi-Soviet Relations 1939-41: Documents from the Archives of the German Foreign Office* (Washington, D. C., 1948), p. 259.

[5] Walter Z. Laqueur, *The Soviet Union and the Middle East* (London, 1959), p. 192.

but doggedly insisted that it was not participating in the vote.[6]

Until 1956, when Egypt recognized the People's Republic of China, the latter had no diplomatic foothold in West Asia. Earlier India had tried without success to persuade Egypt to recognize China. A distinct change in the Arab attitude towards China came at Bandung, where the Arabs made the comforting discovery that there was a promising field, in Asia and Africa, for mobilizing support for the Arab cause in Palestine—a prize which would compensate for the powerful influence of the Zionists in Europe and America. And Chou En-lai was effusively responsive on this point. He also came forward with offers of lucrative trade. Egypt was greatly attracted by the prospect of a sizable market for its cotton, and lost no time in pursuing the matter further with Peking. At Bandung, Chou En-lai also invited the Egyptian Minister of Waqf, Shaykh Hasan al-Baquri (a former Muslim Brother), to visit China and acquaint himself with the conditions of Chinese Muslims. Baquri flew straight from Bandung to Peking and reported back on 29 June 1955 that "the way for co-operation with the Far Eastern nations was wide open". By August, a three-year trade agreement was signed by Egypt and China which facilitated immediate sale of Egyptian cotton worth £8,000,000 at world prices —Egypt's first deal of its kind with China. The next month Egypt set up trade offices in China. By February 1956 the climate in Egypt was propitious enough for China to despatch a cultural mission and an opera troupe. Egypt's recognition of China on 16 May 1956 was the next logical step.

In Damascus, where the Soviet Union had been proffering diplomatic assurances and military hardware to a neutralist Government harassed by the partisans of the Baghdad Pact, influential groups including some cabinet ministers demanded that Syria should emulate Egypt. China responded by sending a 72-member cultural mission to Syria. It also concluded a cultural pact which, among other things, provided for a Chinese exhibition in Damascus—a thoughtful gesture to the fun-loving Damascenes! By the end of 1956, the two countries exchanged diplomatic missions at the ambassadorial level.

Simultaneously, China cultivated the youthful Crown Prince

[6] United Nations General Assembly, *Official Records (GAOR)*, session 5, mtg 327, pp. 695-6.

Muhammad Badr of Yemen. Indeed, China seemed to have a special fascination—like the Soviet Union's in the twenties—for this primitive, isolationist Imamate, which, incidentally, guarded the entrance to the Red Sea and the Indian Ocean. On Badr's initiative, Yemen recognized the People's Republic of China in August 1956.

China's next spectacular success was in Iraq. Within ten days of the 14 July *coup d'état*, Kassem recognized China.[7] The latter responded by sending what some observers called a "massive" diplomatic mission to Baghdad. Iraq's was the first successful *coup d'état* in the Arab East in which the local Communists had played an appreciable rôle. Six months later, the two countries signed a trade pact, according to which China agreed to supply machinery and industrial equipment in return for dates, wool, cotton, and hides. Iraq also became a supplier of crude oil to China.

To sum up, China had evidently made up its mind early in 1955 to make an all-out attempt to win people and make friends in the Arab East. To attain this objective, China shrewdly refrained from peddling its ideological wares. China's approach was outright practical. It harped on the right of the Asians to decide their own fate; showed concern for the Arabs of Palestine; offered prospects of gainful trade; emphasized cultural links between the Arabs and the Chinese Muslims; and, to top it all, made an impressive display of sweet reasonableness. By 1958, China was able to establish active contacts with the Arab East in its own right.

Abortive Experiment in Collective Diplomacy

The image which China projected in the Arab world during 1955-58 was that of an emergent Asian Power, oppressed by colonial Powers in the past but now able to stand on its own feet and eager to make friends with the Arabs. The massive arms and economic aid promised by the Soviet Union to Egypt, Syria, and Iraq doubtless facilitated China's access to the area in the early period. But it was by no means an unqualified blessing. For the Soviet Union bore almost the entire economic and military responsibilities which naturally entitled it to the lion's share in Communist bloc policy-making.

China endeavoured to make up for its deficiency by adding an

[7] Of the remaining states, Jordan, the Lebanon, and Saudi Arabia recognize the Taiwan régime. Kuwait recognizes neither of the two rival Governments.

extra dose of militancy to its vocal propaganda for Arab causes. After the Suez crisis, which was, by coincidence, accompanied by a violent upheaval in Hungary, the Soviet Union condescended to associate China publicly with its West Asian policy. In a strongly worded joint declaration (of 18 January 1957), the two Powers pledged their support to all West Asian countries against "aggression or interference" by Western Powers. It was Moscow's answer to the Eisenhower Doctrine. In a few weeks' time, however, the Soviet Union unilaterally climbed down from the militant posture of the joint declaration and began to reassure the West that it did not really "wish to possess military bases or any kind of concessions in countries of the Near and the Middle East for the purpose of making profits, nor does it seek to obtain any kind of privileges in that area. . . ." Its primary concern was to promote peace in the region "situated in direct proximity to its borders". These observations, contained in a Soviet Note handed over to the United States, Britain, and France on 11 February 1957, were also accompanied by Draft Proposals[8] which stipulated that the four Powers jointly guarantee (a) peaceful settlement of disputes in the region; (b) non-interference in its internal affairs; (c) abolition of military alignments; (d) withdrawal of foreign forces; (e) ban on supply of arms to Middle Eastern countries; and (f) economic assistance without strings.

The logic of the Soviet argument was simple: the Suez War had put an end to Western monopoly in the Arab East. The West should admit this and recognize Soviet interests in the area. It is difficult to say what the Chinese really thought of these proposals except that outwardly at least they looked highly conciliatory in contrast to the fighting stipulations of the Sino-Soviet Declaration of January 1957. Nevertheless, China, as anyone else, could predict that the West would most certainly reject the Soviet proposals and, therefore, saw no harm in hailing them as "a heavy blow to the Eisenhower Doctrine".[9] The Arab neutralists, on their part, were not enamoured of the proposals. Their reactions were pointedly summed up in *Al Qahira's* comment:

It is really strange that both East and West should draw up

[8] Text of the Proposals in *News and Views from the Soviet Union* (New Delhi), vol. 16 (14 February 1957), pp. 2-4.

[9] *Survey of China Mainland Press* (Hong Kong), 20 February 1957, p. 35.

schemes acceptable or otherwise about the Middle East behind the back of the people of the region. . . . Both East and West were now vying with each other in formulating schemes under circumstances of Cold War and in both cases the gains sought by both sides are at our expense.[10]

That China, the Soviet Union, and the Arab neutralists were at cross-purposes became even more evident in the course of the Lebanese crisis. The Chinese seized the occasion to re-stress the "paper tiger" thesis. The *People's Daily* of 30 May 1958 observed: "The Lebanese people provide a further proof of this truth. We are convinced that the Lebanese people. . . will win a brilliant victory." On 29 July, it hailed the military exercises commenced by the Soviet Union and Bulgaria in the Transcaucasus and Black Sea areas and expressed its fervent hope that the Socialist camp "headed by the Soviet Union" would repulse "Anglo-American aggression". The Soviet Union, apparently, had different ideas. And these were broadly spelled out in Khrushchev's letters to Eisenhower, Macmillan, de Gaulle, and Nehru.[11] The Soviet Union hinted that it was not opposed to the interests of the Western Powers in "the petroleum and other raw materials" of the Middle East and was even prepared to consider "the question of putting an end to the deliveries of arms" to the countries of that region. Khrushchev then invited the four Powers to a "summit meeting" in order to iron out existing differences. This idea of a "summit meeting" without China enraged the latter. The *People's Daily* cuttingly wrote: "Begging won't preserve peace. Peace can be won only by militant struggle."[12] Khrushchev immediately rushed to Peking for consultations with Mao. Eventually, China endorsed Khrushchev's "summit meeting" proposals, but only after publicly asserting its right to be consulted.[13]

The Arab neutralists' need for Soviet support was too great at this juncture to permit any candid reaction to the summit idea. But the eventual outcome of the Lebanese crisis turned out to be in their favour. The pro-Western elements were not as thoroughly

[10] Quoted in *Egyptian Gazette* (Cairo), 15 February 1957.
[11] Text of letters in The United Nations Security Council, *Official Records*, yr 13, supplement for July, August, and September.
[12] Quoted in *Peking Review*, vol. 1 (12 August 1958), p. 21.
[13] Sino-Soviet Communiqué, 3 August 1958, ibid., pp. 6-7.

routed as China would have wished. Nor was the Soviet Union able to wrest any concession from the West. The neutralists achieved in the Lebanon what *Pravda* (1 August 1958) had scornfully described as a "semblance of compromise government".

ASPECTS OF SINO-SOVIET DIFFERENCES

About this time, discord between the Soviet Union and the People's Republic of China began to take a serious turn. As we have already seen, China entered the Arab world on its own, and its interests there were not identical with those of the Soviet Union. Perhaps this was also true of the whole range of their international policies. When China found that the policies formulated by the Soviet Union on behalf of the Communist camp did not suit its national interests, it decided to question the ideological soundness of these policies. It is not intended here to go into the origins and ramifications of the Sino-Soviet differences. Some of the basic issues raised referred to the global strategy of the Communist camp *vis-à-vis* the capitalist world. China started by assailing the Soviet thesis on peaceful co-existence and contended that the tremendous advance made by the Communist camp in modern weapons, coupled with its enhanced economic power, called for a global revolutionary posture. The Soviet Union, in turn, pointed out the grave risks involved in this adventurist approach and argued that with the growing military and economic power of the Communist camp, it could triumph, although slowly, through peaceful competition. China quoted chapter and verse from Lenin to establish that the capitalist system would "not crumble of itself".[14] Moscow ascribed this to the infantile mentality of the Chinese, who were stated to be incapable of "creatively applying the revolutionary teaching" of Lenin.[15]

China also challenged the Soviet approach to the emerging states of Asia, Africa, and Latin America, which were neither Communist nor capitalist. As a corollary to revolutionary global strategy, China demanded that the national liberation struggle in the colonial dependencies should be intensified as "an indispensable

[14] See *Red Flag* article on "Long Live Leninism." Extracts in David Floyd, *Mao against Khrushchev* (London, 1963), p. 269.

[15] See Khrushchev's address to the Romanian Congress, 21 June 1960, ibid., pp. 278-81.

weapon in the struggle against imperialism".[16] Again, in China's estimation, it was un-Marxian to be indulgent to the national *bourgeois* rulers of the ex-colonial world. As Wang Chia-hsiang put it, "the national *bourgeoisie* may travel a distance along the road of anti-imperialism", but they will not be able to "effect the transition to Socialism", and "in the final analysis, they can never escape from the control and bondage of imperialism".[17] Moscow rejected this argument on the ground that *bourgeois* nationalism was endowed with two opposite pulls: it intended to resist imperialist domination but was also ready to strike a compromise with it. On the whole, however, it maintained its positive progressive significance. Besides, "the further advance of the independent *bourgeois* countries in the East will be decided not only by the balance of class forces in these countries, but also in the course of competition between systems—the moribund capitalist system and the growing Socialist system".[18] Allied to the issue of national *bourgeoisie*, there was the question of economic aid, and the rôle of Communist parties in non-Socialist countries. In other words, the dispute centred on the question of ways and means of carrying out Socialist transformation in the newly independent states of Asia and Africa. Peking contended that the solution lay in Mao's concept of new democracy, which stipulated a *bourgeois* revolution led by Communist-dominated united front. Moscow countered this argument by saying that the immediate problem before the developing countries was to choose between capitalist and non-capitalist ways of development. The former would draw them into the orbit of capitalism but the non-capitalist way would effect the transition from a semi-feudal economy to a Socialist economy bypassing the stage of mature industrial capitalism. The political form most suited to this kind of development was national democracy which would be operated "not by one class or by one party but by all the patriotic classes joined together in a long-term alliance". It could be led by "any democratic class": the peasantry, the small urban *bourgeoisie*, the in-

---

[16] *People's Daily* (Peking), 30 September 1962. Quoted in *Mizan Newsletter* (London), vol. 5 (March 1963).

[17] Quoted in Donald S. Zagoria, "Sino-Soviet Friction in Under-Developed Areas", *Problems of Communism* (Washington, D. C.), vol. 10 (March-April 1961), p. 8.

[18] G. Levinson, "Two Trends of the National Bourgeoisie", *World Marxist Review* (Prague), vol. 2 (September, 1959), p. 79.

telligentsia, or the revolutionary army officers. Again, economic relations in a national democracy would be governed by an evergrowing State sector, liquidation of imperialism and feudalism, and encouragement to small commodity producers and middle-sized capitalists.[19] And therein lay a positive rôle for the Socialist camp and an ideological explanation for Moscow's aid to developing countries.

China has been somewhat circumspect in its criticism of Soviet economic aid to developing countries. But it has asserted that by following the road of State capitalism (which the Soviet Union prefers to call non-capitalist development) the newly independent states "can hardly free themselves from the oppression and exploitation of imperialism and feudalism".[20] Besides, Mao's new democracy does not consider industrialization to be a necessary prerequisite of Socialist revolution.

We now turn to examine the impact of these Sino-Soviet differences on their respective policies towards the Arab East.

Issue of Liberation Struggle

As a corollary to their militant posture towards the capitalist camp, the Chinese claim that colonial peoples can liberate themselves only by resort to violence. Hence the need for the Communist bloc to support "wars of national liberation". To the theoreticians in Peking, the Lebanese civil war and the Iraqi *coup d'état* of July 1958 were nothing short of wars of liberation.

It will be recalled that when the American marines landed in the Lebanon, the Soviet Union called for a cautious approach to the situation. China, on the other hand, attempted to magnify this event out of all proportion. The *People's Daily* drew a contrast between international support to the American War of Independence and the helplessness of the Lebanese rebels and added:[21]

> We want to ask: Why are they not entitled to the international assistance which the American War of Independence secured? Who dares to say that the French who supported America in those days were aggressors?

[19] "Sobolev's Leap in Theory", *Link* (New Delhi), 24 March 1963, p. 31.
[20] *Red Flag*, 1 October 1959. Quoted in *Mizan Newsletter*, vol. 5 (March 1963), p. 5.
[21] Zagoria, n. 17, p. 7.

It is, however, important to note that in spite of this vocal militancy, China did not go so far as to offer material aid to the Lebanese rebels. It was perhaps intended to push the Soviet Union into active conflict with the West or to humble it in the eyes of the Arabs.

Again in Peking's view, the Iraqi *coup d'état* had "greatly advanced the national liberation movements in Asia, Africa, and Latin America".[22] China forthwith recognized the new régime and set up an over-sized embassy in Baghdad. The situation in Iraq appeared promising for China's forward policy. The *coup d'état* had brought the Communist Party of Iraq to the forefront of political struggle. Unlike its counterpart in Syria, the 7,000-strong Iraqi Party consisted of tough fighters who had survived the rigours of decades of persecution under pro-Western régimes. The inclement political weather of Iraq had never been conducive to "national front" tactics. Besides, the bitter experience of the Communist Party of Syria after the creation of the United Arab Republic (UAR) had demonstrated the utter futility of "national fronts". Peking's militant line, therefore, found warm response in Baghdad. Moscow had its own reasons to hail the change in Iraq. For one thing, it dealt a serious, if not fatal, blow to the Baghdad Pact, which was chiefly directed against the Soviet Union. Secondly, with its small population and considerable mineral and agricultural resources, Iraq could be turned into a model of Soviet-aided economic progress for the neighbouring states to emulate. A friendly Iraq would also lessen the Soviet Union's dependence on Nasser for political support in the Arab East. Peking saw in the Iraqi situation an opportunity to create a Communist-dominated régime which would pave the way for the "liberation of the entire region". To Moscow, on the other hand, the defection of Iraq from the Baghdad Pact strengthened the ranks of the anti-Western forces and was a significant gain by itself. It suited them to encourage and stabilize the neutralist trend in Iraq rather than to indulge in the gamble of liberation.

The Sino-Soviet differences on the issue of liberation struggle were further manifested by the attitude of the two Powers towards the Arab-Israeli conflict since the creation of the Palestine Liberation Organization in 1964. Whereas the Soviet Union counselled moderation to the Arabs, the Chinese encouraged the PLO militants in their plans for a hot war against Israel. In a two-pronged move China

[22] *Peking Review*, n. 12.

reminded the Arabs of the Soviet rôle in the creation of Israel and invited batches of Palestinian commandos for training in guerrilla warfare. Although the long-range implications of this policy still belong to the realm of speculation, it certainly enables China to cause discomfiture to the Soviet Union and to earn Arab goodwill.[23]

National Bourgeoisie

The Iraqi *coup d'état* also reopened the question of the Communist attitude to the national *bourgeoisie*. Khalid Bakdash, the Syrian Communist leader, had followed the Moscow line of co-operation with the national *bourgeoisie* and ended up with the dissolution of his party after Syria's merger with Egypt. This was too high a price even for Khalid Bakdash—an accomplished master of political give and take—to pay. And it was not long before he started publicly giving vent to his resentment. At a symposium held in Prague in June 1958, Bakdash strongly denounced the view propagated by the authorities in the UAR that Socialism in the Arab countries could not be built by the Communists. He then assailed land reforms in Syria and Egypt which, in his view, were merely strengthening "the class of *kulaks*" and concluded that the national *bourgeoisie* had "neither the economic nor the political resources" to adopt more vigorous measures.[24] The Iraqi Communist Party started, perhaps at Moscow's behest, with a moderate programme published within weeks of the July *coup d'état*. It called for the freeing of Iraq from the Sterling Area, some control (not confiscation!) over oil industry and other foreign business, encouragement to national industry and capital, abolition of feudal exploitation, and protection of the working class.[25] But once the nationalist elements in Iraq started their vigorous campaign for union with the UAR, the Communists began to have misgivings about the prospects of fruitful co-operation with the national *bourgeoisie*. The abortive Mosul *coup d'état* of March 1959, which was directed against Kassem and his Communist allies, decided the issue. The Communists ruthlessly suppressed the supporters of the *coup d'état*

[23] For instance, *Al-Hawadith*, a Beirut weekly, commented on 4 June 1965: "The tendency among the Palestinian leaders is to accept the Chinese offer because to neglect such a generous and stringless offer would be a crime."

[24] Khaled Bakdash, "The Crisis and the Problems of the Middle East", *World Marxist Review*, vol. 1 (September 1958), p. 69.

[25] *New Age* (New Delhi), 7 June 1959, pp. 7, 11.

which included Ba'th Socialists, Nasserites, and other nationalists. The conflict between the Communists and nationalists now reached a point of no return. Both Russia and China condemned the Mosul revolt which meant an indirect rebuke to Nasser, who had inspired the rebels. But soon after that, events, or more precisely, the Iraqi Communists, began to get out of Moscow's control. By April it appeared as if the Communists held everything except formal title to government in Iraq. Having eliminated or suppressed their political foes, the Communists were now advancing headlong on the Chinese line which held the national *bourgeoisie* in utter contempt. To seize power, the Communists ordered a general mobilization of trade unions, students, and intellectuals. For a while the People's Resistance Force—a paramilitary adjunct of the Communist Party— seemed to be "stronger than the regular army".[26] On the international plane, the Iraqi Communists publicized their preference for China by setting up an Iraqi-Albanian Friendship Society. They also used their influence over Kassem to establish diplomatic ties with Albania at the ambassadorial level. The Communists then pressed for representation in the cabinet to which Kassem, who had by now alienated nearly all non-Communist elements, had no alternative but to succumb. On 13 July two new ministers known for their Communist leanings were added to the cabinet. In a further attempt to terrorize their rivals, the Communists launched a savage campaign of arson and killing at Kirkuk. That proved to be the last straw for Kassem. On 19 July, he bluntly warned the Communists that those who had "offended against the freedom of the people" at Kirkuk and elsewhere would be "severely punished".[27] This was Kassem's first public criticism of the Iraqi Communists and was followed by a purge of Communists in the army and the administration. Soon it began to dawn on the Communist Party of Iraq that in its adventurist fervour it had overestimated its strength. An enlarged session of the Central Committee, hurriedly summoned in August, reviewed the entire party line and concluded that it had committed serious "Leftist political errors" in its relations with the Government as well as the rank and file, and that in order to

[26] Hans E. Tütsch, "A Report on Iraq", *Swiss Review of World Affairs* (Zurich), vol. 10 (March 1961), pp. 29-30.

[27] The pro-Communist Kurds were reported to have buried 41 anti-Communist Turkomans alive and killed another 79 by other means. *As-Sahafa* (Beirut), 8 August 1959.

14

defeat imperialism, it was essential to "maintain solidarity with the Government and other patriotic forces".[28]

This abrupt *volte face* signified abandonment of the hard line. Peking expressed its displeasure at the turn of events in Baghdad by refusing to publicize the confession of the Iraqi comrades whom they had earlier encouraged to make tall demands on Kassem. On the other hand, although Moscow had earlier played down the demands of the Iraqi Communists, it lost no time in giving wide publicity to their penance for having made them.[29]

It is, however, important to note that the Iraqi example is not representative of the general tenor of China's dealings with the Arab countries. China has been as eager as the Soviet Union, if not more, to cultivate friendly political and economic relations with the Governments of the area. And it has not allowed its ideological reservations to come in the way. Indeed, when it comes to furthering its own interests, China finds no difficulty in exuding warmth and friendliness to the *bourgeois* régimes which it intensely abhors ideologically. This is illustrated by Chou En-lai's tame performance in Cairo in the fall of 1963. His visit was prefaced by a defiant editorial in the official daily *Al-Jumhuriya* (12 December 1963), which invited Chou En-lai "to understand that Arab Socialism can appreciably differ from the Chinese views of its own problems" and added that "a revolution has the right to follow its own way". The visiting dignitary quietly glossed over the rebuke and emphasized "the unity of the ancient civilization embodied by the Great Wall and the Egyptian civilization symbolized by the Pyramids", to which Nasser replied that "the hopes and aspirations of the Arabs are now embodied by the Aswan Dam"—a feat of Soviet economic and technical aid.[30] In sharp contrast to this, Khrushchev received a warm welcome in Cairo and was much less apologetic to his host.[31] The

---

[28] For details see above, ch. 11.

[29] *Kommunist* (Moscow), no. 12 (1959), published it in full and *Pravda* (Moscow) of 17 August 1959 carried extracts of the same document.

[30] *Summary of World Broadcasts* (Reading, England), part I, no. 1551, 12 May 1964, p. 3.

[31] "Shall I tell you", Khrushchev told a distinguished audience at Aswan which included Ben Bella, 'Arif, and Sallal besides President Nasser, "what I want to say or what you want to hear?" And then he proceeded to decry the whole concept of Arab unity: "I have heard your leaders urge Arabs to unite. In such a case, what shall we Russians here do? Go home?" *New York Times*, 18 May 1964.

Egyptians, too, were more indulgent to Khrushchev than to Chou En-lai, which, however, did not imply that they were backing Moscow against Peking. It was just one more proof of the high premium which Cairo put on Soviet amity for obvious political and economic reasons.

On the ideological plane, too, the Soviet Union gained an edge over the Chinese. As against Mao's doctrine of new democracy the Soviet thesis on national democracy found wider acceptance among the Arab Communists.

Economic Aid

Moscow's thesis on the progressive potentialities of the national *bourgeoisie* stipulated active participation of the Socialist countries in the economic development of new nations on an inter-governmental level. It was argued that this would stimulate the development of a State sector, which, in turn, would curb foreign and indigenous monopolies in the recipient states. But apart from ideological considerations, the Soviet Union's political and economic interests demanded that it develop fruitful economic and trade relations with the emerging nations. In the case of Egypt, which was the first recipient of Soviet aid in the Arab East, the Soviet Union's hands were forced by the inexorable logic of events following the withdrawal of the promised American loan for the Aswan Dam. Without Soviet aid, the Arab neutralists would not have the means to sustain their defiance of the West. In November 1957 the Soviet Union offered 700 million roubles to Egypt for industrial projects and 400 million roubles in the following year to cover the foreign exchange cost of the first phase of the Aswan Dam.[32] In January 1960 the Soviet Union promised aid worth £103 million for the second phase of the Dam.[33] Syria received economic credits worth $168 million in 1957 and Yemen $20 million in the following year.[34] After the July *coup d'état*, Iraq also became a significant beneficiary of Soviet aid. Between 1958 and 1961, it received Soviet economic credits worth $183 million.[35] According to one estimate, the Arabs got 25 per cent of the entire Soviet economic aid offered

[32] Robert Loring Allen, *Soviet Economic Warfare* (Washington, D.C., 1960), p. 140.

[33] *Eastern Economist* (New Delhi), 5 February 1960, p. 390.

[34] Allen, n. 32, pp. 141 and 216.

[35] *Commerce* (Bombay), 25 August 1962, p. 310.

to non-Communist countries between 1954 and 1961.[36] The Soviet credits had the additional advantage of a relatively low interest rate (2.5 per cent) and easy terms of repayment. Economic aid accelerated trade between the two sides at such a rapid pace that by 1960 the UAR acquired the fourth position in the Soviet Union's trade with non-Communist countries.[37] It also brought political dividends: the neutralist trend in the Arab world was stabilized and in popular estimation the Soviet Union came to be regarded as a friend of the developing nations.

In the Chinese view, Soviet aid to developing non-Communist nations is a wasteful diversion of resources on which the less developed Socialist states have a prior claim. Secondly, as already pointed out, China feels that Soviet aid stimulates only the growth of State capitalism and offers no safeguards against imperialist and feudal exploitation. It has, however, abstained from a frontal attack on the Soviet Union on this score for fear of antagonizing the recipient states and preferred to express its resentment in subtle ways. In April 1960, when a *New China News Agency (NCNA)* correspondent in Baghdad asked Anastas Mikoyan how the Soviet position on economic aid to Asian-African countries differed from the Western position on that question, the latter sharply retorted that it was just as favourable to the Asian-African peoples as the position of the Chinese Government.[38] In 1961 the Albanians performed this delicate task for China in a more direct fashion.[39] More recently, in the Second Asiatic Economic Forum held at Pyongyang, the leader of the Chinese delegation made an undisguised attack on Soviet economic aid. He said:

> The fact of the matter is that their [i.e. Soviet Union's] "aid" is not only not unselfish but dictated by great-power chauvinism and national ego. In their economic exchanges with Afro-Asian countries it often works out that these contemporary revisionists fail to respect the independence and sove-

[36] Tetsuji Yasuhira, "Soviet Economic Aid to Non-Aligned Countries and the Soviet Programme in South and South-East Asia", in Kurt London, ed., *New Nations in a Divided World* (New York, 1963), p. 211.

[37] M. V. Nesterov, *Trade Between the Soviet Union and Countries of Asia and Africa* (New Delhi, 1960), p. 38.

[38] See W. A. C. Adie, "The Middle East: Sino-Soviet Discords", *Survey* (London), no. 42 (June 1962), p. 144.

[39] *Eastern Economist* (New Delhi), 8 February 1963, p. 210.

reignty of Afro-Asian countries and crudely interfere in their internal affairs. Instead of desiring sincerely to help these countries develop an independent national economy, they demand that one country or another serve by delivering raw materials; and they even establish control over the economy of other countries.

As an alternative to Soviet economic aid, which is virtually equated with neo-colonialism, China put forward the slogan of "reliance on one's own strength".[40]

China's ideological posture on the issue of economic aid serves to cover up its inability to compete with the Soviet Union in this sphere. At the same time, China is eager to make judicious use of its own meagre resources in order to win friends in the non-Communist world. In 1958 China singled out the strategically situated Imamate of Yemen for economic aid worth £4½ million. It also took advantage of the Soviet breakthrough in the Arab East in the mid-fifties to expand rapidly its trade with the area.[41]

Struggle for Leadership

Perhaps the most pressing urge behind China's ideological dispute was the desire to wrest leadership of the world Communist movement from Moscow's hands. Here, the Soviet Union possesses the initial advantage of having long-standing contacts with the Arab Communist parties. Many of their leaders have been trained in Moscow and have mastered the art of adapting themselves to the vagaries of the Soviet party line. Their contacts with the Chinese Communists, on the other hand, have been indirect and are of recent origin. Hence the instinctive reaction of the Arab Communists to the Sino-Soviet controversy was to side with Moscow. But that was not all. The Soviet Union's stand on the attitude the Communists should adopt towards the *bourgeois* nationalist régimes had

---

[40] *Ekonomicheskava Gazeta* (Moscow), 22 August 1964, quoted in US Department of Commerce, *Translations on International Communist Developments*, no. 642, 15 September 1964, pp. 4 and 9.

[41] The exports of Arab countries to China rose from $10.9 million in 1953 to $52.8 million in 1958 and imports increased from $5.8 million to $7.7 million. This trade was apparently more beneficial to the Arab countries than to China and was politically motivated. See Latif Ahmad Sherwani, "Sino-Soviet Aid Programme in Asia", in Kurt London, ed., *Unity and Contradiction: Major Aspects of Sino-Soviet Relations* (New York, 1962), p. 325.

more than a theoretical significance for the Arab Communists. The Soviet Union's close alliance with Nasser in Egypt, with the radical nationalists in Syria, and with Kassem in Iraq was a millstone round the neck of Arab Communism. Although the Soviet Union helped Nasser with arms and economic aid, the latter continued to suppress local Communists with unabated zeal; and after the creation of the UAR, he extended this policy to Syria as well. After a short-lived honeymoon with the Iraqi Communists, Kassem, too, dropped them like a hot brick. In these conditions, the Soviet pledge of "protracted co-operation with the national *bourgeoisie*" promised a bleak future for the Arab Communists.

As the squeeze tightened on the Arab Communists, they tended to take shelter behind China's tough line. After Nasser's forceful condemnation of the Arab Communists in 1958, the Egyptian Communists started a heated debate inside prison camps on the question of whether or not to support the existing régime in Egypt and this ended in a rift between those who thought that Nasser had progressive potentialities and those who condemned him as a plain reactionary. In Syria, Khalid Bakdash left the country in disgust immediately after the creation of the UAR and began to take a fresh look at the Soviet line. "We must not forget", he reminded his comrades, "that the national bourgeoisie often uses the assistance rendered by the Socialist camp in bargaining with the imperialists for favourable terms."[42] A year later, the Chinese offered him their official platform to launch a frontal attack on Nasser's domestic and foreign policies.[43] The Iraqi Communists, as we have already noted, even resorted to violence in their abortive attempt to dislodge Kassem's *bourgeois* régime. Afterwards they publicly repented of this "Left-sectarian" adventure but were never wholly reconciled to the Moscow line. "The dual nature", wrote an Iraqi Communist in the fall of 1961, "of the national bourgeoisie—especially its anti-democratic aspects—was not probably understood by the public and *even by many revolutionaries*, long accustomed to concentrate attention mainly on the positive aspects of the *bourgeoisie* which were typical for the pre-revolutionary period."[44]

[42] Bakdash, n. 24.

[43] For details of Bakdash's speech in Peking on 27 September 1959, see *Mideast Mirror* (Beirut), 4 October 1959, pp. 2-3.

[44] Mohammad Salim, "Three Years After the Iraqi Revolution", *World Marxist Review*, vol. 4 (October 1961), p. 37. Emphasis added.

Notwithstanding these broad indications, it would be erroneous to conclude that the Soviet Union has completely abandoned the West Asian Communists to the mercy of the existing nationalist régimes or that China has emerged as their sole champion and saviour. On more than one occasion there have been sharp exchanges between Moscow and Cairo on the question of the treatment meted out to Egyptian and Syrian Communists by Nasser. Indeed Khruschchev did not announce his acceptance of Nasser's invitation to visit the UAR until Nasser decided to release the bulk of the Egyptian Communists from prison.[45] Moscow also took exception to the massacre of Iraqi Communists at the hands of the Ba'thists following the February 1963 *coup d'état*. It was indeed one week after the Soviet Union had started the campaign condemning the slaughter that Peking felt induced to join in. Again, while Moscow frowned on the Ba'thist *coup d'état* in Syria in March, the Chinese Press preferred to gloss over the event. The Peking Government lost no time in extending recognition to the new Syrian régime. In June, *Pravda* went so far as to hint that the actions of the Baghdad authorities might prejudice the future of Soviet economic aid to Iraq.[46] While the Soviet Union was busy exerting diplomatic and propaganda pressures on Damascus and Baghdad, the Chinese used the opportunity to win the friendship of the Ba'thists.[47]

It is, therefore, not surprising that in spite of Moscow's active cooperation with several anti-Communist régimes in the Arab East, it has been able to retain the loyalty of the local Communists. On the official plane, the Communist parties of Egypt, Iraq, Jordan, the Lebanon, and Syria have extended unqualified support to the Soviet Union in the Moscow-Peking ideological controversy. A joint resolution adopted by the Arab Communist parties in April 1965 condemned "the revisionist views of the Chinese leadership" as well as its "disruptive and splitting activity".[48] Earlier Khalid Bakdash wrote that "every patriot and revolutionary in the Arab world, be he a Communist, a Socialist, or just a progressive, experiences a

[45] In July 1963 Nasser told *Le Monde* (Paris) that all political prisoners (most of them were Communists) would be released by the end of the year. Khrushchev visited Cairo in May 1964.

[46] *Pravda*, 20 June 1963. Quoted in *Mizan Newsletter*, vol. 5 (July-August 1963), p. 33.

[47] *Sunday Telegraph* (London), 24 May 1964.

[48] Text of the resolution in *Information Bulletin* (Prague), no. 15 (1964), pp. 797-807. See also *An-Nida* (Beirut), 18 August 1964.

feeling of repugnance, dissatisfaction, condemnation, and anger towards the people who have sunk to their necks in the mire of nationalism". He denied Peking's charge that the Arab Communist parties were mere "pawns in the game of Soviet diplomatic chess" but hastened to add that "the friendship between the Arab and Soviet Communists, and what is more important, the Arab-Soviet friendship in the widest possible sense, has become a rock on which those who try to destroy it will crack their heads".[49]

But on the rank-and-file level, the sharp divisions between the gradualists and those who want to go the whole hog continue to exist. The latter resent Moscow's softness to the existing régimes at *their* expense; and are lured by Peking's fire-eating bellicosity. Moscow's sway over the Arab Communists is, therefore, not absolute. Peking has made inroads upon it and, in all probability, will continue to do so. Pro-Peking groups already exist in Egypt, Iraq, and the Lebanon. The anti-Nasser plot by Mustafa Agha and his accomplices, uncovered by the Egyptian authorities in 1965, was believed to have been inspired by the Chinese Embassy in Cairo. That it came close on the heels of the voluntary dissolution of the pro-Moscow Communist Party of Egypt was a clear indication of China's disapproval of Communist co-operation with Nasser. In Iraq, the militants of the Kassem era have not completely acquiesced in the pro-Moscow line followed by the newly constituted Central Committee of the Communist Party. The differences between pro-Moscow and pro-Peking Communists in the Lebanon have resulted in the latter forming a rival Communist faction headed by Nasib Nimr, formerly editor of the Communist weekly *Al-Akhbar*. Nimr's faction has started its own weekly organ called *Ila'l Amam*, which also serves as a mouthpiece of Peking.

Retrospect and Prospect

Whereas Russia has been a factor in the politics of the Arab East since the Tsarist times, China entered the stage only recently. In the initial years, the latter benefited from its alliance with the Soviet Union, but through painstaking diplomacy and skilful salesmanship, it was soon able to carve out a place for itself.

In the early years of the Sino-Soviet breakthrough in the Arab

[49] *Pravda*, 27 June 1964. English Translation in US Department of Commerce, *Translations on International Communist Developments* (Washington, D.C.), no. 626, 29 July 1964, pp. 59-64.

East, the two Powers worked in harmonious co-operation. After the Suez War, Moscow tried to use its newly acquired prestige and influence to strike a deal with the West. It offered to neutralize the entire region if the West agreed on its part to liquidate the Baghdad Pact. This move, motivated chiefly by the Soviet Union's security interests and repeated at the time of the Lebanese crisis, was not to the liking of Peking. As the wider ideological differences between Moscow and Peking came out in the open, the Chinese also began to question the validity of the entire Soviet line in regard to the neutralist nations of the Arab East. While the Soviet Union endeavoured to woo them through diplomatic support, delivery of arms, and economic credits, China called for intensification of Arab-Western frictions, exercise of diplomatic and economic pressures on *bourgeois* nationalist rulers, and stimulation of local Communist activities.

But China itself seldom practised what it blatantly preached to the Soviet Union, with the single, if spectacular, exception of the Iraqi incident. The ideological warfare, however, served to throw into bold relief the two Powers' overriding urge to pursue their divergent national interests. But divergence of interests did not rule out borrowing from each other's experience and tactics.

Both the Soviet Union and China have had to reckon with re-surgent nationalism in the area. In the twenties Soviet advance was hindered by a youthful Kemalist Turkey and Reza Shah's Iran. In the fifties, the Soviet Union as well as China came to terms with re-surgent Arab nationalism in order to acquire a foothold in the Arab East. They endorsed Arab neutralism and pledged non-interference in the internal affairs of the Arabs.

Secondly, in their dealings with the indigenous Communists, both the Soviet Union and China have been at their Stalinist best, that is, they have had no compunction in throwing the local Communists to the wolves if it served their national interests. Besides, they could not obviously maintain close relations with the existing régimes and at the same time seek to undermine them through the local Communists. Objective conditions in the region also favoured this approach. The Communist movement there has been uneven and diffused. And even in its strongholds like Syria and Iraq the Communists do not seem to possess a monopoly of political and economic cures, nor the means to apply them, even if they possessed one. In fact, with pragmatists like Nasser having taken the wind out of the Communist sails, the present trends are not at all propitious for the Soviet Union or China to set store by prospective Communist revolutions in the area.

Thirdly, recent experience has shown that Arab Governments have no desire to take sides in the Moscow-Peking controversy. On the other hand, the Soviet Union and China seem to have realized that while some of the Arab nations might be revolutionary in their own way, they certainly do not make good Marxists. What they want from their more powerful friends is cash and credit, not political creed.

Finally, the Chinese practice in the Arab East has not been inhibited by its ideological dogmatism. In their actual dealings with the rulers of the area, Peking has not been less flexible or accommodating than Moscow. This deviation is sanctified by Mao's dictum that the Communists should respect the enemy tactically but detest him strategically. Besides, Mao also admits that practice is the decisive criterion, and in practice almost everything is different from theory.

Notwithstanding this parallelism, the fact remains that China's interests in Arab East are not identical with those of the Soviet Union. Soviet interests stem from its concern for the security of its southern flank. The Chinese drive in the region on the other hand is motivated by its dominant impulse to reduce isolation and achieve Great-Power status. This diversity of interests explains the friction in their policies. If the global estrangement between Moscow and Peking continues unabated, their friction in the Arab East will acquire greater intensity and scope and affect the pattern of power-relationship in the area.

The Soviet Union today wields greater influence than China in the Arab world because of its economic superiority and geographical proximity. None the less, some Arabs are dismayed by the growing signs of a *rapprochement* between the Soviet Union and the United States. For more than a decade they have been leaning on the Soviet Union in their perennial quarrels with the Western Powers and Israel. But now they feel uncertain about the future. Indeed it was Khrushchev's suggestion to Anthony Eden during the former's visit to London in 1956 regarding control of arms supplies to the Middle East that prompted Nasser to recognize the People's Republic of China.[50] More recently, an Egyptian com-

[50] Nasser's interview to Robert Stephens and Patrick Seale on 4 July 1964. See *Observer* (London), 5 July 1964.

mentator observed that the balance of power in the world might now change and that as a result of the Sino-Soviet conflict, the Soviet Union might publicly take the side of the West.[51] Hence the Arabs' anxiety to preserve and promote their contacts with China.

[51] Muhammad Musa in *Al-Akhbar* (Cairo), 4 September 1963.

CHAPTER SIXTEEN

CONCLUSION

THE purpose of this chapter is to summarize briefly the distinctive features of the Communist movements covered in this study and to analyse the character and consequences of their interaction with the local, regional, and international environments.

The areas where Communism has triumphed in its endeavour to seize State power can be broadly divided into two categories: the countries where its advance was largely self-sustained as in the case of Russia, China, Yugoslavia, and North Vietnam; and the countries where it prevailed as a result of direct foreign intervention or assistance as evidenced by Mongolia, North Korea, and the East European countries. Between these two categories lies an intermediate region where Communism has been too weak or inept or else physically detached from the centre of Communist power to attain political supremacy but potent enough to cause social and political radicalization in an appreciable measure. The Arab East belongs to this last category.

One of the cardinal shortcomings of Arab Communism has been its general failure to relate the Marxian doctrine to the specific conditions and requirements of the Arab East. Lenin once spoke of the necessity for a Marxist to "take cognizance of real life, of the true facts of *reality*" and not to "cling to a theory of yesterday, which like all theories, at best only outlines the main and the general, only *comes near* to embracing life in all its complexity".[1] The history of Arab Communism affords little evidence of sustained creative interaction between abstract theory and concrete reality. Much of the theoretical writings of the Arab Communists are either fragmentary or based on changing interpretations of Marxian theory periodically advanced by the international Communist movement. As such, they are mostly couched in slogans and clichés which afford little insight into the inner structure of the Arab society and can only serve as a hazardous basis for any revolutionary action. That no Arab Marxist has yet offered a sustained analysis of the

[1] V. I. Lenin, "Letters on Tactics", *Collected Works* (Moscow, 1964), vol. 24, p. 45. Emphasis in the original.

peculiar complexities of Arab society derived from a mature comprehension of the Marxian doctrine in part explains the erratic course of Arab Communism.

The predominantly middle-class character of Communist leaderships in the Arab East is a commonplace fact which need not be laboured here. It must, nevertheless, be stated that Arab Communism is by no means unique in this respect. It was true, in the past, of the Communist parties of Russia and China; and it fully applies to many a present-day Communist movement elsewhere in Asia. Lenin indeed[2] sought to give ideological sanction to this awkward phenomenon when he argued that the working class by itself was incapable of developing its own ideology which was to be brought to them from the outside by middle-class intellectuals, the so-called "professional revolutionaries". But the anomaly of Arab Communism is that in an essentially agrarian society it has remained an exclusively urban movement. With their clientele drawn largely from the intelligentsia, the modern professional classes, the exuberant student community, and, to a lesser extent, the expanding industrial proletariat, the Arab Communist parties have left the far more numerous and oppressed but acquiescent peasantry practically untouched. Khalid Bakdash's frank admission, while reporting to his central committee in 1951, that the party's efforts had not been "expended in the circles where it should be expended"[3] was not the first or the last instance of Communist autocriticism on this score. But it scarcely, if at all, made any difference to Communist practice.

In the urban Arab East too the Communists have had to contend with serious rivals. The early generation of Arab nationalist leadership virtually bypassed the Bolshevik Revolution. There was indeed no Arab counterpart of Sun Yat-sen to say: "We no longer look to the West. Our faces are turned towards Russia." During the thirties the mushroom growth of Fascist or semi-Fascist organizations relegated Communism to the background. The forties witnessed the tide of Islamic revivalism on the one hand and the rise of the pan-Arab Ba'th Socialism on the other. Whereas the former strove to purge Islamic society of all modernizing influences, the latter claimed

---

[2] V. I. Lenin, "What Is to Be Done?", *Selected Works* (Moscow, 1960), vol. 1, pp. 216 ff.

[3] Text of the report in *Middle East Journal* (Washington, D.C.), vol. 7 (Spring 1953), p. 209.

to provide a nationalist and non-materialistic socialist alternative to Communism. In the fifties, Arab Communism confronted a far more formidable rival in the Egyptian Revolution. By contracting the arms deal with Czechoslovakia and nationalizing the Suez Canal Company, it blasted the Communist argument that the *bourgeois* nationalist specialized only in surrender and compromise. More recently, by undertaking a daring programme of far-reaching socio-economic transformation, the pragmatists of the Egyptian Revolution have demonstrated that doctrinaire Communism, far from having a monopoly of radical solutions to the problems of Arab society, is, in fact, unequal to the challenges it posed. Doubtless, the Egyptian Revolution has not been an unqualified success. But few Communist or non-Communist régimes that attempted to take so much on hand have done much better.

Although Communism failed to become a dominant force even in the urban sector, its appeal to the Arab mind as an innovating model of special relevance to the developing societies can hardly be exaggerated. The driving force behind all modernist movements in the Arab East has been the consuming passion to catch up with the industrialized, powerful, and affluent West. The early modernists looked to Europe, whether consciously or otherwise, as the ideal type to be emulated by the backward East. But Europe's irksome colonial connexion with the Arab East together with its moral and material decline in the course of the thirties and the forties disposed the Arabs to look elsewhere for models of progress and change. It was in this context that the Soviet system which displayed the capacity to construct a highly industrialized and powerful society on the ruins of an outmoded feudal order began to engage the attention of Arab modernists. The Soviet Union's striking victories in the latter part of the Second World War and its subsequent emergence as a major world Power further enhanced the attraction of the Communist model. This development sharpened the effect of local Communist propaganda and secured for the Arab Communist parties a wider support among diverse political groups hitherto allergic to Marxist ideas. It also served to create a climate of opinion in favour of land reform, progressive labour legislation, and social justice. These ideas indeed found ready acceptance among political groups representing a wide spectrum of diverse interests. Nasserism—and to some extent Ba'th Socialism—went much further by drawing extensively on Communist practice though formally rejecting the latter's ideological trappings. This indirect achievement of Communism is a far more significant fact of modern Arab history than the sundry exploits directly attributed to it.

The question whether Islam constitutes a barrier or bridge to Communism in the Arab East has been the subject of much speculation and comment in recent years. It is commonly believed that the cleavage between the value systems of monotheistic Islam and atheistic Communism affords a credible guarantee against the latter's inroads upon the Islamic lands. A more ingenious view, held by some experts, is that far from being a bulwark against Communism traditional Islam may facilitate the transition to it by substituting a Communist party in place of the religious hierarchy or by merely shifting the emphasis from things spiritual to things temporal.[4] The actual Arab experience would, however, suggest that Islam is not a barrier or bridgehead to Communism any more than Orthodox Christianity was in the case of Russia. With the single, if significant, exception of the Muslim Brothers, Islam has seldom offered any sustained resistance to Communism. Nor did Communism always project itself as a godless antithesis of Islam. Indeed the popular image of Communism in the Arab East depicts it more as an ardent champion of social justice and a guarantor of rapid economic progress than as militant atheism.

Likewise, the issue of Communism v. nationalism is more apparent than real in the Arab context. This is not to underrate the significance of occasional confrontations between the two. Indeed the example of the Syrian Communist Party's collaboration with the French during the Second World War and of general Communist support of the partition of Palestine, outraging genuine nationalist sentiment in both cases, underscore the serious potentialities of factors that divide the two creeds. Besides, many a nationalist leader has viewed with distaste the Communist slogan of class struggle on the ground that it impaired national unity. In actual practice, however, the dividing line between nationalism and Communism is often blurred by the simple fact that for many decades both encountered a common foe in the colonial and capitalist West. Nor did the Communist appeal to class interest always fail to evoke responsive chords in nationalist hearts. Indeed, to many Arabs

[4] See Bernard Lewis, "Communism and Islam", *International Affairs* (London), vol. 30 (January 1954); and Nabih Amin Faris, "Islam and the Appeals of Communism", *Middle East Forum* (Beirut), vol. 31 (Summer 1956).

Communism represented an extreme variant of nationalism, not its antithesis. But this brand of nationalism has always been in a minority in the region. More representative of the modern generation of nationalists are the Nasserites and the Ba'thists. And it was to close collaboration with these forces that the Communists largely owed their spectacular successes in Syria and Egypt in the mid-fifties and in Iraq immediately before the July 1958 *coup d'état*. In the current phase, the partnership between Communism and radical nationalism has been revived in Egypt and the entire Fertile Crescent and with no dissimilar results. In the process, however, Communism has had to shed much of its dogmatism and reconcile to a junior position in the new Socialist patterns being evolved in the Arab East. Will Communism be content with this subordinate rôle? Or is it yet another facet of the meandering strategy and tactics of Arab Communism? Previous experience would suggest that whereas prospects, real or imaginary, of an imminent revolution tend to evoke sectarianism and violence among the Communists, the recession of the goal invariably induces a spirit of moderation and compromise. If the Communists change their present course, a showdown between them and the radical nationalists cannot be averted. Such an eventuality would seriously undermine the position of the entire Arab Left and clear the way for the ascendancy of conservative forces. Conversely, if the partnership endures, it may act as a coolant of Communist doctrinarianism and, in turn, permeate the nationalist tradition with the revolutionary ideals and moral fervour of the Marxist creed.

Finally, the relevance of Communist international polycentrism to the Arab situation. The Sino-Soviet discord has doubtless put an end to Moscow's incontestable hold on the Arab Communist parties. A frantic race between Peking and Moscow for winning Communist loyalties in the Arab East is already under way. This, in turn, tends to accentuate the latent differences between the "Rightist" and "Leftist" factions in the Communist parties of the region. These divisions had been there even before the Communists seized power in China. But the Sino-Soviet rift offers them the advantage of alternative rallying points. The Soviet Union and China are no less eager to exploit these factions to the best of their abilities. At present, Moscow has an edge over Peking in this battle for loyalties. This may or may not last long. But if the past is taken as a guide to the future, the outcome of this battle is not likely to have any decisive impact on the Arab East. Moreover, in spite of its present advantage, the Soviet Union does not seek to achieve its goals in the region mainly through local Communist channels. And there is no evidence to suggest that China will not follow the conventional methods of Great Powers, which have potentialities as well as limitations of their own.

POSTSCRIPT

IT IS perhaps too early to assess the full consequences of the June 1967 Arab-Israeli conflict for Arab Communism or for Soviet prestige and influence in the Arab East. But there is no doubt that the crippling defeat of the Arab armies at the hands of the Israelis has a direct bearing on both. Of the three Arab states involved in large-scale hostilities, namely the United Arab Republic, Syria, and Jordan, the first two had leaned heavily on Soviet military, economic, and diplomatic support, and were joined by the third through a defence pact hastily concluded on the eve of the war. Besides, both in Syria and in the UAR local Communist elements enjoyed a measure of respectability which gave them the status of an auxiliary power *élite*. Hence neither the Soviet Union nor the local Communists could evade reproof for the Arab disaster.

For a short while, after the cease-fire, it appeared that the Soviet-backed radical régimes of the UAR and Syria were on the verge of collapse and that Soviet as well as Arab Communist prestige had suffered a severe set-back. But contrary to these early forebodings the Soviet Union rallied back from the initial blow and the Arab Communists discovered new opportunities to improve their prospects in the area.

Arab Communist theoreticians came forward with a twofold explanation of the causes and consequences of the six-day war. First, they argued that the Arab-Israeli conflict belonged to the series of worldwide confrontations between the imperialist and revolutionary forces, that Israel being subservient to the imperialist Powers, the main object of its aggression was to topple the existing progressive régimes of the UAR and Syria and to undermine Arab-Soviet friendship, and that the imperialists eventually failed in achieving their object. In other words, the defeat of Arab arms did not in fact amount to a victory for the imperialists. On a different plane they ascribed Arab defeat to the internal shortcomings of the progressive régimes, in particular to their misplaced reliance on "reactionary officers" and pitiable failure to rally the masses both before and during the battle. Hence "elimination of the consequences of aggression"—a phrase borrowed from Nasser—required radical changes in the structure, policies, and ideologies of the political systems prevailing in "the liberated Arab states". Moscow's massive arms and economic aid to the war-ravaged UAR and Syria in the face of unconcealed American solicitude for Israel lent plausibility to the first thesis; the large-scale arrests and trials of leading Egyptian army and intelligence officers seemingly vindicated the second.

The Communists combined these ideological explanations with marked initiative and drive in handling the new political situation. In the UAR, they played a significant rôle in sustaining the pro-Nasser demonstrations that followed Nasser's resignation speech. The humiliation of the army, which was the chief prop of Nasser's régime until the June war, and the absence of any other organized force to replace it, tempted the Communists to step into the resultant vacuum. An obvious course open to them was to strengthen their position in the Arab Socialist Union, the only political organization in the country. This was facilitated by the appointment of the Left-leaning 'Ali Sabri as its Secretary-General. The Communist-inspired demonstrations by students and workers to protest against the "lenient" sentences meted out to military commanders blamed for the June débâcle forced Nasser's hands to make further concessions to the Left. Nasser's "March 30 Programme" offered to mobilize mass support to protect the revolution and to liberate the occupied areas. This was to be achieved by recasting the Arab Socialist Union as a "socialist vanguard". In Syria, military defeat impelled the ruling Left-wing faction of the Ba'th Socialist Party to accord a wider berth to the Communists than before. While Samir 'Atiya, a party member, retained his place in the cabinet, Khalid Bakdash pleaded for a national front which would facilitate, within the framework of the existing régime, exchange of views on the political situation and joint efforts to realize "tangible national goals". Curiously, the Communist Party of Syria not only insisted on its right to be consulted but assumed the rôle of a moderator of the adventurist slogans and perilous warlike postures of the Ba'thist leadership. Bakdash blamed the Arabs for being swayed by excessive emotion and urged for "a patient and farsighted policy which steers clear of demagogic slogans" that cannot be translated into action. At the same time, the Communist Party commended recourse to political struggle and Arab co-operation as against military confrontation with Israel and continued progressive-conservative discord among the Arabs as the most effective means of regaining lost Arab lands—an approach which fully conforms to current Soviet policy. The Communists in Jordan joined with other Left-wing and militant groups to form the "National Coalition" dedicated to "popular resistance" to Zionism and imperialism "in all its forms". The amnesty granted to the Communists after the six-day war enabled Fu'ad Nassar, the Secretary-General of the Jordanian Communist Party, to return to Amman after ten years of exile in Eastern Europe. In the Lebanon, the Communist alliance with the Ba'thists, the Nasserites, and Kamal Junblat's Progressive Socialist Party under the label of "Front of Progressive Political Parties, Organizations and Independent Personalities", originally formed in 1966, has been further cemented. The Communist Party of Iraq is still under a cloud but has indirectly gained from the growing unpopularity of those in power. All in all, the June conflict did not adversely affect the fortunes of Arab Communism; on the contrary, it afforded new openings for advancement which the Communists have been deftly turning to account.

The outbreak of the Arab-Israeli war apparently caught the Soviet Union unawares. Hence the despair, confusion, and indecision that characterized Moscow's reactions in the early phase of the conflict. Earlier, the Soviet Union had started by giving cautious support to Nasser's moves; but on 24 May 1967 an official Soviet statement proclaimed that "should anyone try to unleash aggression in the Near East, he would be met not only with the united strength of the Arab countries, but also with strong opposition to aggression from the Soviet Union and all peace-loving states". Two days later, the Soviet Ambassador in Moscow sought and obtained an assurance from Nasser that he would not fire the first shot. This background led many Arabs to expect firm Soviet action in the event of an Israeli attack. That such action did not materialize caused much disappointment in the Arab world. Moscow's subsequent endorsement of the Security Council resolution for an unconditional cease-fire turned Arab disappointment into frank indignation. For the first time since 1955 an anti-Soviet demonstration was held outside the Soviet Embassy in Cairo on 10 June 1967; and some leading columnists of the Government-controlled UAR Press sharply taunted Moscow for doing next to nothing "to repel the new tripartite aggression". But the Soviet Union moved expeditiously to retrieve lost ground; and in doing so it was greatly helped by the moral and material incapacitation of the vanquished Arab states. The Moscow conference of seven Socialist states pledged "full and complete solidarity" with the Arabs and offered them "aid in repelling aggression and defending their national independence and territorial integrity". Following this, the Soviet Union broke off diplomatic relations with Israel and dispatched a large consignment of arms and military technicians to rebuild the UAR and Syrian armies. On the international plane, the Soviet Union urged for an emergency session of the General Assembly. While the efforts in the United Nations did not yield any positive results, the massive arms and economic aid to the UAR and Syria forfitied the Soviet position in the Arab East. Besides, there were some side gains with both immediate and long-range implications. The Soviet warships which were rushed to the Mediterranean on the eve of the June war came to stay and have since been reinforced. Moscow still does not possess air or naval bases in the Mediterranean area; but has set up stores and ground installations at Latakia, Alexandria, and Mers al-Kabir. The influx of large numbers of Soviet military technicians into the UAR and Syria is another significant portent. Current estimates of their numbers in the UAR alone range from 1,500 to 7,000. This gives Moscow a rare opportunity to influence the new officer corps now under training in these countries.

All this does not mean that the Communists or the Soviet Union emerged unscathed from the Arab military catastrophe. The discreditable performance of the UAR and Syrian armed forces has not unnaturally emboldened the conservative elements to blame the disaster on the Arab Left. It also clearly upset, if not entirely reversed, the balance of power between the radical-nationalist and the conservative-revivalist forces. For the first time in recent years the radicals were impelled to be on the defensive in their own strongholds and in full retreat elsewhere (e.g. the two Yemens and the Gulf area). The Soviet Union's ineffective rôle during the hostilities caused tremors in the Arab Communist ranks as well. In Syria, the opponents of Bakdash began to press for an early party congress, never held since 1943, and a firm line on Israeli aggression. Major-General 'Afif Bizri, ex-Chief of Staff of the Syrian Army, reappeared on the political scene as a spokesman of national Marxism. The inner party split was even more pronounced in the Lebanon, where George Hawi, 'Abdul Samad, Amin 'Awar.

Khalil Dibs, and their followers openly rebelled against the old guard headed by Niqula Shawi. They argued that the original Soviet endorsement of the partition of Palestine was unprincipled and that Moscow should make amends by withdrawing its recognition of Israel. They held Bakdash and Shawi responsible for the "Stalinist stagnation" of Arab Communism and demanded that "scientific socialism" must grow "on the national soil like the farmer sowing his new seeds in his own land". This marked the second split in the Lebanese Communist Party since Nasib Nimr broke away in 1964. As in the previous case the dissidents derived inspiration from Peking. The Chinese allegations of Moscow's "complicity with the imperialists" and offers of material aid to the Arabs had an even wider impact. Indeed Mao's doctrine of war of liberation found new adherents among students and intellectuals, who were irked by Moscow's counsels for moderation. Even so, China was too remote and lacking in resources to make a serious dent in the Soviet position. This also helped the moderate pro-Moscow Communists to retain the edge over their extremist rivals. Another factor favourable to the Arab Communists and the Soviet Union is the inflexible commitment of the United States to Israel. At the same time, the growing conviction in Arab capitals that Washington, rather than Moscow, holds the key to the present Arab-Israeli deadlock is a pointed reminder that Soviet military and political support has its own definite limitations.

SELECT BIBLIOGRAPHY

ARABIC

Documents and Books

'AMIR ABDULLAH, *Qadaya 'Arabiya* (Beirut, 1959)

'AMIR ABDULLAH, *At-Tariq at-Tarikhi li Wahda al-Ummah* (Beirut, 1959)

'ABD AL-WAHID AHMAD, *Limaza Ayyadana-al Ittihad as-Sawfiti* (Cairo, 1947)

'AHMAD FUAD AHWANI AND OTHERS, *Ash-Shuyu'iya: al-Yawm wa Ghadan* (Cairo, n.d.)

'ABBAS MAHMUD AL-'AQQAD, *La Shuyu'iya wa la Isti'mar* (Cairo, 1957)

S. AYYUB, *Al-Hizb ash-Shuyu 'i fi Suriya wa Lubnan: 1922-1958* (Beirut, n.d.)

'AZIZ AL-HAJ, *Ayna yaqifun? Wa Ayna yaqif al-'Iraq?* (Beirut, 1959)

'AZIZ AL-HAJ, *Al-qawmiya al-'Arabiya wa'd Dimuqratiya* (Beirut, 1959)

KHALID BAKDASH, *Fi Sabil Hurriyat ash-Sha'b al-Wataniya wa'd Dimuqratiya* (n.p. or d.)

KHALID BAKDASH, *Hizb al-'Ummal wa'l Fallahin* (Beirut, 1955)

KHALID BAKDASH, *Tariq al-Istiqlal* (Damascus, 1939)

KHALID BAKDASH, *Tariq al-Istiqlal wa'd Dimuqratiya wa'l Wahda* (Beirut, n.d.)

KHALID BAKDASH, *Al-Hizb ash-Shuyu'i fi'l Nidal li ajli'l Istiqlal wa's Siyada wa'l Wataniya* (Damascus, 1955)

KHALID BAKDASH, *Nidal ash-Shu'ub al-'Arabiya fi Sabili'l Jila' wa'l Istiqlal* (Baghdad, 1959)

KHALID BAKDASH, "Nidal ash-Shu'ub al-'Arabiya", *At-Tariq*, vol. 6, March 1947, pp. 83-105

KHALID BAKDASH, "As-Siyasa al-Britaniya fi'sh Sharq al-'Arabi" *At-Tariq*, vol. 6, January 1947, pp. 27-45

KHALID BAKDASH, *Ba'd Masa'ilina al-Wataniya* (n.p., 1943)

KHALID BAKDASH, *Al-Hizb ash-Shuyu'i fi Suriya wa Lubnan: Siyasatuhu al-Wataniya wa Barnamyuhu* (n.p. or d.)

RASHID BAKTASH, *Ma'arakat al-Qawmiya al-'Arabiya* (Baghdad, 1959)

'ABD AR-RAHMAN AL BAZZAZ, *Safhat min al-Ams al-Qarib* (Beirut, 1960)

'AFIF AL-BIZRI, *Nass al-Bayan Sadara fi Damishq* (n.p. or d.), 14 June 1962

COMMUNIST PARTY OF SYRIA, "Statement on Syria's Secession", *An-Nida* (Beirut), 4 October 1961

COMMUNIST PARTY OF SYRIA AND LEBANON, *Qararat al-Mu'tamar al-Watani: 31 December 1943—2 January 1944* (n.p., 1944)

AL-HAKM DARWAZA, *Ash-Shuyu'iya al-Mahalliya wa Ma'arakat al-'Arab al-Qawmiya* (Beirut, 1963), edn 2

FARJALLAH, *Al-Islah ad-Dakhili wa Matalib ash-Sha'b* (Matabi' al-Kashshaf, n.p., 1944)

NIHAD GHADIRI, *Didd ash-Shuyu'iya* (Cairo, 1959)

GEORGE HANNA, *Ma'na al-Qawmiya al-'Arabiya* (Beirut, 1957)

MUHAMMAD ABUL HASAN (OF AZHAR), *Dawruna fi Kifah al-Watani* (n.p. or d.)

MUHAMMAD HASANAYN HAYKAL, "Communism and Communists in Egypt and the Arab World", *Al-Ahram*, 29 January 1965

"IBN KHALDUN", pseud. "Muhawala fi Fahmin Waqi'iyin l'il Qawmiya al-'Arabiya', *Ath-Thaqafa al-Wataniya*, vol. 6, June 1957, pp. 16-18, 62-65 and July 1957, pp. 9-11 and 62-64

MUHAMMAD JALAL, *Al-Jabha ash-Sha'biya* (Cairo, 1951)

MAHMUD AL-JUNDI, *Al-Tahrifiya al-'Arabiya* (Baghdad, 1959)

RA'IF KHURI, "Al-Jawhar at-Taqaddumi fi'n Nahda al-'Arabiya al-Qadima", *At-Tariq*, vol. 5, December 1946, pp. 3-4

MUNIB AL-MADI AND SULAYMAN MUSA, *Tarikh al-Urdun fi'l Qarn al-'Ishrin* (n.p., 1959)

RAFIQ MA'LUF, *At-Taghalghul ash-Shuyu'i fi'sh Sharq al-Awsat* (Beirut, 1959)

ILYAS MARQAS, *Al-Marksiya fi 'Asrina* (Beirut, 1965)

ILYAS MARQAS, *Tarikh al-Ahzab ash-Shuyu 'iya fi'l Watan al-'Arabi* (Beirut, 1964)

HILAL NAJI, *Al-Qawmiya wa'l Ishtirakiya fi'sh Shi'r ar-Risafi* (Beirut, 1959)

MAHIR NASIM, *Al-Qawmiya al-'Arabiya wa'sh Shu 'ubiya* (Cairo, 1959)

MAHIR NASIM, *Ash-Shuyu'iya ... wa'l Isti 'mar* (Cairo, 1957)

MAHIR NASIM, *An-Nizam ash-Shuyu'i* (Cairo, n.d.)

NASIB NIMR, *Muhtawa al-Qawmiya al-'Arabiya* (Beirut, 1959)

QADRI QAL'AJI, *Tajraba 'Arabi-fi'l Hizb ash-Shuyu'i* (Beirut, n.d.)

ADNAN AR-RAWI, *Min al-Qahira ila Mu'taqal Qasim* (Beirut, 1963)

SALAMA MUSA, *Tarbiya Salama Musa* (Cairo, n.d.)

AMIN SHAKIR AND OTHERS, *Haqiqat ash-Shuyu'iya* (Cairo, 1959)

FATHI SALIM SHARAB, *Ana wa'sh Shuyu'iya* (Beirut, n.d.)

SHUHDI 'ATIYA ASH-SHAFI 'I, *Tatawwur al-Haraka al-Wataniya al-Misriya 1882-1956* (Cairo, 1957)

MUHAMMAD 'ALI ZARQA AND ILYAS MARQAS, *Khiyana Bakdash li'l Qawmiya al-'Arabiya* (Cairo, 1959)

ZIYAD, "Ba'd Wujuh al-Mushkila az-Zira'iya fi Suriya", *At-Tariq*, vol. 8, July 1949, pp. 68-89

Newspapers and Periodicals

Al-Ahali (Baghdad)
Al-Ahram (Cairo)
Al-Akhbar (Beirut)
Al-Ayyam (Damascus)
Ad-Difa' (Jerusalem)
Al-Hadhara (Baghdad)
Al-Hayat (Beirut)
Al-Ittihad (Haifa)
Ittihad ash-Sha'b (Baghdad)
Al-Mabda' (Baghdad)
Al-Misri (Cairo)
An-Nida (Beirut)
An-Nur (Damascus)
As-Sahafa (Beirut)
Sawt al-Ahrar (Baghdad)
At-Tariq (Beirut)
Ath-Thaqafa al-Wataniya (Beirut)

OTHER LANGUAGES

Documents and Books

ROBERT LORING ALLEN, *Soviet Economic Warfare* (Washington, D.C., 1960)

ANWAR ABDEL-MALEK, *Egypte: Société Militaire* (Paris, 1962)

ARAB COMMUNIST PARTIES, "Statement on Arab Unity," *Information Bulletin*, vol. 15 (1964), pp. 797-807

HASAN ARFA, *The Kurds: An Historical and Political Study* (London, 1966)

KHALED BAKDACHE, *La Charte Nationale du Parti Communiste en Syrie et au Liban*, (Beyrouth: Editions "Saout ul-Chaab", n.d.), p. 50

KHALID BAKDASH, "For the Successful Struggle for Peace, National Independence and Democracy We Must Resolutely Turn towards Workers and Peasants", *Middle East Journal*, vol. 7, Spring 1953, pp. 206-221

ZBIGNIEW BRZEZINSKI, ed., *Africa and the Communist World* (Stanford, Calif., 1963)

Communist Party of Egypt, "Program of Action of the Communist Party of Egypt", *Middle East Journal*, vol. 10, Autumn 1956, pp. 427-37

Communist Party of Iraq, "Important Event in the Life of Iraqi Communist Party", *Peace, Freedom and Socialism*, vol. 7, November 1964, pp. 82-85

Communist Party of Iraq, "Text of Statement Issued on the Occasion of the Fourth Anniversary of the 1958 Revolution", *New Age* (Weekly), 24 February 1963

Communist Party of Iraq, "Statement of the Iraqi Communist Party", *Information Bulletin*, vol. 7 (1964), pp. 268-70

Communist Party of Iraq, "Role of Parties in Iraq", *New Age* (Monthly) (New Delhi), vol. 8, July 1959, pp. 12-20

Communist Party of Syria, "Manifesto (Extracts) March", *Orient*, vol. 5 (1961), pp. 207-10

Communist Party of Syria, "Statement", *For a Lasting Peace, For a People's Democracy*, 8 April 1955

Communist Party of Syria, Central Committee, "Resolution on the Arab National Liberation and World Communist Movement", *Information Bulletin*, vol. 21 (1964), pp. 1129-39

Communist Party of Syria, "Platform of the Syrian Communist Party", *World Marxist Review*, vol. 2, February 1959, pp. 61-63

Communist Party of Syria and Lebanon, "On Task of Party Organization", *For a Lasting Peace, For a People's Democracy*, 30 September 1955

ROBERT V. DANIELS, ed., *A Documentary History of Communism* (New York, N.Y., 1960)

Democratic Party of Kurdistan, "Programme and Administrative Regulations", *Middle East Journal*, vol. 15, Autumn 1961, pp. 445-59

DAVID FLOYD, *Mao Against Khrushchev: A Short History of Sino-Soviet Conflict* (London, 1964)

MANFRED HALPERN, "Middle East and North Africa", in Cyril E. Black and

Thomas P. Thornton, eds, *Communism and Revolution: The Strategic Uses of Political Violence* (Princeton, N.J., 1964), pp. 303-329

ALBERT HOURANI, *Arabic Thought in the Liberal Age, 1798-1939* (London, 1962)

J. C. HUREWITZ, *The Struggle for Palestine* (New York, N.Y., 1950)

Information Department, Government of the UAR, *The Charter (Draft)* (Cairo, 1962)

R. K. KARANJIA, *Dawn or Darkness* (Bombay, 1959)

JEAN AND SIMONNE LACOUTURE, *Egypt in Transition* (London, 1958)

WALTER Z. LAQUEUR, *The Soviet Union and the Middle East* (London, 1959)

WALTER Z. LAQUEUR, *Communism and Nationalism in the Middle East* (London, 1957), edn. 2

WALTER Z. LAQUEUR, ed., *The Middle East in Transition* (London, 1958)

V. I. LENIN, *Selected Works* (Moscow, vols 1-2, [1960] vol. 3 [1961])

V. I. LENIN, *The National-Liberation Movements in the East* (Moscow, 1957)

Kurt London, ed., *New Nations in a Divided World* (New York, N.Y., 1963)

Kurt London. ed., *Unity and Contradiction: Major Aspects of Sino-Soviet Relations* (New York, N.Y., 1962)

A. B. MAGIL, *Israel in Crisis* (New York, N.Y., 1950)

M. V. NESTEROV, *Trade Between the Soviet Union and Countries of Asia and Africa* (New Delhi, 1960)

Revolutionary Movement in the Colonies and Semi-Colonies: Thesis Adopted by the Sixth Congress of the Communist International, 1928 (Bombay, 1948)

William Sands, ed., *New Look at the Middle East* (Washington, D.C., 1957)

William Sands, ed., *Tensions in the Middle East* (Washington, D.C., 1956)

DANA ADAMS SCHMIDT, *Journey among Brave Men* (Boston, Mass., 1964)

PATRICK SEALE; *The Struggle for Syria: A Study of Post-War Arab Politics, 1945-1958* (London, 1965)

BENJAMIN SHWADRAN, *The Power Struggle in Iraq* (New York, N.Y., 1960)

IVAR SPECTOR, *The Soviet Union and the Muslim World, 1917-1956* (Washington, D.C., 1956)

JOSEPH V. STALIN, *Problems of Leninism* (Moscow, 1947)

JOSEPH V. STALIN, *Marxism and the National and Colonial Question* (London, 1947)

GORDON H. TORREY, *Syrian Politics and the Military: 1945-1958* (Ohio State University Press, 1964)

United Nations General Assembly, *Official Records*, session 2, supplement 11, vol. 3, annex A, *Oral Evidence Presented at Public Meetings to the United Nations Special Committee on Palestine*

United States Congress, House Committee on Foreign Affairs, *Report on Strategy and Tactics of World Communism, Supplement IV, Five Hundred Leading Communists* (Washington, D.C., 1948)

United States Congress, House Committee on Foreign Affairs, *Strategy and Tactics of World Communism: Report of Sub-Committee No. 5, National and International Movements* (Washington, D.C., 1949)

Articles

W. A. C. ADIE, "The Middle East: Sino-Soviet Discords", *Survey*, no. 42, June 1962, pp. 132-147

SAADI ALI, "Events in Iraqi Kurdistan", *World Marxist Review*, vol. 5, March 1962, pp. 85-86

ROBERT LORING ALLEN, "Report on the Middle East and the Communist World", in William Sands, ed., *Middle East Report 1959*, (Washington, D.C., 1959), pp. 77-87

A. AZIZ ALLOUNI, "The Labour Movement in Syria", *Middle East Journal*, vol. 13, Winter 1959, pp. 64-76

AZIZ AL-HAJJ, "The Agrarian Problem and the National Liberation Movement", *World Marxist Review*, vol. 4, March 1961, pp. 63-65

AZIZ AL-HAJJ, Khalid Bagdash etc., "Problems of the National-Liberation Movement of the Arab Peoples", *Peace, Freedom and Socialism*, vol. 7, July 1964, pp. 74-82, and September 1964, pp. 51-61

KHALID BAGDACHE, "The October Revolution and the Arab East", *For a Lasting Peace, For a People's Democracy*, 20 May 1955

KHALID BAGDACHE, "Two Trends in the Arab National Movement", *World Marxist Review*, vol. 2, November 1959, pp. 26-32

KHALED BAGDASH, "Syria's New Road", *Peace, Freedom and Socialism*, vol. 8, March 1965, pp. 4-10

KHALED BAGDASH, "Some Problems of the National Liberation Movement", *Peace, Freedom and Socialism*, vol. 7, August 1964, pp. 48-56

A. BENNIGSEN, "The 'National Front' in Communist Strategy in the Middle East", in Walter Z. Laqueur, ed., *The Middle East in Transition* (London, 1958), pp. 360-69

LARBI BOUHALI, "The Building of Communism and the Liberation Struggle of the Arab Peoples", *World Marxist Review*, vol. 5, January 1962, pp. 20-25

JOEL CARMICHAEL, "The Nationalist-Communist Symbiosis", *Problems of Communism*, vol. 8, May-June 1959, pp. 35-41

MARTIN EBON, "Communist Tactics in Palestine", *Middle East Journal*, vol. 2, July 1948, pp. 255-69

C. J. EDMONDS, "The Kurds and the Revolution in Iraq", *The Middle East Journal*, vol. 13, Winter 1959, pp. 1-10

ISMAIL EGE, "The Extent and Significance of Soviet Penetration in the Middle East", in William Sands, ed., *New Look at the Middle East* (Washington, D.C., 1957), p. 12

MAHMUD M. AL-HABIB, "The Labour Movement in Iraq", *Middle Eastern Affairs*, vol. 7, April 1956, pp. 137-43

G. AL-HAIDARI, "Communist Movement and the Youth", *World Marxist Review*, vol. 5, February 1962, p. 75

ARNOLD HOTTINGER, "Moscow's Influence in the Arab World", *Swiss Review of World Affairs*, vol. 15, April 1965, pp. 11-12

KING HUSSAIN OF JORDAN, "Exclusive Interview with King Hussain of Jordan: How One Arab Ruler Stopped the Reds", *U. S. News and World Reports* (Washington, D.C.), 5 July 1957

LAMICE HUSSEIN, "South Arabian People's Fight for Freedom", *Peace, Freedom and Socialism*, vol. 7, October 1964, pp. 71-73

G. A. HUTT, "Egyptian Nationalism and the Class Struggle", *Labour Monthly*, vol. 4, April 1923, pp. 286-99

"Iraqi Communists Combat Opportunism", *World Marxist Review*, vol. 3, April 1960, pp. 63-65

K. IVANOV, "The Middle Eastern Situation", *International Affairs* (Moscow), January 1959, pp. 76-81

JABBAR ALI, "The Iraqi Communist Party and the Kurdish Question", *World Marxist Review*, vol. 5, August 1962, pp. 18-24

AMNON KAPELIUK, "The Debate between Khaled Baghdash and President Nasser", *New Outlook* (Tel Aviv), vol. 2, March-April 1959, pp. 24-29

LOTFI EL KHOLI, "Perspectives of Cooperation and Unity of the Progressive Forces in the Arab Countries", *Peace, Freedom and Socialism*, vol. 9, October 1966, pp. 27-29

M. KREWNYOV, "The UAR: Its Progress and Its Problems", *Peace, Freedom and Socialism*, vol. 7, July 1964, pp. 83-91

WALTER Z. LAQUEUR, "The Appeal of Communism in the Middle East", *Middle East Journal*, vol. 9, Winter 1955, pp. 17-27

WALTER Z. LAQUEUR, "Middle East Irreconcilables", *New Republic* (Washington, D.C.), 5 January 1959, pp. 15-17

WALTER Z. LAQUEUR, "The Iraqi Cockpit", *New Leader* (New York N.Y.), 1 February 1960, pp. 7-8

WALTER Z. LAQUEUR, "The 'National Bourgeoisie': A Soviet Dilemma in the Middle East", *International Affairs* (London), vol. 35, July 1959, pp. 324-31

WALTER Z. LAQUEUR, "Nasserism and Communism", *World Today*, vol. 12, October 1956, pp. 390-98

WALTER Z. LAQUEUR, "Communism in North Africa", in S. Hamrell and C. G. Widstrand, eds, *The Soviet Bloc, China and Africa* (Uppasala, 1964), pp. 64-74

WALTER Z. LAQUEUR, "Arab Unity vs. Soviet Expansion", *Problems of Communism*, vol. 8, May-June 1959, pp. 42-48

WALTER Z. LAQUEUR, "Communism in Jordan", *World Today*, vol. 12, March 1956, pp. 109-19

JOSEPH LAWRENCE, "The Levant Chooses 'Socialism' ", *Middle Eastern Affairs* vol. 9, May 1958, pp. 172-78

V. B. LUTSKII, "The Revolution of July 1952 in Egypt", in Walter Z. Laqueur, ed., *The Middle East in Transition* (London, 1958), pp. 496-502

F. MANSOUR, "In Defence of Political Prisoners in Saudi Arabia", *Peace, Freedom and Socialism*, vol. 9, September 1966, p. 48

GEORGE S. MASANNAT, "Sino-Arab Relations", *Asian Survey* (Berkeley, Cali.), vol. 6, April 1966, pp. 216-26

S. MIKUNIS, "Against Israel's Joining an Imperialist Alliance", *For a Lasting Peace, For a People's Democracy*, 27 January 1956

S. MIKUNIS, "The Peoples of Palestine Struggle for National Independence", *For a Lasting Peace, For a People's Democracy*, 15 April 1947

PAOLO MINGANTI, "Political Parties in Lebanon", *New Outlook* (Tel Aviv), vol. 2, September 1959, pp. 13-23

K. MOHEI EL-DIN, "The Course of the Egyptian Revolution and its Future", *Peace, Freedom and Socialism*, vol. 9, August 1956, pp. 19-24

MOUNIR AHMID, "The Situation in Iraq and the Policy of the Communist Party", *Peace, Freedom and Socialism*, vol. 7, December 1964, pp. 34-38

S. NADER, "Lebanon: Paths of Development of Newly Independent Countries", *World Marxist Review*, vol. 5, June 1962, pp. 81-82

NADJI, "The Situation in Iraq and the Position of the Communist Party", *Peace, Freedom and Socialism*, vol. 8, June 1965, pp. 58-59

FU'AD NASSAR, "Anti-Imperialist Struggle of the Arab People", *Peace, Freedom and Socialism*, vol. 6, September 1966, pp. 15-20

FU'AD NASSAR, "On Arab Unity", *Peace, Freedom and Socialism*, vol. 7, February 1964, pp. 16-22

HARRY J. PSOMIADES, "Soviet Russia and the Orthodox Church in the Middle East", *Middle East Journal*, vol. 11, Autumn 1957, pp. 371-81

MAURICE SALIBI, "Syrian Communists in the Fight for Social Progress", *Peace, Freedom and Socialism*, vol. 8, November 1965, pp. 54-56

MOHAMMAD SALIM, "Three Years after the Iraqi Revolution", *World Marxist Review*, vol. 4, October 1961, pp. 35-41

AMIN SALIMOV, "Iraqi Coup: Cause and Effect", *International Affairs* (Moscow) (September 1963), pp. 38-45

SAMI MAHMUD, "Combating the Terror in Iraq", *World Marxist Review*, vol. 4, June 1961, pp. 90-92

A. V. SHERMAN, "Nationalism and Communism in the Arab World: A Reappraisal", in Walter Z. Laqueur, ed., *The Middle East in Transition* (London 1958), pp. 444-61

HANS E. TÜTSCH, "Nasser's Communist Rivals", *Swiss Review of World Affairs* (Zurich), vol. 8 (February 1959), pp. 5-6

HANS E. TÜTSCH, "A Report on Iraq", *Swiss Review of World Affairs*, vol. 10, March 1961, pp. 25-32 and 38-40

L. N. VATOLINA, "The Growth of National Consciousness among the Arab Peoples, 1945-1955", in Walter Z. Laqueur, ed., *The Middle East in Transition* (London, 1958), pp. 487-96

GAVRIEL WARBURG, "Lebanon's Trade Union Federations", *New Outlook*, vol. 7, March-April 1964, pp. 59-70

DONALD S. ZAGORIA, "Sino-Soviet Friction in Underdeveloped Areas", *Problems of Communism*, vol. 10, March-April 1961, pp. 1-13

ROBERT F. ZEIDNER, "Kurdish Nationalism and the New Iraq Government", *Middle Eastern Affairs*, vol. 19, January 1959, pp. 24-31

Newspapers and Periodicals

Daily Star (Beirut)
For a Lasting Peace, For a People's Democracy (Bucharest)
Information Bulletin (Prague)
International Affairs (London)
International Affairs (Moscow)
Iraq Times (Baghdad)
Labour Monthly (London)
L'Orient (Beirut)
Middle East Forum (Beirut)
Middle Eastern Affairs (New York, N.Y.)
Middle East Journal (Washington, D.C.)

Mideast Mirror (Beirut)
Mizan Newsletter (London)
New Age (New Delhi) (Weekly)
New Times (Moscow)
Peace, Freedom and Socialism (Prague)
Peking Review (Peking)
Problems of Communism (Washington, D.C.)
Soviet News (London)
Summary of World Broadcasts (Reading, England)
Survey (London)
World Marxist Review (Prague)
World News and Views (London)
World Today (London)

INDEX

Abasov, B., 84n
Abaza, Fikri, 83
'Abbas, 'Abdul 'Amir, 135n
Abbas Bridge incident, 45
'Abbasi, Muhammad Saleh al-, 144n
'Abd al-Fattah, Ibrahim, 65
'Abd al-Ilah, 133
'Abdi, Major-General Ahmad Salah al-, 122, 126, 131
'Abdullah, Amir, 42, 135n
'Abdullah, Hamza, 69, 147-48
Abi Shahla, Habib, 25
Abi 'Ubayda: See Kawsi
Abu Hajla, 'Abd al-Majid, 73, 74n
Abu Khatir, Midhat, 101
Abukir, 46
Abu Nuwar, Major-General, 'Ali, 153-4
Abu Sha'r, George, 101
Achduh Avodah ("Unity of Work"): See Palestine
Al-Adab (Beirut), 171
Adie, W.A.C., 116n, 212n
'Adil, Salam, 173n
Afghanistan, 198
'Aflaq-Bitar-Razzaz faction, 175
Africa, 200, 204, 207
Agha, Mustafa, 216
Al-Ahali (Baghdad), 119, 122
Ahmad, Ahmad Sulayman al-, 123n
Ahmad Husayn, 32, 47, 162
Ahmad, Ibrahim, 69, 70, 148, 149
Ahmid, Mounir, 192n, 194n
Al-Ahram (Cairo), 86, 94, 100, 122
Ahrar (Liberal) Party: See Iraq
'Ajlani, Munir al-, 87
Al-Akhbar (Beirut), 102, 109, 111, 216
Al-Akhbar (Cairo), 172
Al-'Alam (Damascus), 154
'Alam, Mahmud Amin al-, 80n
'Alamuddin, 25
'Alawis: See Syria
Albania, 209, 212

Alexandretta, 19
Algeria, 145, 157, 164, 193, 194
Allied Middle East Command, 47
Allied Powers, 22-23
Alluni, A. Aziz, 53n
Amara, 68
American War of Independence, 206
Amili, Husayn Ahmad al-, 125n
Amin, Colonel Majid Muhammad, 116, 139
Amin, Muhammad, 99
Amin, Mustafa, 90
'Ammarin, Wadi' Michael, 156
'Ammun, Fu'ad, 106n
Anglo-American Committee (Palestine), 36
Anglo-Egyptian Financial Deal, 100
Anglo-Egyptian Treaty (1936), 8, 32, 47
Anglo-Iraqi Joint Defence Board, 66
Anglo-Iraqi Treaty (1930), 34
Anglo-Jordanian Treaty (1948), 150-52
Anqar, Jabra al-, 74n
Anti-Zionist League: See Iraq
Arab Communism,
  and Arab-Israeli war (1948), 42-3
  and Arab-Israeli war (1967), 227-30
  and Arab nationalism, 157, 161-70, 172-6, 183-4, 223-4
  character and consequences of, 220-5
  and colonialism, 181-2
  and Comintern, 41
  extremist posture, 186-8
  and Fascism, 181
  on future role of working class, 193-4
  ideology, strategy, and tactics, 177-95
  and Islam, 223
  and Nasserism, 50-1, 81-6, 95, 98-100, 103-5, 108, 110, 118-20, 172, 214

and national *bourgeoisie*, 181-2, 184, 186-7, 208
and national democratic state, 194-5
and national fronts, 181-6, 192
and national liberation struggle, 182, 190-1
and neutralism, 167-70, 185, 188
on "new road" to Socialism, 189-91, 193
and partition of Palestine, 40-1, 43
phases of, 177-81
pro-Peking activities, 110, 195
and Sino-Soviet controversy, 213-9, 224-5
and Syro-Egyptian Union, 170-1
Arab East,
and China, 196, 199-210
and Great Powers, 196-9
international significance of, 196
and the Korean crisis, 199
political polarization in, 155-7
and Sino-Soviet discord, 203-19
and Soviet Union, 196-9, 218
Arab Higher Committee, 31, 38; and Communists, 12, 30, 38, 39, 179
Arabia, 197
Arabian Peninsula, 163
Arab-Israeli Conflict, 42-3, 207, 227-31
Arab League, 53, 166, 167
Arab Legion, *See* Jordan
Arab Nationalism, 16, 25, 26, 34, 35, 41, 42, 53n, 84, 141, 147, 216
and Communism, 161-76, 197, 199, 223-4
evolution of, 162-3
influence of Fascism on, 21
Soviet image of, 24
Arab Neutralism, 216; achievement of, 203-4
Arab Socialist Institute: *See* Egypt
Arab Socialist Party, 183
Arab Socialist Union: *See* Egypt, Iraq
Arab Solidarity Agreement, 152-3
Arfa, Hasan, 69n, 147n
'Arif, 'Abd as-Salam, 116-8, 121n, 128, 144-6
'Aris, Mustafa al-, 19, 53
Armenians, 15, 54, 165

Arshidat, Nabih, 74n
'Asali, Sabri al-, 60, 62
Ashhab, 'Awdat al-, 41
Asia, 200, 204, 207, 220
Asian-African, 51, 57, 111, 189, 212
Assyrians: *See* Syria
Aswan Dam, 210, 211
Atasi, 'Adnan al-, 87
Atasi, Faydi al-, 87
Atasi, Hashim al-, 17
'Atiya, Samir, 228
Atrash, Amir Hasan, al-, 87
Avakov, R.M., 85n
'Awadatallah, Tu'mih al-, 94
'Awar, Amin, 230
'Awn Allah, Salih, 74n
'Awni, Yusuf, 138
Awqati, Air Commodore Jalal al-, 139n
Axis Powers, 22, 24, 33, 35
'Ays, Muhammad Husayn 'Abd al-, 135n, 143
Azerbaijan, 68
'Aziz al-Haj, 85n, 119, 121, 141, 146, 171, 174n
'Azm, Khalid al-, 54, 58, 60, 88, 90, 95, 186

BADR, MUHAMMAD, 210
Badrossian, Krikor, 33
Baghdad Pact, 43, 57, 58, 62, 73n, 114, 121, 183, 198-200, 207, 216; withdrawal of Iraq from, 122; and Jordan, 74
Bahr al-'Ulum, Muhammad Salih, 67n
Bakdash, Khalid, 16-9, 22-8, 52-4, 85, 87, 97, 99, 100-1, 103-5, 122, 141, 164, 166-73, 174n, 181-2, 184n, 186-8, 192-3, 208, 214-6, 228, 230
Bakr, Ibrahim, 74n
Bakri, Ahmad al-, 49
Baku, 198; Baku Congress, 177, 197
Ba'lbak, 55
Balfour Declaration, 9, 12
Bandung, 200; Conference, 51; declarations, 80
Bani, Wasfi al-, 49n, 55n, 99, 102
Banna, Hasan al-, 32

Baquri, Shaykh Hasan al-, 200
Barazani, Mulla Mustufa, 69, 117, 147-9
Barazanis, 68, 69n
Basim, Zaki, 33, 66, 67
Ba'th Socialists, 56-61, 68, 73, 84, 87, 92, 94, 104-5, 110, 114-5, 122, 128-30, 133, 142-4, 146, 150-7, 174-5, 183, 187, 191, 215, 221-2, 224; and Communists, 128-9, 142-4, 146, 174, 186, 222
Bayya, 'Abdullah Sulayman al-, 156
Bazzaz, 'Abd ar-Rahman al-, 64n, 118n
Ben Bella, 174
Berger, Joseph, 14
Bindari Pasha, Muhammad Kamil, 46
Bizri, 'Afif, al-, 88, 94, 97, 122, 230
Bizri, Salah al-, 94
Blum, Léon, 17, 19
Bolshevik Revolution, 3, 4, 12, 14, 34, 161, 162, 177
Bolshevism, 147, 221
Brazil, 53n
Bukhari, Muhammad al-, 102n
Bulganin, N. A., 81, 92, 107
Bulgaria, 171, 203
Burma, 194
Bustani, 'Abd al-Qadir Isma'il al-, 139, 141, 143
Butrus, 55n

CAIRO-DAMASCUS-RIYADH AXIS, 152
Catroux, General, 22-3
Chadirchi, Kamil al-, 20, 65, 66
Chalabi, Dr Ahmad al-, 125n
Charter (1962): See Egypt
China, Kuomintang, 6-7, 199, 200
China, People's Republic of, 80, 97, 153, 220
  and Arab Communists, 110, 144, 201n, 204-10, 212-3, 215-8
  and Arab East, 198-203, 206, 207, 216-9
  and Arab-Israeli conflict, 207-8, 231
  and Arab neutralists, 204
  Communist Party, 200
  and Egypt, 81, 199, 200, 216

  and Eisenhower Doctrine, 202
  and Iraq, 98, 206, 207
  and Jordan, 153, 201n
  and Kuwait, 201
  and Lebanon, 199, 203, 204, 206, 207
  and Saudi Arabia, 199, 200, 201n
  Sino-Soviet rift, 204-8, 212-3, 216-7, 224-5
  and Syria, 199, 200, 215, 217
  trade with Arabs, 213
  and USSR, 202-8, 212-3, 216-7
  and Yemen, 200, 201, 213
Chinese Muslims, 200, 201
Chou En-lai, 200; visit to Cairo, 210
Churchill, Winston, S., 30
Citadelle: See Egypt (Communists)
Coghill, Colonel Sir Patrick, 75
Cold War, 182-3, 203
Cominform, 183
Comintern, 7, 21, 35, 37, 179-80
  dissolved, 24, 26
  and Egyptian Communist Party, 4, 7, 8
  Seventh Congress, 181
  Sixth Congress, 177
  thesis on national bourgeoisie, 16; and Zionism, 11, 41
Comité Francais de la Libération Nationale, 28
Communist Manifesto, first Arabic translation, 17
Curiel, Henry, 32, 45, 47-8
Czechoslovakia, 222; arms deal with Egypt, 51, 62, 183; and Syria, 89

DAJNANI, MUSA, 41
Dalal, Sason, 66
Da'ud, Karim Ahmad ad-, 135n
Dawalibi, Ma'ruf ad-, 58
Dayrani, Ilyan, 101, 102
de Gaulle, Charles, 23, 203
Delbos, Yvon, 17
Demchenko, P., 143
Democratic Bloc: See Syria
Dentz, General, 22
Dibs, Khalil, 230
Dinshwai Tragedy, 99

Druze, 179
Dulaymi, Dr Nasiha, 67n, 128, 138

EASTERN EUROPE, 9, 91,220; treatment of Jews in, 11
Eden, Anthony, 166, 218
Egypt, 55, 86, 89, 95, 97, 103, 155, 164, 166-7, 170-1, 175, 184, 186-7, 193-4, 197-8, 207-8, 210, 216, 224, 227-8, 230
    Abu Z'abal camp, 79; and Arab-Israeli war (1967), 227-30
    Arab Socialist Institute, 86
    Arab Socialist Union, 175, 228
    and Arab Solidarity Agreement, 152
    and Britain, 8, 32, 44, 46, 47, 49, 50, 62, 100n
    Canal Zone Question, 44-7, 49-51
    Charter (1962), 84-96, 190, 193
    and China, 80, 81, 199, 200
    Confederation of Trade Unions, 5-6
    Congress of Workers Union, 44
    Constitution, 80
    coup d'état, 47
    Czech arms deal, 51, 62, 79
    Dinshwai tragedy, 49
    Faruq, King, 32, 45, 46, 49
    First Army, 97
    Free Officers, 48
    IBRD loans to, 100; and India, 200
    and Iraq, Co-ordination Agreement with, 145
    and Jordan, 73n, 150; July Laws, 84, 85
    League of Egyptian Industries, 8
    Marxist Study groups, 32
    Misr Bank, 8, 100
    Muslim Brothers, 32, 46, 47, 51
    Nile Valley, 44, 45
    non-alignment, 51
    and Palestine war, 46
    Press and radio, 120, 128-9, 150, 172; Revolution, 191, 222
    Revolutionary Command Council (RCC), 49-51, 81
    Socialist economy in, 189-91, 193
    Socialist Party of, 3-4, 32, 47, 182
    and Soviet bloc, 51, 79, 81

Suez Canal nationalization, 80
Suez War, 80-2
    and Syria, 79, 82, 84, 92, 93, 95-6, 103
    At-Tali'a, 17, 32, 86
    and tripartite attack on, 80
    and visits of Chou En-lai, Khrushchev, 210-11
    Wafd Party, 4-8, 32, 33, 45-7, 49, 51-2, 52-8, 80, 179
    and USSR, 79, 81-5, 92, 198, 201, 211-2; and US, 89
    Watani Party, 46
    and West Germany, 100
Egypt, Communist Party of, Communists in, 3, 50n, 51, 55, 80, 172, 222, 227
    activities, 33, 45-8, 51
    On agrarian revolution, 180
    and Arab League, 166; and ASU, 86, 193
    and Arab Unity, 166, 168-70
    character of, 47, 165
    and Charter, July Laws, 84
    Citadelle, 32
    and Comintern, 40
    and Constitution (1956), 80
    and Czech arms deal, 79, 80
    disbanding of party, 86
    factionalism in, 49, 81, 216; Al-Fajr al-Jadid, 32
    and Faruq rule, 48
    gains, 80, 81, 84-6, 185-6
    and Government, 45, 81-2, 86, 187
    influence, 33, 45-6
    initial phase, 179
    and Iraqi Communists, 81
    Iskra, 32, 42n, 44-5
    Kafr Dawr incident, 49-50; Manifesto (1921), 4
    and Moscow-Peking controversy, 215
    and Mosul Revolt, 82
    Mouvement Democratique du Libération Nationale (MDLN), 42, 45-7, 80, 81
    Mouvement Egyptien de Libération

Nationale (MELN), 32, 33, 42n, 44-5, 182
and Muslim Brothers, 46-8, 50, 182
on Naguib, 50
and Nahas, 32, 45-6
and Nasser, 50, 82-3
on national *bourgeoisie*, 186
National Committee for the Defence of Peace, 46
National Committee of Workers and Students, 44
on national front, 193-4
National Peace Council, 86n
and Power blocs, 194
Programme, 4-5, 180, 191
Pro-Peking group in, 216
and RCC, 49-50
rebirth of, 31
and Socialist Party, 47, 182
and Suez Canal nationalization, 80
Tahrir ash-Sha'b, 32
and tripartite attack, 80-1
and Wafd, 5-8, 33, 44-5, 47, 179
Eisenhower, Dwight D., 91, 107, 203
Eisenhower Doctrine, 122, 153-4, 156, 202

FABIANISM, 20
Fahd: *See* Yusuf Salman Yusuf
Al-Fajr al-Jadid (New Dawn), 32
Fakhuri, 'Umar, 17, 25
Falahi, Sadiq al-, 132
Fara, Munir, 101
Faranjiya, Hamid, 106n
Far'un, Henri, 106n
Faruq, King, 32, 45, 46, 49, 50
Faruqi, Sulayaman Haj, 72
Fascism, 13, 17-8, 21, 28-30, 32, 35, 47, 50, 53, 64, 181
Fertile Crescent, 53n, 87, 163, 164, 166, 182, 198, 224
France, 15, 17-9, 22, 23, 27, 28, 35, 52-6, 81, 107, 163-4, 167, 196, 202
Franco-Syrian Treaty, 17-9
François Sagan, 97
Free Officers' Movement: *See* Egypt and Jordan
French Revolution, 177

GAYLANI, RASHID 'ALI AL-, 35, 64, 121n, 128; *coup d'état,* 113
Gaza, 31
Germany, 12, 13, 21-3, 30, 32, 35, 36, 181-2, 196
Ghabban, Muhammad, 139
Al-Ghad, 37
Ghana, 194
Ghanimah, Subhi Abu, 71
Ghufri, Nasuh al-, 99
Glubb Pasha, Sir John Bagot, 74, 75n, 152
Goldobin, A. M., 50n, 51n
"Greater Syria", 53, 55, 166
Great Wall of China, 210
Greek Orthodox, 17n
Gromyko, A., 39, 40, 42
Guatemala, 91n

HABBANIYA AIR BASE: *See* Iraq
Hablb, K., 47n, 48n
Habibi, Emile, 41
Haddad, Jamil, 174n
HADETU: See MDLN under Egypt (Communist Party)
Al-Hadhara (Baghdad), 139
Hadi, 'Awin Bey 'Abd al-, 12n
Hadid, Muhammad, 20, 115n
Hafiz, Lieutenant-General Amin al-, 104
Hakim, Mahmud, 101
Hakim, Muhammad al-, 99
Hakim, Muhsin al-, 139
Hamadun, Captain Mustafa, 94
Hamarneh, Juris, 74n
Hamud, Ahmad al-, 74n
Hamudah, Yahya, 74n, 123n
Hanna, George, 123n, 185
Haqiqat group (Iraq), 66
Harrison, Earl, 36
Hasan, Na'if al-, 125n
Hasani, Shaykh Taj ad-Din al-, 22
Hashim, Ibrahim, 75, 154
Hashimi, Butrus, 14
Hashomer Hatzair: See Palestine
Al-Hawadith, 208
Hawi, George, 230
Hawrani, Akram al-, 60, 87, 183

Haydari, Jamal al-, 144n
Haykal, Muhammad Hasanayan, 85, 94, 96n, 97n; on release of Egyptian Communists, 85; on Michael Wright, 116; on two kinds of "Left", 189-90
Henderson, Loy W., 91, 92
Hilal, Fida ("Um Sulayman"), 102
Hilu, Charles, 106n
Hilu, Farjallah, 17, 19, 22, 25-6, 28-9, 102, 108
Hilu, Ridwan, 71
Hindiyya, 129
Hinnawi, Sami, 54-55
Histadrut: See Palestine
Hitler, Adolf, 12, 13, 21, 29, 32, 36, 53
Hiwa (Hope) Party: See Iraq
Hizb al-Ittihad ash-Sha'b: See Iraq
Hizb ash-Sha'b: See Syria
Hizb ash-Sha'b al-Lubnani, 14, 15
Hizb al-Watani: See Syria
Hukstep, 46
Hulagu, 130
Hungary, 202
Hungarian Party Congress, 103, 173
Husayn (King of Jordan): See Jordan
Husayn, Karim, 144n
Husayn, Yunus, 156
Husayni, Ahmad ar-Rifa'i al-, 102n
Husayni, Amin al- (Mufti of Jerusalem), 10, 12
Husayni, Hamdi al-, 12
Husayni, Colonel Ibrahim, 91
Hutton, Brigadier William, 75
Huzayyin, Yusuf, 105

IBN SA'UD, 197
Ibrahim, 'Abd al-Fatah, 20, 137n
Ibrahim, Habib A., 55
IBRD, 100
'Id al-adha, 126
Ila'l Amam (Beirut), 111
Ilyan, Mika'il, 87
'Inani, Muhammed 'Abdullah al-, 3
India, 7, 20, 80n; and Egypt, 200
Indian Ocean, 201
Indonesia, 80n
Iran, 68, 91n, 197, 216

Kurds in, 68
Kurdish Democratic Party, 69
and Turkey, 69
and US, 90
and USSR, 198
Iraq, 47, 55, 82-4, 98, 99, 123, 137, 143, 164, 166-7, 173, 188, 208
Ahrar (Liberal) Party, 65n
Arab Socialist Union, 146
pan-Arabists, 34, 35, 141, 147
Armenians, 123
Assyrians, 123
Baghdad Pact, 199
Ba'thists, 68, 114-5, 118, 122, 128-9, 130n, 133, 142, 142-4, 146, 174, 187
Ba'thist National Guards, 188
and Britain, 66, 67, 113, 123; and China, 199, 201
"Committee for the Defence of the Republic", 131
Committee for the Protection of Republic, 121
Coup d'état (1958), 113, 115, 186, 206
Coup d'état (February 1963), 142-3
Coup d'état (November 1963), 144
Date Association, 128n
Development Board, 114
and Egypt, 118, 145
and Eisenhower Doctrine, 122
Electoral Law, 67, 68
External Policy, 113-4
General Federation of Peasants Associations, 125
General Federation of Trade Unions, 132
General Students' Union, 123, 129, 133, 139
Hiwa (Hope) Party in, 69
Istiqlal Party, 68, 114-5, 118, 122, 130n, 183, 187
and Jordan, 73n
Journalists' Union, 132
Kirkuk incident, 65, 84, 120, 129, 131, 133, 140, 142, 187
Kurdish Democratic Party (KDP), 69, 70, 117, 130n, 147-9
Kurds, 68-9, 141, 148, 165

Land Reform Law, 119
Land Settlement Law, 113
Law of Association and Parties, 134-5
Lawyers' Union, 132
League for the Defence of Women's Rights, 128
"League of Peasants", 121
Leftists in, 65, 66
Mosul Revolt, 82, 120, 121, 123, 147, 173
Nasserites, 129n, 132-3, 142, 157
National Congress, 67n
National Council of the Iraqi Revolution, 143
National Democratic Party (NDP), 19-20, 34, 64, 66-8, 114-5, 119, 122, 124-6, 130n, 136, 141, 183, 187
National Guards, 143-4
National Oil Company Law, 145
National Union (*Ittihad al-Watani*), 65
Oil industry, 113, 118
Partisans of Peace, 67, 120, 123-4, 126, 138
Party of People's Unity, 135
Peasants' Association, 138
People's Court, 116-7, 121n, 123, 139
"People's Defence Committees", 121
People's (*Sha'b*) Party, 65, 66
People's Resistance Force (PRF), 117, 120, 121-2, 126, 131, 144, 209
political parties, 64, 68, 114, 124, 127, 133-4
political system, 19, 113
Press, 65, 139
Progressive KDP, 69; Republic Party, 137
Republican Law, 117
Rightists, 131-3
Shi'is, 141
"Soldiers' Committees", 121
Sovereignty Council, 115
Teachers' Union, 128
Tobacco Workers' Union, 139
Tripartite Unity Charter, 143

Turkoman Liberation Party, 128
Turkomans, 209
United National Front (UNF), 68, 114-5, 124-5, 127, 130, 187
and US, 90
and USSR, 148, 201, 207, 211, 215, 217
"Vigilance Squads", 121
Women's League, 139
Iraq, Communist Party of, 19, 33-5, 41, 42, 64-7, 69, 104, 115, 119-21, 124, 127, 132-3, 135, 139, 145-6, 165, 229
and Albania, 209
and Arab nationalism, 131-2, 147, 208, 209
and 'Arif, 118, 144-5
and Army, 115-6
and Baghdad Pact, 123
and Ba'th, 115, 128-9, 142-4, 208-9
and Britain, 35, 66, 114
and Cairo-Baghdad tussle, 118, 145
Charter, 33-4
and China, 145-6, 205, 209
and Congress of Partisans of Peace, 120, 123-4
and *coup d'état* (1958), 113, 117, 201, 207; *coup d'état* (November 1963), 144-5
demands, 121-5
and Egyptian Communists, 81
and Electoral Law, 67
extremist posture, 187
factionalism, 33, 66, 134-8, 216
failures, 140-2
front organizations, 121, 123, 125, 128, 129, 131-3, 135, 138-9
gains, 115, 140-2
and Gaylani's *coup d'état*, 35
and government, 115-6, 127-8, 136-7
influence, 35, 66, 119, 139-40
and Istiqlal, 115, 183
and KDP, 117, 147-8
and Kassem, 115, 116, 118, 120-2, 126-7, 130-40, 142, 205, 214
supports Kassem against Nasser, 120-1
Khayri group, 134-8

and Khrushchev-Nasser exchanges, 120
and Kirkuk incident, 128, 129, 131, 133, 205
and Kurds, 117, 141, 165
and Land Reform Law, 119
and Mosul Revolt, 120
and NDP, 34, 122, 124-6, 136, 183
and Nasserism, 85, 120-1, 157, 208-9
on national bourgeoisie, 187
on national front, 194
on neutralism, 119
and Palestine partition, 41, 42
pro-Peking group, 216
and People's court, 116-7, 139
PRF, 116-7, 120-2, 126, 131, 144, 209
policy, 145-6, 209-10
political claims, 117
on Portsmouth Treaty, 66
present position of, 149
programme, 208
re-organization, 33
and Rightists, 131-2; Sayigh group, 134-6, 138
supports Republic, 127
secret meeting, 144
self-criticism, 130-1
and Shi'is, 141
and Sino-Soviet rift, 145, 215
and Soviet line, 145-6, 214
splits, 131, 134-6, 146
Taharrur al-Watani, 65
Turkoman Liberation Party, 128
underground activity, 140
United National Front (UNF), 68, 70, 114, 125, 127, 130n, 194
Iraqi-Albanian Society, 209
Iraqi Communist Brotherhood, 134n
Iraqi Communist League, 33
Iraqi Development Board, 114
Iraqi-Jordanian Federation, 171
Iraqi Kurdistan, 149
Iraqi National Front, 185
'Isa, Rashad, 102
'Isha, Hasan Abu, 41
Iskra: See Egypt (Communist Party)
Islam, 52; and Communism, 223
Islamic revivalism, 221-22

Isma'il, 'Abdul Qadir, 20, 135n
Isma'ilia, 47
Israel, 71, 81, 94, 107, 218
and Arab Communists, 40-1; Arab-Israeli war (1967), 227-31
creation of, 36, 42, 167
and Jewish Communists, 40
and US, 36
and USSR, 36, 42, 43
Israel, Communist Party, 41
Istiqlal Party: See Iraq, Palestine, and Transjordan
Italy, 15, 30, 48, 164-5, 196
Al-Ittihad, 30
Ittihad ash-Sha'b (Baghdad), 115, 121-2, 124
Ivanov, K., 170-1
'Izza, Nimr Hasan al-, 74n
Al-Jabha ash-Sha'biya, 47n
Al-Jabha al-Wataniya: See Jordan (Communist Party)

Jabir, Mahmud, 156
Jabr, Salih, 66
Jabrah, Ratib, 101
Jadid, Ghassan, 61
Jalal, Muhammad, 47n
Jamali, 'Abdul Baqi, 82n, 101, 102
Jamali, Fadhil al-, 64n
Jamali, Samih al-, 99
Jami'at al-'Ummal al-'Arabiya al Falistiniya: See Palestine (Communist Party)
Jamil, Dr Khalil, 67n
Jamil Mardam Bey, 17
Jassim, Kazim al-, 135n
Jawad, Dr Khalil Jamil al-, 135n
Jawahiri, Muhammad Mahdi al-, 67n, 132, 137n
Jesus, 14
Jews in Palestine, 9-13, 29, 31, 32, 36-42
Jewish Agency, 38
Jewish National Home, 9
Johnson, Paul, 90
Jordan, 40, 42, 55, 71, 122-3, 185, 227, 229
Abdullah (King), 71, 72

annexation of West Bank, 71
Arab Legion, 74, 75
Army Intelligence Department, 75
and Baghdad Pact, 74
Ba'thists, 73, 150-1, 154-7; Bedouin army, 152, 154
and Britain, 72, 73, 75
and China, 201n, 153
and Egypt, 150
elections, 72, 73, 151
"Free Officers", 153
and "Greater Syria", 166
Husayn (King), 71, 74, 75, 150-2, 154, 157
Istiqlal Party, 71
martial law, 154
Nabulsi Cabinet, 151-3, 155; "National Coalition", 229
National Socialist Party, 73, 150-1, 154-6
rôle of Palestinians, 71, 158
Parliament, 72, 74, 154
political parties, 154
trade unions, 154
and US, 154
and USSR, 153, 157
Jordan, Communist Party (League of National Liberation)
Arab Students' Congress, 154
balance sheet, 155
and Ba'th, 73, 156-7; Committee on National Guidance, 154
and elections, 73, 151
and front tactics, 150-1
growth of, 71
Al-Jabha, 74
against military alliance, 74, 75, 150
and Nabulsi Cabinet, 151
and Nasserism, 85
National Bloc, 72, 73
National Front, 74, 183, 187, 194, 215
new line, 157-8
Partisans of Peace, 72
People's Resistance, 72
prospects, 158
repression, 73, 156
shift in tactics, 72

and Zionism, 72
Jordan River, 71
Jumard, 'Abd al-Jabbar, 116n
Al-Jumhuriya (Cairo), 93, 210
Junblat, Kamal, 56, 106, 229

KAFR DAWR, 49, 50
Kamil, Sa'd, 46
Karim, 'Ali 'Abdul, 123n
Kassem, 'Abd al-Karim, 82, 83, 104, 147, 165
and Ba'th, 133
and China, 201
and Communists, 115-42, 205, 209, 214
execution of, 143
and Nasser, 116, 120-3, 132-3
and restoration of political parties, 128, 134-5
Al-Katib, 50
Kawsi, 'Abd as-Sattar, 146
Kayid, Turki al-, 74n
Kayyali, Hasib, 101
Kazamayn, 143
Kerensky, 8
Khalid Muhi ad-Din, 49, 50, 51n, 81, 82, 86, 101, 191
Khalis, Dr Salah, 125n
Khamis, Mustafa, 49
Khayma, Shubra al-, 33
Khayr, Muhammad, 123n
Khayri, Zaki, 33, 66, 135, 141, 146
Khrushchev, N. S., 85, 92, 93, 107, 108, 116, 203, 204n, 210, 218
on Arab unity, 172-3, 210n
and China, 203
and Iraqi Communists, 120
and Nasser, 83, 120
"Khrushchev Doctrine", 95
Khuli, Lutfi al-, 86, 192, 175, 194n
Khuri, Bishara, al-, 28, 54
Khuri, Faris al-, 60, 62
Khuri, Ra'if, 52n, 102
Kirkuk, 35, 65, 120, 128-9, 131, 140, 142, 149, 187
Kohri, Ilyas Hanna, 135n
Kol Haam ("Voice of the People"), 29, 30

Korean crisis, 199-200
Kotov, Vice-Admiral V. F., 92
Kubba, Ibrahim, 115, 118, 138, 144
Kubba, Mahdi, 115n
Kubra, Mahalla al-, 33
Kuomintang, 7, 199
Kurdish Democratic Party: See Iran and Iraq
Kurds: See Iran, Iraq, Soviet Armenia, Syria, and Turkey
Kutla al-Wataniya ("National Bloc"), 72, 73
Kuwait, 122, 201
Kuzbari, Mamun al-, 103

LACOUTURE, JEAN AND SIMONNE, 31, 49
Laqueur, Walter Z., 12, 31
Laski, Harold, 20
Latin America, 204, 207
Law, John, 154
League of National Liberation (LNL): See Jordan (Communist Party)
Lebanese Syndicate of Labour Unions, 53
Lebanon, 14, 15, 18, 24, 25, 54, 87, 94, 99, 106, 122-3, 165-6, 203; crisis (1958), 106
  and Eisenhower Doctrine, 106
  and France, 17, 22, 23, 27
  Front of Progressive Political Parties, Organizations, and Independent Personalities, 229
  Maronites, 26
  and USSR, 29, 107-8, 198
  United National Front, 106
Lebanon, Communist Party (See also Communist Party of Syria and Lebanon), and Arab nationalism, 26, 52, 53, 108, 168-9, 229-30
  and Armenian emigration, 54; and Ba'thists, 229
  separation from CPSL, 25-7
  and crisis of 1958, 106
  and elections, 109
  and France, 28
  membership, 29, 182
  and Nasserism, 85, 109, 229
  and Palestine, 42, 54

Partisans of Peace, 53-5
Party organs, 109
  and PPS, 110
  Programme, 26, 56, 182
  and Progressive Socialist Party, 56
  sectarianism, 57
  self-criticism, 56
  and Sham'un, 107, 108
  and Sino-Soviet rift, 109-12, 215-6, 231
  suppression, 54, 109
  tribune of Arab Communism, 106
  united front, 56, 57
  United National Front, 106, 107
  and Western Powers, 53, 55, 107
Lenin, V. I., 14, 204, 220
  on Colonial East, 180
  on middle class leadership, 221
  on national liberation, 177
Levant, 3, 23
Lodge, Henry Cabot, 93
Lumumba, Patrice, 108

MABDA', AL-, 134, 136
Macmillan, H., 203
Madnat, 'Isa, 158
Madoyan, Artin, 15, 17, 102
Mahabad Republic, 68
Mahdawi, Colonel Fadhil 'Abbas al-, 116, 122-3, 139, 143
Mahfil, Ahmad, 99
Mahmud, Ibrahim Yusuf, 156
Mahmud, Majid, 139
Mahmud, Sami, 141n
Mahmud al-'Abd Khayr ad-Din, 74n
Majali, Hazza', 74, 75
Majdalani, Nasim, 106n
Malik, Anwar 'Abd al-, 48n, 79n, 86, 191
Maliki, 'Adnan al-, 60-1
Mallory, Lester D., 154
Mandates, 163-4
Mongolia, 220
Mao Tse-tung, 203, 205, 211, 231
Maqsud, Clovis, 185n
Maroni, 'Adnan, 101
Maronite Christians, 26
Marqa, Fakhri, 74n

Marun, Antun, 5-6
Marxism, 5, 14, 20, 23, 37, 47, 181, 190, 220, 224
Marxism-Leninism, 14, 36, 37, 194
Al-Masa' (Cairo), 82
Mas'ad, Mayar, 25
Mashta, 'Allama Shaykh 'Abd al-Karim al-, 67n
Mas'ud, 'Abdullah, 33
Maswadi, Rashad, 74
Matran, Nakhla, 123n
Ma'ushi, Paul, 106
Mawsali, Bishar al-, 99
May Day, 97
Mediterranean, 19, 91, 197
Menderes, Adnan, 92
Middle East: See Arab East
Midfa'i, Jamil, 64n
Mifleget Poalim Sozialistim Ivrin (Jewish Socialist Workers' Party): See Palestine (Communist Party)
Mikoyan, Anastas, 212
Mikunis, Samuel, 30, 38, 40
Milhim, Qasim, 71
Misr al-Fatat ("Young Egypt"), 32, 47n
Molotov, V. M., 21, 62, 198
Mopsi: See Palestine (Communist Party)
Morocco, 6
Moscow, 11, 22, 46, 51-2, 62, 78, 81, 92, 93, 95-7, 103, 104, 111, 170, 173, 185; Conference of Communist Parties, 185, 189
Mosul Revolt: See Iraq
Mount Lebanon, 25
Mouvement Democratique du Libération Nationale (MDLN): See Egypt (Communist Party)
Mouvement Egyptien de Libération Nationale (MELN): See Egypt (Communist Party)
Mufti of Ba'lbak and Buqa', 55
Muhammad, 14
Muhammad, Tawfiq Ahmad, 135n
Mulhami, 'Abdul Hakim, 101
Munir, Tawfiq, 67n
Al-Muqawima ash-Sha'biya (People's Resistance): See Jordan (Communist Party)
Muruwwah, Husayn, 123n
"Musa", 12, 30
Musa, Muhammad, 219n
Musa, Mustafa, 44
Musa, Salama, 3, 4n, 80, 81n
Al-Musawwar (Cairo), 83
Muslim Brothers, 52, 53, 64, 223: See also Egypt
Mustafa, Anwar, 174n
Mu'tamar Mukafihat al-Fasistiya (Anti-Fascist League), 18
Mu'tamar al-'Ummal al-'Arab (Arab Workers' Congress): See Palestine.
Mutlaq, Mahmud, 73

NABULSI, SULAYMAN, 72, 73, 151, 155
Naccache, Alfred, 22
Nadir, Sami, 33
Nadji, 144n, 146n
Nafih, Amal, 158.
Nafuri, Amin al-, 94
Naguib, Muhammad, 50, 81
Nahas, Mustafa, 8, 33, 46, 47, 198-9
Naqrat as-Salman, 67
Naqshbandis, 69n, 102
Nashashibi, Raghib Bey, 10
Nassar, Fu'ad, 13, 71n, 73, 156-8, 174n, 175n, 193-4, 229
Nasser, Gamal 'Abd al-, 35, 50-1, 58, 60, 80, 97, 116, 122n, 142n, 150, 170, 172-3, 186, 207, 210, 216, 218
  and Arab-Israeli war (1967), 228-9
  and Ba'thists, 84
  and Communists, 50, 81-6, 95, 98-100, 103, 105, 108, 118, 120, 173-4, 186, 214
  and Kassem, 116, 120
  and Socialism, 189-90
  and union with Syria, 84, 96
  (See also Egypt)
Nasserism, 129n, 132-3, 142, 175, 224; and Communists, 83-85, 222
National Bloc: See Syria and Jordan
National Democratic Party: See Iraq

National Liberation Front (FLN), 174
National Socialist Party: *See* Jordan
Nazi-Soviet Non-Aggression Pact, 13, 21, 22, 181
Nehru, Jawaharlal, 203
New China News Agency (NCNA), 212
New Statesman (London), 90
New York Times, 92
An-Nida (Beirut), 103, 109
Nile, 44
Nimr, Nasib, 104, 109, 111, 216
Nizam ad-Din, General, 88
North Korea, 220
North Vietnam, 220
An-Nur (Damascus), 82, 84, 97, 101-2
Nur ad-Din, General, 68

ORTHODOX CHRISTIANITY, 223
Ottoman Empire, 3, 163, 196

PALESTINE, 9, 10, 13, 29, 39, 46, 71, 166, 197, 200-1, 223
  Achduh Avodah("Unity of Work"), 9
  Arab armies in, 42
  Arab-Jewish conflict, 9-12, 29, 37-9
  Balfour Declaration, 9, 12
  and Britain, 9, 11-3, 29, 30
  Hashomer Hatzair("YoungGuard"), 37
  Histadrut (Confederation of Jewish Labour), 30
  Istiqlal Party, 12, 71
  Jewish immigration, 9-10
  partition, 36, 39
  Poale Zion ("Workers of Zion"), 9
  and US, 39
  and USSR, 39, 40; and Zionism, 9-10
Palestine Arab Higher Committee, 12-3, 179
Palestine Arab Workers' Society, 31
Palestine, Communist Party of, 9-11, 13, 15, 30-1, 37-40, 42, 71n, 179
  on agrarian policy, 11, 180
  and Arab Higher Committee, 12, 13, 179
  and Arab-Israeli war, 42
  and Arab-Jewish conflict, 11
  and Arab-Jewish State, 38
  and Arab nationalism, 163-4; Arab Writers' Council, 37
  and Balfour Declaration, 12
  bifurcation of, 30
  birth of, 9
  and Britain, 10-13, 29, 30
  factionalism, 37
  and Fascism, 13
  Federation of Arab Trade Unions and Labour Societies, 31
  Al-Ghad (Tomorrow), 37
  growth, 10, 12, 37
  and *Histadrut*, 10, 11, 30
  influence of, 37
  and Istiqlal Party, 12
  and Jewish Agency, 38
  and Jewish immigration, 9
  and Jewish rights, 37
  League for National Liberation (LNL), 30-1, 37-41
  Mifleget Poalim Sozialistim Ivrin ("Jewish Socialist Workers' Party"), 9
  Mopsi, 9
  Palestine Communist Union, 37, 38
  Partisans of Peace, 183
  and partition, 36, 39, 40
  and Syria and Lebanon, 14
  and UNSCOP, 38
  and USSR, 39, 40, 42
  and Zionism, 9, 11
Palestine Liberation Organization, 157-8, 207-8
Pan-Arabism: *See* Arab nationalism
Pan-Islamists, 104
Partaw, Dr Faruq, 67n
Parti Populaire Syrien (PPS): *See* Syria
People's Court: *See* Iraq
People's Daily (Peking), 203
People's Resistance Force (PRF): *See* Iraq.
Persian Gulf, 197
Poale Zion: *See* Palestine
Popular Resistance Force: *See* Syria
Portsmouth Treaty: *See* Iraq

Pravda, 83, 143, 203, 215-6
Preminger, 38
Progressive KDP: *See* Iraq
Progressive Socialist Party, 56, 106, 229
Pyongyang, 212
Pyramids, 210

QADI, 'ISAM AL-, 144n
Qadi, Mahmud al-, 74n
Qadir, Ahmad Mulla, 135n
Al-Qahira, 202
Qal'aji, Qadri, 17
Qash'ami, Ilyas, 14
Qaswat, Rifah, 101
Qazanji, Kamil, 66
Qibya incident, 74
Qudsi, Nazim al-, 18
Quwatli, Murad, 174n
Quwatli, Shukri al-, 17-8, 52, 89

RABITA AL-MUTHAQQAFIN, AR-, ("Arab Writers' Council), 37
Radhi, Husayn Ahmad ar-, 135n
Rashid, 'Abdullah, 144n
"Red Axis", 154
"Red Fertile Crescent", 122
Red Sea, 201
Republic Party: *See* Iraq
Reston, James, 92
Revolutionary Command Council (RCC): *See* Egypt
Reza Shah, 216
Rida, 'Abd as-Sattar Mahdi Muhammad, 144n
Rida, Rafiq, 16, 18-9, 101, 102
Rida, Rashid, 161
Ridwan, Fathi, 46
Rifa'i, Sa'id Sulayman ar-, 45, 48
Rifa'is, 102
Rikabi, Fu'ad, 115n, 117n
Riyad, Mahmud, 60
Riyashi, Iskander al-, 14
Romanian Party Congress, 204n
Rosenthal, Joseph, 5
Russia (Tsarist), 197: *See* also USSR

SA'ADA, ANTUN, 53n

Sa'ati, Najah as-, 123n
Sabit, 55n
Sabri, 'Ali, 228
Sabri, Zuhayr, 6
Sa'd, Muhammad Sa'id, 156
Sa'da, Muhammad Mahmud, 156
Sa'd ad-Din, Ibrahim, 86
Sadiq, Colonel Yusuf, 49, 50
As-Sahafi at-Ta'ih (The Wandering Journalist), 14
Sa'id, Farid, 174n
Sa'id, Nuri as-, 64n, 113, 115, 142, 144, 166
Salam, 'Adil, 141, 143
Salam, Sa'ib, 106n
Saleh, Asma', 102
Salih, 'Abd al-Qadir, 74
Salim, Mohammad, 141n, 188n, 214n
Salimov, Amin, 140
Samad, 'Abdul, 230
Samarrai, Fa'iq as-, 142n
Samir, Faysal as-, 128, 138
Sanhuri, 'Abdul Razzaq, 46
Sarkis, Ihsan, 170
Sarraj, Colonel 'Abdul Hamid, 60, 62, 87, 92, 94, 103
Sa'ud, King, 93, 152
Saudi Arabia, 55, 93, 123, 150, 152, 197, 199-201
Sawaya, 174n
Sawdi, Sulayman as-, 74n
Sawt al-Ahrar (Baghdad), 115, 121, 124, 133
Sawt ash-Sha'b (Beirut), 19, 22, 23, 25, 28, 29, 42; *Sawt ash-Sha'b* (Baghdad), 143
Sayf, Malik, 33
Sayigh, Da'ud as-, 33, 134-5
Seale, Patrick, 91
Sha'b (People's) Party: *See* Syria
Shabib, 'Abd al-Razzaq, 132
Shabib, 'Abdul Qadir, 151
Shabibi, Muhammad al-, 67
Shafi'i, Shuhdi 'Atiya ash-, 33n
Shafiq, Doria, 46
Shahin, Rushdi, 71, 73
Sham'un, President, 107-9
Shanshal, Siddiq, 115n

Sharab, Fathi Salim, 30n, 31n, 40n
Sharafuddin, Shaykh 'Abd al-Husayn, 55
Sharara,Ash-, 33
Sharif, 'Abd ar-Rahim, 135n
Sharif, 'Aziz, 65, 66, 123, 132
Sharif, Mulla, 33
Sharif of Mecca, 3
Shawi, Niqula, 17, 22, 29, 102, 108-9, 231
Shawwaf, 'Abd al-Latif, 128n, 138
Shawwaf, Colonel 'Abdul Wahab ash-, 82, 120
Shaykh, 'Aziz Ahmad ash-, 135n
Shaykh, Sharif ash-, 33, 66
Shepilov, M. Dimitri, 62
Shimali, Fu'ad ash-, 14, 16
Shishakli, Adib, 54, 55, 57, 58, 87, 183
Shumail, Ibrahim Najib, 66
Shuqayr, 'Abd ar-Rahman, 74n, 123n, 158
Shwartz, Hillel, 32, 45
Siba'i, Badruddin as-, 97
Siba'i, 'Umar, 174n
Siddiq, Ibrahim, 67
Sidqi, Bakr, 20
Sidqi, Isma'il, 45
Sino-Soviet Declaration, 202
Sino-Soviet rift: *See* Arab Communism, China, and USSR
Siris, 'Abd al-Jalil, 25
Sirri, Colonel Mustafa Rif'at, 133n
Sixth Fleet, 91, 154, 156
Socialist Party of Egypt, 3
Soviet Armenia, 54, 68
Soviet bloc, 51, 79, 81, 87
Spain, 15, 21, 164
Spartacus Party, 15
Stalin, Joseph V., on colonialism, 6-7
  on nationalities, 17
  on neutralism, 196
  on strategy and tactics, 177-8
  on united front, 56-7
Stalingrad, 24, 32, 198
Stockholm Peace Appeal, 46, 55, 72
Stone, Howard E., 91
Sudan, 5, 44, 45, 91n, 123

Suez Canal, 5, 51, 82, 183, 222: *See* also Egypt
Suez War, 62, 75, 87, 107, 152, 202, 216
Sulayman, Sidqi, 34
Sulh, Riad as-, 27
Sun Yat-sen, 221
Surur, Shaykh Ha'il as-, 87
Suwaydi, 64, 65
Sweeny, Colonel James, 154
Syria, 14, 17-9, 24, 25, 47, 83, 103, 122-3, 155, 164, 166, 170, 175, 183, 185-6, 194-5, 197-8, 224
  'Alawis, 101; and Arab-Israeli war (1967), 227-8, 230
  Arab Socialist Party, 183, 185-6
  Arab Solidarity Agreement, 152
  Armenians, 15, 101
  Assyrians, 101
  Ba'th Socialists, 56-8, 60-2, 84, 92-4, 104-5, 110, 174-5, 191, 228
  Central Bank of Issue, 191
  and China, 62, 199, 200
  Constitution, 87
  crisis (1957), 88-95
  coup d'état, 54, 60
  and Czechoslovakia, 89
  Democratic Bloc, 60n
  and East-West confrontation, 88, 89, 92
  and Egypt, 82, 84, 87, 92, 95, 96, 101, 103, 208
  and France, 17
  Hizb al-Sha'b, 58, 60, 61
  Hizb al-Watani, 58, 61
  Iraqi plot, 87, 88
  and Jordan, 150
  Kurds, 68, 101
  Kutla ("National Bloc"), 16-7, 54, 179; labour code, 99
  Naqshbandis, 102
  National Front, 88, 93, 94
  nationalists, 23, 25-6, 61, 92
  Parti Populaire Syrien (PPS), 52, 53, 58, 60, 61, 87, 110, 168
  Peasants' Organization, 102
  Popular Resistance Force, 94, 101
  positive neutralism, 63

radicalization of politics, 60
reforms, 191-3
Rifa'is, 102
Teachers' Association, 101
Trade Union Laws, 53
and Turkey, 19, 91-3
and US, 88-92, 95
and USSR, 29, 58, 62, 87-92, 95,
    103-5, 173, 198, 201, 211, 214-5
Vichy rule in, 22
Western pressure on, 58
Syria, Communist Party of (since
    1943), 27, 54-6, 59, 63, 94, 95, 97-
    9, 103-4, 170, 183, 185-6, 197, 223
on Anglo-American rivalry, 55; and
    Arab-Israeli war (1967), 227-8,
    230
on Arab nationalism, 23, 26, 52, 163,
    168-9
on Arab neutralism, 58, 63
and Arab Socialist Party, 183, 185-6
and Armenians, 54
and Army, 94, 95
and 'Azm group, 60
and Ba'th, 56-8, 60, 61, 94-7, 104-5,
    183, 185-6
and Britain, 53, 55
Charter, 26
crisis (1957), 88, 93-5
defections, 82, 100-3
and Egypt, 57-8, 105, 207
and elections, 57, 58, 61
failures, 56
and France, 28, 29
gains, 82, 88, 94, 95, 105
and Greater Syria, 55
growth, 29
and Iraqi coup d'état (1958), 98
and Islam, 52
and Lebanese Communists, 42, 53
membership, 182
and Mosul revolt, 99
and Muslim Brothers, 52, 57-8
and Nasserism, 58, 82, 83, 85, 95,
    98-100, 103-5
National Democratic Front, 55n
and national front, 56, 57, 89, 93-4,
    186

and National Union, 58
and Palestine, 42
and PPS, 52, 60, 61
pro-Peking faction, 104, 110
and PRF, 94, 101
programme, 56, 182
and secession, 103
and Sha'b Party, 60
and Shishakli, 57
and Sino-Soviet rift, 215-6
suppression, 54, 105
on Syro-Egyptian Union, 96, 97,
    103, 171, 173
on Syro-Iraqi entente, 55
on Syro-Lebanese unity, 26
and US, 52, 53, 61
and USSR, 42, 54, 57, 58, 63, 95, 105
and Watani Party, 61
and Western moves, 52, 53, 58
Women's Organization, 102
Writers' Association, 101-2
and Za'im group, 55
Syria and Lebanon, Communist Party
    of (up to 1943), 14-9, 23, 24, 29,
    165, 181
on Arab solidarity, 165
bifurcation of, 25, 26
and Bolshevik Revolution, 177
and Catroux, 23
and Comintern, 15, 24
and Druze revolt, 15
and elections, 23, 25
and Fascism, 18, 22
formation of, 15
and France, 18, 19, 22, 23
and Franco-Syrian Treaty, 17, 18
growth, 15, 29
Hizb ash-Sha'b al-Lubnani, 14, 15
and National Bloc, 17, 179
and national unity, 23, 25
and Nazi-Soviet Pact, 21n, 22
origins, 13, 16
and Palestine Communist Party, 14,
    15
Peace Committee, 90
on peasants' role, 179
and Popular Front, 17, 19
programme, 179

17

Spartacus Party, 15
Syro-Egyptian Mutual Defence Pact, 221

TABAQCHALI, BRIGADIER NAZIM AT-, 120, 133
Taha, Samir, 31
Taharrur al-Watani (National Liberation) Party: *See* Iraq
Taha Shaykh Ahmad, Brigadier, 139, 143
Tahir, Fazal at-, 74n
Tahir, Wasfi, 116, 122, 139, 141, 143
Tahrir ash-Sha'b
Taiwan, 199
Talbani, Jalal, 149
At-Tali'a, 17, 32, 86
Ta'mir, 'Abid, 33
At-Taqaddum, 158
Tashkent Conference, 97
Tashnak Party, 15n
Tass, 153
Tehran-Riyad-Amman Axis, 104
Tel Aviv, 87
Thabit, Antun, 18, 57n, 110n
Thabit, M., 6
Thawra, Ath-, 136
The Times (London), 89
Timman, Ja'far Abu, 20
Trablusi, Sa'id, 174n
Transcaucasus, 203
Transjordan: *See* Jordan
Trotsky, Leon, 9
Truman, Harry S., 36
Tsarapkin, 39
Tuma, Emile, 30, 41
Tu'ma, Farid, 14
Tuqan, Qadri, 74
Turkey, 54n, 68, 69, 90-3, 165, 197-8, 216
Turko-Iraqi Pact: *See* Baghdad Pact
Turkoman Liberation Party, 128

'UDA, NIMR, 13
'Umar, Jabir al-, 117n
'Umari, Arshad al-, 64n, 65
'Umari, Mustafa al-, 68
"Um Sulayman": *See* Hilal

United Arab Republic: *See* Egypt
United Arab States, 171
United Kingdom, 3, 6, 10n, 11-3, 15, 22, 29, 30-3, 44-7, 49n, 50, 53, 55, 56, 62, 64, 66, 72, 73, 75, 81, 100n, 107, 123, 150, 152, 163-5, 167, 179, 197, 202
United National Front: *See* Iraq and Lebanon
United Nations (UN), 36-8, 93, 107n, 199, 200, 203n, 230
United States (US), 3, 14, 36, 56, 61, 107, 146, 152-3, 183, 199, 200, 202, 206, 218
  Allied Middle East Command (proposal), 47
  American Jewry and Palestine, 36
  and Arab East, 196
  and Arab-Israeli war (1967), 228, 231
  Eisenhower Doctrine, 89-91
  and Jordan, 154
  and Syria, 87, 88, 90-2, 95
  and Syro-Lebanese Communists, 53-5
  and USSR, 89, 90, 92, 95
'Urabi, Husni al-, 3-5
'Usayran, 'Adil, 106n
USSR, 8, 14, 23, 33, 35, 51, 52, 54, 68, 102, 146, 151, 161, 183-4, 194, 202
  and Afghanistan, 198
  and Arab Communists, 40-2, 213-8, 222, 224-5
  and Arab East, 39-40, 42, 197-9, 202-3, 211-2, 216-9
  and Arab-Israeli conflict, 198, 207, 227-31
  and Arab neutralism, 43, 198
  and pan-Arabism, 165, 167, 170
  and Asian-African countries, 189, 190
  and Baghdad Pact, 198
  Bolshevik Revolution, 3, 4
  and China, 202-9, 211-3, 216-9, 224-5
  Communist bloc, 201
  Communist Party of, 105n, 220

on economic aid, 188
and Egypt, 45, 51, 62, 79, 81, 82-5, 198, 201, 211-2
and European Jews, 39
and Germany, 13, 21, 22, 24, 32
and Iran, 198
and Iraq, 35, 148, 201, 207, 211, 215, 217
and Israel, 36, 198, 230
and Jordan, 157
and Kassem, 120
and Lebanon, 29, 107-8, 198
and Mahabad Republic, 69
and Nasser, 51; naval presence in the Mediterranean, 230
and Palestine, 12, 39-42
and Saudi Arabia, 197
and Syria, 29, 54, 57, 58, 62, 63, 68, 87-9, 90, 92, 95, 103-5, 173, 198, 201, 211, 215
and Syro-Egyptian Union, 96
and Turkey, 92, 93, 198
and US, 89, 90, 92, 95
and Yemen, 211
'Uwayni, Hasan, 143

VATOLINA, L. N., 51
Vichy, 22
Vilner, Meir, 38

WADI', MICHAEL, 156
Wafd Party, 5, 8, 33, 44, 45, 47, 179
Wahbi, 'Abd al-Jabbar, 144n
Wang Chia-hsiang, 205
Wardi, Dr Husayn 'Ali al-, 135n
Wardi, Dr Jalil al-, 125n
Warrad, Fa'iq, 74n, 154
Warrad, Fayid, 158
Watani Party: See Syria

West Asia, 22, 200: See also Arab East
Western Powers, 71, 95, 202
Wilson, Woodrow, 3
Windawi, 'Abd al-Majid al-, 125n
World Federation of Trade Unions (WFTU), 44, 53
World Peace Council, 110n
World War, the First, 3, 8, 54n, 165
World War, the Second, 7, 19, 22, 181, 199, 222-3
Wright, Michael, 116

YAFI, 'ABDULLAH, 106n
Yaghmour, 'Abdul Khaliq, 154
Yahya, Muhamad al-, 74
Yahya, Tahir, 144
Ya'qub Zia ad-Din, 154
Yazbak, Yusuf Ibrahim, 14, 17
Yemen, and China, 199 201, 213
   and United Arab States, 171
   and USSR, 197-211
Yugoslavia, 220
Yunus, Hajj, 61
Yusuf, Abu Sayf, 82
Yusuf, 'Awni, 128n
Yusuf, Naji, 125n
Yusuf, Yusuf Salman, 19, 33, 65, 66

ZAGHLUL, SA'D, 6, 8
Zahir, 'Abd as-Samad, 105n, 174n
Za'im, Husni, 54
Zaqiq, Khalid, 102
Zarqa, 154
Zarqa, Muhammed 'Ali, 26n, 165n
Zionism, 9, 36, 82, 99, 168, 179, 200
   and Communism, 9-11, 30, 36, 37, 39-41
Ziyadni, Yaqub, 158